KU-175-506

VEGGIE & ORGANIC LONDON

Russell Rose

Photography by Natalie Pecht

Veggie & Organic London
Written by Russell Rose

Photography by Natalie Pecht
Edited by Abigail Willis
Maps by Lesley Gilmour
Design by Susi Koch & Lesley Gilmour

All rights reserved. No part of this publication may be reproduced, stored in a retrieval system or transmitted in any form or by any means electronic, mechanical, photocopying, recording or otherwise without the prior consent of the publishers and copyright owners. Every effort has been made to ensure the accuracy of this book; however, due to the nature of the subject the publishers cannot accept responsibility for any errors which occur, or their consequences.

Published in 2005 by
Metro Publications
PO Box 6336
London
N1 6PY

Printed and bound in India by Thomson Press Ltd

© 2005 Russell Rose

British Library Cataloguing in Publication Data.
A catalogue record for this book is available from the British Library.

ISBN   1 902910 21 4

Dedicated to the memory of my parents Lily and Sydney Rose

ACKNOWLEDGEMENTS

Special thanks to my wife, Tracy Rose, a quintessential dining partner, who enthusiastically encouraged and supported me in writing this book.

I must also thank publisher Andrew Kershman at Metro Publications for recognising the need for this book, Susi Koch for making the book look so appetising and Lesley Gilmour for her delicious maps. I'm also very grateful to Abigail Willis for her editing expertise and Natalie Pecht for her wonderful photography.

Thanks are due also to the Vegetarian Society, the Vegan Society and the Soil Association for their useful information and to Frances Schwartz at East London Organic Gardeners for her help in putting me in touch with various organic organisations.

ABOUT THE AUTHOR

Russell Rose has been eating his way through London as a restaurant reviewer since 1998 and was a contributor to Metro Crushguide 2002, Sainsbury's Carlton Taste Restaurant Reviews 2003 and restaurant correspondent for Health Eating Magazine and Mondo. He writes on health, food, nutrition and lifestyle for The Daily Express, The Daily Mail, BBC Good Food, Now Magazine, Olive and has written for Organic Living and Allergy Free. He has co-written and presented a specialist exercise and diet video, Curvenetics, and been a guest food critic on Channel 5 television and London Tonight Channel 3.

Contents

Eat and Two Veg

INTRODUCTION

The London Vegetarian Scene

London is now the hottest city on the planet for vegetarian and organic cuisine. The range of choice, quality and creativity is simply mind boggling. At the top end of the spectrum are first class restaurants run by some of the most innovative chefs in the UK. At Nahm in the fabulously chic Halkin Hotel, David Thompson is creating miraculous Thai vegetarian dishes and indeed made it the first Thai restaurant ever to be awarded a Michelin Star. In Pimlico, Alexis Gautier at Roussillon offers a spectacular vegetarian multi-course tasting menu possibly only equalled by Morgan Meuniere at Morgan M in Highbury and Chef Paul Gaylor at the Conservatory at the luxuriously elegant Lanesborough Hotel.

Vegetarian tasting menus are one of the hottest things to happen on the London vegetarian scene. They really let great chefs rip with their virtuosity and experimentation and the diner will often have a memory to savour that lasts a lifetime. Even the super-celebrity TV chefs, Jamie Oliver at Fifteen and Gordon Ramsay at Claridges include vegetarian tasting menus in their repertoire. Everyone should try at least one of these gastronomic journeys during their lifetime!

The other major advance on the London scene is the advent of the 'Vegetarian Diner' as exemplified by Eat and Two Veg in Marylebone. Here, mock carnivore dishes reach their zenith with a burger and fries on a par with Hard Rock and Planet Hollywood. Peking Palace, a superb Chinese eaterie in Archway continues to develop mock fish Chinese dishes – although it's hard to see how much more it is possible to improve upon them. Good Earth in Knightsbridge and Mulan on Haverstock Hill are also cooking great mock Chinese cuisine.

Indian vegetarian food, too, continues to get better and better. At one of the swankiest new Indian restaurants to hit the London scene, Deya on Portman Square, Chef Sanjay Dwivedi is combining Asian herbs and spices that give completely new twists to Indian classics. In the suburbs, the big shift is towards full scale Indian buffets of which perhaps the best is Rani in Finchley where the standards of presentation, hygiene and quality are supreme. The great thing about vegetarian buffets is the opportunity to taste so many different dishes and if you don't like one, hey what the heck there's another sixty to choose from. Certainly the guys down at Drummond Street in Euston, Diwana, Ravi Shankar and Chutney and Sakonis in Forest Gate have racked the prices right down making quality vegetarian banquets affordable to anyone.

One of the biggest worries for several established vegetarian restaurateurs, but a gift for their vegetarian customers, is the fantastic proliferation of Thai/Chinese outlets like Tai Buffet and Joi – offering £3 meal boxes and £5 eat as much as you like deals. These are popping up all over the place. How these good looking self-service places do it, I don't know. But the food is good and my recommendation if you are looking for a quality cheapeat.

Mediterranean vegetarian food has always been marvellous from a health standpoint and The Greenery at West Smithfield and Futures! near Eastcheap continue to make wonderful flavoursome classics for hungry veggie City workers. In writing this book I must have downed over 150 falafels and can safely say the London falafel scene is most definitely alive and well. Maoz in Soho and Taboon in Golders Green are just two outfits specialising in this delicious veggie snack.

Italian vegetarian grub remains ever popular with pastas and pizzas available along just about every shopping parade in London. The Pizza Organic chain is going down well with the eco-conscious concerned about GM, pesticides and preservatives but who like their fast food inexpensive and delicious.

The most successful organic-orientated restaurants follow the classic cuisine formats. Pizzas at Pizza Organic on Gloucester Road, organic burgers, Lancashire hot pot, sausage and mash at Eat and Two Veg, Asian oriental salads at mycafé Aveda Covent Garden, traditional brunches at Heartstone in Camden. On the pub circuit, The Duke of Cambridge in Islington and The Crown in Hackney both follow classic gastropub formats and stock a seriously respectable array of organic beers and organic wines.

Many vegetarian restaurateurs I spoke to would love to use organic completely but because of difficulties in consistent supply and the greater expense are holding back and adopting a 'use-organic-where-possible' stance.

As organic becomes more mainstream there is every reason to think that more and more restaurants will adopt it Major organic supermarkets Planet Organic and Fresh & Wild already run 100% organic canteen eateries and all the main supermarket chains and food stores such as Waitrose, Marks and Spencer, Tesco, Sainsbury's and Asda have committed to stocking a growing proportion of organic food ranges. Indeed, Marks and Spencer now have a good quality health and beauty product range with a high content of organic ingredients.

Café Cicero

Where beauty and cosmetics are concerned, getting it right with quality and organic ingredients is a difficult juggling act for manufacturers. However, good inroads are being made by Green People, Jurlique and Dr Hauschka whose products are selling well in London's most upscale shops and stores and are cruelty-free. To satisfy the demand of the new urban 'Metrosexual man', in June 2004 Jurlique launched a new range of men's organic skin care and grooming products available in upscale stores such as Space NK, Dickins & Jones and Fresh & Wild.

Talking to vegetarians about their reasons for following this lifestyle decision, it seems that health comes out top. Whereas years ago, animal welfare and rights was a big determinant, nowadays people are really thinking about what meats saturates are doing to to their heart and arteries. Perhaps the Government's 'Eat Five A Day' campaign of eating five portions of fruit or veg a day is beginning to kick in. People are certainly becoming more aware of the health benefits of antioxidants and vitamins in fruit and veg and their possible role in reducing cancer incidence. Hardly a week goes by without a report appearing in the press about some particular fruit or vegetable containing an antioxidant that is deemed to have a beneficial affect on our health and well being. Whilst supplement manufacturers have been keen to offer solutions to our

3

dietary problems in a pill, research shows that eating wholefoods with natural combinations of beneficial antioxidants and other substances has a better synergistic effect than those found in supplements.

For London vegetarians and the eco-aware there are many contact organisations for keeping up to date on the latest issues and research. The most important national organisations are The Vegetarian Society, The Vegan Society and the Soil Association. For a full listing of useful veggie and organic organisation see pages 281-287.

London also has a good range of vegetarian caterers most of which have their own eateries. Organic and vegetarian caterers of note include Manna (North London) and Organic Express (Central and South London)

Café Pacifico

Organic Londoners

The highest concentration of organic Londoners are to be found around the affluent areas of Notting Hill, Soho, Camden, Hampstead and Islington. Up and coming districts such as Stoke Newington, Crouch End and Hoxton are also attracting the organically minded. However, in every neighbourhood there are people on a spectrum of incomes buying organic in the supermarkets. People are also growing their own organic fruit, veg, herbs and plants at home and on allotments. There are a number of London based organisations there to help the green fingered including ELOG in East London, Growing Communities in Stoke Newington, Spitalfield City Farm in Spitalfields and the Spa Hill Organic Gardening Group (SHOGG). Many of these community run projects use volunteers and some do very good work for charities and those with learning disabilities. A list of organic contact organisations is given on pages 285-287.

For some, being involved with an organic allotment is a form of therapy, a way of combating the strains of modern day life and simultaneously involving oneself with nature. For others such as the Bangladeshi women of the Coriander Club at Spitalfields City Farm, it's a way of cultivating essential nutritional sustenance for themselves. In South London, the Spa Hill Organic Gardening Group run well-supervised practical organic gardening courses and hold regular meetings on organic issues.

On my travels around London, I found amongst organic food enthusiasts a mindset of concern. People are buying organic for health reasons and to allay their fears about chemicals such as pesticides, herbicides and fungicides. Some are obsessed and will eat nothing but organic, while others take things on a more casual basis.

Have a conversation with a passionate organic Londoner and the topic will soon turn to GM, superbugs, fair trade, biodynamic farming, damage to the countryside and a sustainable future. These are people who really care about the environment.

In 2003, organic food sales in the UK hit £1.12 billion having tripled in five years. With new branches of organic supermarkets such as Planet Organic and Fresh & Wild opening all the time and the support of the major supermarkets and individual wholefood shops around London, interest in organic seems to be ever increasing.

How to use this book

Explanation of café/restaurant ratings

People are always asking me 'what's your favourite restaurant? what's the best meal you've ever had?' These are always difficult questions to answer because there are always so many considerations. Taste, choice, price, nationality and how do you compare a meal with modern dishes against a classic one? In an attempt to give an assessment I've included a star rating system to supplement my comments in the reviews based on impressions gained during my visit to the venue. In addition, at the end of the book the Veggie and Organic London Hot List gives a quick guide to help you pick the type of restaurant you want.

Vegetarian choice

★★★★★ – complete vegetarian menu with good vegan choices

★★★★ – over 50% of menu is vegetarian or has a Vegetarian Tasting Menu

★★★ – at least three vegetarian choice of main dishes on menu

★★ – less than three vegetarian choices

★ – don't worry the chef will throw a green salad together for you!

Organic choice

★★★★★ – complete organic menu

★★★★ – over 50% of menu is organic

★★★ – at least 3 organic choices on menu or many organic ingredients

★★ – less than three organic choices

★ – we used to do organic – I'll go and see if the chef has got anything

Taste

★★★★★ – Exceptional

★★★★ – Very Good

★★★ – Good

★★ – Okay

★ – Poor

Price (Inc. main course & one other course eg. starter or dessert, without drinks)

£	under £10
££	£10–15
£££	£15–20
££££	£20–25
£££££	£25+

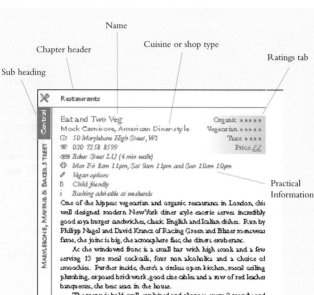

Name

Chapter header

Cuisine or shop type

Ratings tab

Sub heading

Practical Information

Review

✂ Restaurants

Central

MARYLEBONE, MAYFAIR & BAKER STREET

Eat and Two Veg
Mock Carnivore, American Diner-style
⌚ 50 Marylebone High Street, W1
☎ 020 7258 8599
🚇 Baker Street LU (4 min walk)
🕐 Mon-Fri 8am-11pm, Sat 9am-11pm and Sun 10am-10pm
🌱 Vegan options
Ⓑ Child friendly
i Booking advisable at weekends

Organic ★★★★★
Vegetarian ★★★★★
Taste ★★★★
Price ££

One of the hippest vegetarian and organic restaurants in London, this well designed modern New York diner style eacerie serves incredibly good soya burger sandwiches, classic English and Italian dishes. Run by Philipp Nagel and David Krantz of Racing Green and Blazer menswear fame, the joint is big, the atmosphere fine, the diners exuberant.

At the windowed front is a small bar with high stools and a few serving 13 pre meal cocktails, four non alcoholics and a choice of smoothies. Further inside, there's a tireless open kitchen, metal ceiling plumbing, exposed brickwork, good size cables and a row of red leather banquettes, the best seats in the house.

The menu is bold, well explained and changes every 2 months and tries to use organic and GM free produce across the board. The average cost per head is £25 with drinks and the service, courtesy of the t shirted young waiting staff, is hyper attentive.

No less than eight salads are on offer here and the Nuc Nicoise is recommended. In scarcer portion size it's still big and comes with maxi nated organic tofu, tiny pieces of avocado, leaves, green beans, potatoes, delicious capers and a free range organic hard boiled egg. Pan fried Polenta is a very comfortable sized opener and is topped with button mushrooms and sun blushed tomatoes in pesto red wine sauce with melted cheese. The EatV Burger is highly recommended and has the wow factor, it looks just like a real chargrilled burger meal with a decent sesame bun, caramelised onions, tomatoes, lettuce and match stick french fries — the best mock burger in London.

There are 10 main course with English stalwarts such as Lancashire Hot Pot, Sausage and Mash and a Shepherd's Pie that's indistinguishable from the real thing and delicious.

The vegan Seasonal Fruit Crumble with berries, rhubarb and thin soya custard is unfortunately not so good but the Tiramisu, a biscuity dessert with coffee liqueur and Malibu cream cheese, arrives in a short sundae glass and slides down well.

40

Restaurants

Hugo's

CENTRAL LONDON

World Food Café

BLOOMSBURY & RUSSELL SQUARE

Restaurants
1) Alara Wholefoods p.12
2) Mary Ward Vegetarian Café p.13
3) Planet Organic p.14
4) The Vegetarian's Paradise p.14
5) Wagamama p.15

Shops
a) Alara Wholefoods p.223
b) Planet Organic p.224

Bloomsbury and Russell Square are central, smart and have some charming unspoilt streets and shops. Below are reviews for a wide range of vegetarian restaurants from the ultra stylish Wagamama to the cheap Italian veggie outlet – Mary Ward in Bloomsbury. There are only two vegetarian/wholefood shops in the area but both Alara Wholefood and Planet Organic are great shops - well worth going out of your way to visit and both serve good veggie and organic food.

11

Alara Wholefoods
International, Classic

🖃 *258-260 Marchmont Street, WC1*
☎ *0207 837 1172*
🚌 *Russell Square LU (1 min walk)*
🕐 *Lunch served 11.30am-4pm, Mon-Sat*
☀ *Outside seating*
i *Eat in & Takeaway (outside catering also)*

Organic ★★★★★
Vegetarian ★★★★★
Taste ★★
Price £

Bargain priced organic hot and cold help-yourself buffet, with a varied selection of juices, smoothies and hot drinks at this large neighbourhood vegetarian, health food and alternative remedy shop.

It's all a bit of a squeeze at lunchtime at the various serving stations but people are friendly and with a bit of luck you won't get somebody's elbow in your carton which you fill up as you like and pay for by weight (85p/100g). Our two cartons of hot food totalled £4.80, making it possibly the cheapest veggie organic lunch to be had in London.

On a fine day, get an outside table looking out onto busy Marchmont Street and the Vegetarian Paradise opposite (see below). Alara is a bit of a hang out for students and lecturers and folk from the BMA (British Medical Association) but also attracts some shirt and tie clad businessmen and a fair few vegetarian tourists staying at the hotels around Russell Square. At the back of the shop amongst the unpacked bottles of organic juices are additional stools around a long narrow table where you can eat lunch on the cardboard plates provided.

The salad station is quite appealing and don't miss out on the choice of organic balsamic vinegar or Tomari organic soya sauce to enhance the enjoyment of your meal. Food here changes every day but hummous, Greek salad and cottage cheese remain longstanding regulars. There are also some organic bread choices for extra hungry souls for only an additional 30p.

Over on the hot buffet, the warm Moussaka was okay whilst the Lasagne – one of the house specials – is a quiet reasonable affair. The Fusilli pasta with broccoli and Roquefort cheese was the favourite of our choices. Coffees here are inexpensive and there are some delicious sweets such as Crayves Date and Walnut cake or the Apple and Cinnamon cake as well as a tempting selection of ice-creams. Alara Wholefoods buy in bulk to their shop enabling them to sell the organic buffet at a highly competitive price. Which just goes to show satisfying organic meals can be offered at bargain basement prices. For Alara's Organic Shop see page 223.

Mary Ward Vegetarian Café
International, Classic

Vegetarian ★★★★★
Taste ★★★
Price £

⌨ *42 Queen Square, WC1*
☎ *020 7831 7711*
🚌 *Russell Square or Holborn LU (5 min walk)*
🕐 *Mon-Thur 9.30am-8.50pm, Fri 9.30am-8.30pm, Sat 9.30am-4pm*
🌶 *Vegan options*
i *Counter service*

Bargain Italian and Portuguese vegetarian food forms the menu at this adult education centre canteen that's also open to the public. Opened in 1998, the café itself is privately owned by Helena and Daniella who devise this 100% vegetarian selection. Helena became a vegetarian 25 years ago when she came over from Portugal and found there was a meat scare here.

The café is a hive of activity with enough seats for 48. At midday, there may be committee group discussing its agenda, a doctor chilling out, some nurses queuing up asking about salt content in the cheese. Apart from students it's popular with nurses, doctors and staff from the hospitals on Queen Square and also attracts people of all ages and often strict dietary requirements. Paintings are exhibited on the walls and the best tables are by the window boxes with a pleasant view overlooking Queen's Square.

The blackboard menu changes twice daily and includes light snacks such as soup and bread, baguettes and sandwiches through to hearty mains such as Penne Pasta with Veg, Layered Potato pieces with cheese or polenta. The tasty Tortilla is a mega-wedge Spanish Omelette of egg, caramelised onion and potato with a side-salad of coleslaw, red cabbage, lettuce and mung beans and olive oil dressing. The roasted Vegetable Risotto turns out to be not a true risotto as it uses ordinary white rice instead of arborio but it's not bad at £3 although the carrots and parsnip veg could have been cut smaller to be more manageable.

Breakfast runs until 11.30am and is a basic toast, butter and jam affair although they do bake their own bread. Virtually all the food is made on the premises except the cakes which come from Portuguese bakers Lisboa Patisserie (at 57 Golborne Road, W10, tel 020 8968 5242). Their speciality are the custard tarts called pasteis de nata although there is also carrot and walnut cake, passion cake and almond tart to choose from. Soya milk is available for coffees. A good inexpensive veggie eaterie.

Planet Organic

Organic Vegetarian, International

Organic ★★★★★
Vegetarian ★★★★★
Taste ★★★
Price £

- ▦ *22 Torrington Place, WC1*
- ☎ *0207436 1929*
- 🚌 *Goode Street LU (5 min walk)*
- 🕓 *Mon-Fri 8.45am-8pm, Sat 11am-6pm, Sun 12noon-6pm*
- ◊ *Child friendly*
- i *Eat in (counter service) & Takeaway*

See Planet Organic, Westbourne Grove branch for food review (page 173) and store review on page 249.

The Vegetarian's Paradise

Indian, Classic

Vegetarian ★★★★★
Price £

- ▦ *Bhel Poori House, 59 Marchmont Street, WC1*
- ☎ *020 7278 6881*
- 🚌 *Russell Square LU (1 min walk)*
- 🕓 *Daily lunch served 12noon-3pm & dinner served 5pm-11pm*
- 🥕 *Vegan options*
- i *Eat in (table service) & Takeaway*

A good value lunchtime destination with an eat-as-much-as-you-like buffet for £4.50. Situated opposite Alara Wholefoods, the chocolate coloured exterior is hardly a fitting entrance to 'paradise'. Still, for bargain hunting vegetarians the £2.50 buffet takeout box makes up for any deficiencies in the décor.

The help yourself buffet consists of twelve choices some of which are a classic selection of Indian chutneys. The buffet changes daily and may include a chickpea and potato curry, a mixed vegetable curry with herbs and spices, wholemeal puri bread, naan and basmati rice.

The evening menu features all the Western and Southern Indian stalwarts with a three course deluxe thali at £6.95. Food here is of reasonable quality but requires a little more work before reaching the status of 'paradise'.

Wagamama
Japanese, Modern

Vegetarian ★★★★
Taste ★★★★
Price £

🖼 *4 Streatham Street, WC1*

☎ *020 78960 5757*

🚌 *Tottenham Court Road LU (10 min walk)*

🕐 *Tue-Sat 5pm-11.30pm*

Popular student and budget conscious diners' venue. For review see Wagamama (Wigmore Street branch) page 47. Also a branch in Camden, see page 121.

COVENT GARDEN, LEICESTER SQUARE & THE STRAND

Restaurants

Shops

In vibrant Covent Garden there's inventive country-style Indian at Mela, vivacious Mexican party atmosphere at Café Pacifico, an opera-themed restaurant at Sarastro and exquisite Pacific rim cuisine at East@West. For stylish food in a stylish environment mycafé Aveda is a great choice. Around the famous Neal's Yard, vegetarians are spoilt for choice with Neal's Yard Salad Bar, World Food Café, Neal's Yard Bakery, bargain meals at Food for Thought or, for fine Italian dining, Carluccio's Neal Street Restaurant. For great Turkish food with plenty of veggie choices try Sofra in Covent Garden. For Thai food there are several outlets from which to choose and for great Indian vegetarian food a branch of Woodlands. Nearby too, serving excellent organic coffee is the Monmouth Street Coffee Company and First Out, a meeting point for gay vegetarians.

Café Pacifico
Mexican, Classic

	Vegetarian ★★★
	Taste ★★★★
	Price ££

🖼 *5 Langley Street, WC2*
☎ *020 7379 7728*
🚇 *Covent Garden LU (1 min walk)*
🕐 *Mon-Sat 12noon-11.45pm, Sun 12noon-10.45pm*
    (bookings only Sun-Thur and Fri & Sat daytime,
    other times first come first served)
🥕 *Vegan options*
⌀ *Child friendly*

A famously joyous eaterie with several good veggie choices on its omnivore menu. Opened in 1982, Café Pacifico is drenched in Mexican atmosphere with its dark, decadent décor, heavy wooden tables and chairs and lots of interesting Mexican posters. The place has a strong vegetarian clientele and makes a great party venue, with a well-stocked bar.

Veggie options are marked on the menu. Nachos Rancheros is simply superb and arrives as corn chips covered with beans, melted cheese, ranchera sauce, tomato, lettuce and onion, masses of heavenly sour cream and guacamole. The Spicy Vegetarian Tostada main consists of two tortillas laden with artichoke hearts, balsamic onions, avocado slices, soft cheeses and salad and is fab fun food. Fajita fans can opt for the Wild Mushroom and Artichoke special. Desserts? Forget them. This is really a starter and main place. Order more side plates and party-on!

Carluccio's Caffé
Italian, Classic

Vegetarian ★★
Price £££££

▯ *26 Neal Street, WC2*
☎ *020 7836 8368*
🚌 *Covent Garden LU (3 min walk)*
🕐 *Mon-Sat lunch 12noon-2.30pm & dinner 6pm-11pm*
🍴 *Vegan options*
🍼 *Child friendly*
i *Booking advised in evenings; outside catering (tel 020 7629 0699)*

Carluccio's Neal Street Restaurant is the fine dining version of the Carluccio's Caffé chain. The difference in menu prices reflects this and the fact that you are getting recipes created by one of the best Italian chefs in the world.

The set menu is £21 for two courses and £25 for three courses. Whilst vegetarian choices are limited here the Roast Pepper Soup is highly regarded and the Fresh Tuscan Salad with tomatoes, celery, green olives, bread and capers very tempting. This may be followed by a Mushroom Risotto which is recommended given Mr Carluccio's expertise in this area. Check with the waitress to find out what desserts are vegetarian, although there is a cheese selection served with pears and walnuts.

The à la carte menu includes mixed sautéed mushrooms of the day or a decent salad, a soup suitable for vegetarians and main of courgette flowers stuffed with ewe's milk ricotta, served with chilled tomato and basil sauce. The Neal Street Restaurant is perhaps the best Italian in the Covent Garden area and attracts business people and shoppers at lunchtime. In the evenings it is candlelit and makes a refined pre-theatre and post- theatre dining spot.

Chi
Thai, Chinese, Classic

Vegetarian ★★★★★
Taste ★★★
Price £

▯ *56 St Martin's Lane, WC2*
☎ *020 7836 3434*
🚌 *Leicester Square LU (5 min walk)*
🕐 *Daily 11am-11pm*
🍴 *Vegan menu*

Bargain £5 all you can eat vegan Thai/Chinese cuisine. For food review see Tai Buffet (Camden branch) page 120.

East@West
Vietnamese, Japanese, Chinese, Modern

🔲 *13-15 West Street, WC2*
☎ *020 7010 8600*
🚇 *Leicester Square LU (5 min walk)*

Organic ★★★
Vegetarian ★★★★
Taste ★★★★
Price *£££££*

East@West

🕓 *Dinner Mon-Sat 5.30pm-12midnight*

East@West is part of the bijou West Street Hotel (see page 297 for hotel details) and has developed quite a following since opening in 2003, not least for its enjoyable Pacific Rim vegetarian tasting menu.

Situated a few yards from the Ivy, this plush oriental styled place features a bar over two floors and a sumptuously Eastern Asian looking restaurant. The bar is large and impressive and comes complete with subdued lighting, backless leather sofas, DJ and a 20's/30's crowd. East@West draws a mix of middle of the road socialites with a fair sprinkling of Australians, many of whom are fans of the Australian chef

Central

COVENT GARDEN, LEICESTER SQUARE & THE STRAND

here, Christine Manfield.

Before dining they seat you in the bar for a half an hour and take your order. The vibes are good and the pre-meal drinks get you into a relaxed mood after which they take you upstairs to the equally cool dining room, with its sophisticated strips of orange lighting. Tell them you are vegetarian and two Nori sushi vegetarian canapés with a mustardy sauce will appear.

There are four tasting menus, which includes one vegetarian option (called Delicious) which consists of five small courses and costs £40 or you can order single à la carte tastes at £9 each. Altogether a dinner for two with wine and service runs to about £120. Judging by comments overheard on other tables when the bill came along the lines of "this is very reasonable for what we had," "the food here is great, worth it," there's a real feel-good factor to this place and some consensus that it's good value for money.

I didn't go for the whole shooting match not fancying the fried quail's egg and instead ordered four tasters from the à la carte. Asparagus Tempura made with lotus root, toasted seaweed and a wasabi avocado cream was beautifully crafted but overly mustardy, suppressing some of the other flavours. Spiced turmeric lemongrass broth is about half the size of a normal bowl of soup and bursting with intense flavours that exquisitely linger in your mouth for ten minutes after. Indeed, this may be the best vegetarian soup in London.

Fried Bean Skin Pastry is a drop dead gorgeous couple of small pasty rolls encapsulating a delectable tofu with micro nameko mushroom salad in a scrummy yellow bean sauce.

All the desserts are vegetarian-friendly and the remarkably sculptured Caramelised Ginger Cream with intense candied ginger and lychee and mangosteen salad is a fantastic twist on crème caramel. The Hazelnut Chocolate Pyramid comes recommended although it does bear the puzzling name 'Golden Gaytime'.

East@West does get busy in the evenings and isn't what most people would call inexpensive, but it does offer a special pre-theatre deal 5.30pm-6.30pm, with two courses and a glass of wine for £15. A good evening out.

First Out
International

Vegetarian ★★★★★
Taste ★★★
Price £

- 52 St Giles High Street, WC2
- ☎ 020 7240 8042
- Tottenham Court Road LU (1 min walk)
- Mon-Sat 10am-11pm, Sun 11am-10.30pm
- ☀ Outside seating

i   Counter service

Located opposite Centrepoint, this all-vegetarian, gay and lesbian café is a veritable meeting/pickup place that's been running for 18 years. It's friendly, big on eye contact, but also mellow with a lot of solitary grazers reading the free pamphlets and mags. An intellectual-looking woman gazes at the tempting serving-counter of salads, cold pastas and mezzes and orders a doorstop sized quiche. "Four-ninety five! For quiche! Too much" she exclaims and settles for a smoothie. In fact the mains, all under a fiver, represent good value and the choice incudes Mexican Nachos and bean burgers, seven jacket potatoes, pre-packaged rolls and on Sundays there's a brunch of veggie sausage, garlic and mushrooms. Quiches here are delicious and come served with a green salad. Coffee is good and the cakes are highly inviting and enough for two.

Decked out in biscuit, vanilla and a petrol-grey, the walls are hung with paintings for sale such as Neon Blue Kiss for £75. The specials change daily and the blackboard menu changes seasonally. Downstairs is a cosy bar suitable for veggie smokers.

Food For Thought

International, Classic

Vegetarian ★★★★★
Taste ★★★
Price £

⌨ *31 Neal Street, WC2*

☎ *020 7836 9072*

🚌 *Covent Garden LU (5 min walk)*

🕐 *Mon-Sat, breakfast 9.30am-11.30am, lunch 12noon-4pm,*
   dinner 4pm-8.30pm; Sunday 12pm-5pm

🖉 *Vegan options*

i *Eat in (counter service) & Takeaway, outside catering available*

Food For Thought is a remarkable bargain basement vegetarian eaterie in the heart of crowded Covent Garden shopping area. Forget the couple of tables as you go in, the main event is all downstairs. Of course, first you'll have to join the queue on the stairs, a time-honoured tradition that goes back to '74. However, the queue moves fast and before you can say Cauliflower and Dill Quiche you're at the serving counter being ladled up with stir fry veg, tagine with cous cous and leek soup. Armed with your meal, find a vacant seat sharpish as they do get snapped up quickly. Although a 40-seater, space is tight, so expect to share a table.

The menu changes daily and each evening there's a special. The Thai Plate Special (£6.50) is a big platter of delicious vegan Thai Curry served with fragrant white rice. The Special bit is that on the same plate you get a starter of cold bean sprout salad, spring rolls and chilli sauce. The salad is fine and the sauce excellent but the spring rolls are a taste-less waste of space as they were virtually filled with air. Green Spinach and Chick Pea Savoury Crumble (£4) is a substantial hunger buster of chick peas, spinach, aubergine and courgettes in a sundried tomato sauce with a parsley and cheese crumble topping – of variable temperature but otherwise quite good. Fresh Fruit Salad is available and looks a better bet for dessert than the Strawberry and Banana Scrunch.

The atmosphere is informal and the place is a magnet for blue-jeaned vegetarian students, backpacking tourists and even the odd suited price-conscious business-types doing a veggie pre-theatre bite.

Food For Thought is not a place to linger long but despite the crush it is one to recommend to your friends. Whilst the food is not organic, their mantra is 'they never knowingly use GM foods in any of their dishes.' For a real cheapo bite, right in the middle of London's theatre-land, it's tough to beat.

Mela
Indian

Vegetarian ★★★★
Taste ★★★★★
Price £££

🏠 152-156 Shaftesbury Avenue, WC2

☎ 020 7836 8635

🚌 Leicester Square LU,
Tottenham Court Road LU (10 min walk)

🕐 Mon-Wed 12noon-11.30pm, Thur-Sat 12noon-11.45pm,
Sun 12noon-10.30pm

🥕 Vegan options

ⓞ Child friendly

i Eat in & Takeaway; function room available

Upscale popular Indian restaurant serving highly creative and wonderfully tasty country style dishes. Brightly coloured in décor, it won Indian Restaurant of the Year 2001 at the Carlton, Evening Standard, Moet & Chandon awards.

The menu has three vegetarian starters, four tandoor dishes, eight mains, three rice dishes and seven breads. Dishes are rich in aroma and a magnificent treat for the taste buds. There's a wonderful tandoor main, Subz Thal, a mix of peppers stuffed with cumin flavoured vegetables, tomatoes with spiced dal, cottage cheese skewered with capsicums, stuffed potatoes and other veg and is served with a mint chutney.

Mirch Baingan Ka Salan, is a deliciously traditional spicy aubergine dish with red chillies in a peanut flavoured yogurt type sauce. This with Jeero Pulao, basmati rice with cumin, a naan and a Roomali Roti, a fat-free flat bread on a dome shaped Tawa, is excellent. The set three course vegetarian menu is £24.95 (2 persons). Non-vegetarian dishes are available.

Bargain tip: the lunchtime deals are £1.95-£4.95 on the Paratha Pavilion Menu that's inspired by Old Delhi's historic Parathey Wali Gali, a street well known for its distinctive rural street food. Your lunch comes in a box with a pickle and chutney accompaniment – all you do is choose your bread, filling and curry and leave the rest to the chef.

Mela also has sister restaurants, Chowki and Soho Spice.

World Food Café

mycafé Aveda Covent Garden
International, Modern

Organic ★★★★★
Vegetarian ★★★★
Taste ★★★★★
Price ££

⌨ *174 High Holborn, WC1*
☎ *020 7759 7352*
🚇 *Covent Garden LU*
🕐 *Mon-Sat 9am-6pm*
🥕 *Vegan options*
i *Table service (order at counter)*

Join the high maintenance beautiful people for the perfect post hairdo/stress-relieving beauty treatment chow down at this fab organic eaterie. Mycafé is a front of house ultra-chic modern café at the Aveda Hairdressing Institute opposite the Shaftesbury Theatre. This is where health and diet-conscious ladies-who-lunch lunch, along with a smattering of well-groomed tourists and local business folk.

The combined breakfast-lunch menu is stacked with gems of healthy nutritional info and is 98% organic. Papaya, lime and passion fruit plate is a delicious detoxing daily kickstarter and the orange juice is exquisite. More exotic juice concoctions are available as is mycafé's own breakfast smoothie, muesli and muffins.

Lunchtimes are busy especially late week but the ambience remains relaxed. Spinach, Lime and Lentil Broth is a delightful visual treat and comes accented with mint and lemon and is strongly recommended. Raw foodists should go for the Asparagus, Enoki Mushroom and Spearmint Wrap, a wonderfully crunchy, well-crafted light lunch. The other vegetarian wrap is called Happy Chicken, a chicken-less wheat flour tortilla wrap of organic eggs, mayonnaise, basil and cress and tastes fine. It was given its name because the chickens are free-roaming and eat only organic food – unhappy chickens as they say, can't make good eggs!

For coeliacs, the Wheat-Free Baby open sandwich of rye, amaranth and quinoa bread topped with baby spinach leaves, tomato and sesame seeds is a tasty option.

Of the three vegetarian salads, my favourite is the New Greek that comes with a satisfyingly tangy organic feta and kalamata olives. The Salad of Life with five different seeds and sprouts, shoots and leaves with tahini dressing is a rare treat and well worth a whirl.

Organic Mango sorbet is a refreshing way to finish but there are also cakes from Crayves organic bakery. A few non-vegetarian dishes are available. Mycafé is to be commended for its well-presented healthy and organic vegetarian selection and good service.

Neal's Yard Bakery
Café

Organic ★★★★
Vegetarian ★★★★★
Taste ★★★
Price £

🖾 *6 Neal's Yard, WC2*
☎ *020 7836 5199*
🚌 *Covent Garden LU (5 min walk)*
🕐 *Mon-Sat 10.30am-5pm*
🌱 *Vegan options*
◓ *Child friendly*
i *Eat in (table service) & Takeaway*

Opened in 1980 when things really started happening in Neal's Yard, this organic bakery sells the most delicious Three Seeds Bread (organic linseed, poppyseed and sesame) although their plain wholemeal remains their bestseller to this day. They wholesale to the likes of Fresh & Wild and Harvey Nicks whilst upstairs the café serves soups, salads and sarnies. Everything is vegetarian and the beanburger is vegan. The five cakes are all organic vegetarian and they do organic scones and biscuits.

Neal's Yard Bakery

Neal's Yard Salad Bar
Café

⌗ *2 Neal's Yard, WC2*
☎ *020 7836 3233*
🚇 *Covent Garden LU (5 min walk)*
🕐 *Mon-Sat 10am-8pm, Sun 10am-5pm*
🌶 *Vegan options*
◌ *Child friendly*
☀ *Outside seating*
i *Eat in & Takeaway*

Vegetarian ★★★★★
Taste ★★★
Price £

Opened in 1982 this all home-made vegetarian/vegan eaterie serves hot meals, soups and salads small or large at £2.50-£4. Don't be fooled by the hamburgers on the menu, they're soya!

Pick a sunny day and loll around under the parasols outside. Otherwise chow down inside the two newly refurbished eating areas. Also serves exotic fruit juices.

Sarastro
Mediterranean, Classic

⌗ *126 Drury Lane, WC2*
☎ *020 7836 0101*
🚇 *Covent Garden LU (2 min walk) & Holborn LU (5 min walk)*
🕐 *Daily lunch 12noon-3pm & dinner 5pm-11pm*
🌶 *Vegan options*
◌ *Child friendly*
i *Booking essential*

Vegetarian ★★★
Taste ★★★
Price ££

Vegetarian actress Celia Imrie introduced me to Sarastro as a must eat at destination in London's theatre district, and I love it. Inside it's opera themed, so go in a group and reserve an upstairs semi-private opera box and toast the other diners in their boxes who will toast you back. The décor is exuberant with recycled wall-mounted opera boxes draped with gold lamé, crushed velvet tablecloths and napkins, gilt furnishings and brocade upholstered chairs. At ground level, there's more seating for dating couples and a central reservation for parties of 20 or more.

Upbeat Bizet, Mozart and Verdi opera anthems, cheerful service, birthday party groups and big smiles all round announce this is hedonistic dining with a vengeance. And oh yes, there's erotic wallpaper in the toilets – don't say you haven't been warned!

Chilli sauce, ginger and tomato dip with olive bread is a complimentary and rather good overture from the management. Asparagus starter with olive oil and lemon is recommended as is the Cheese Börek, warm triangulated pasties filled with cheese. Hummous, here, is also done well.

There are four veggie mains of which the Pancake Special filled with stirfried spinach, cucumber, mushroom and creamy sauce slides down easily. Even better is the Vegetarian Bake with a mix of haloumi, parmesan and cheddar that can be made cheese-free with aubergine for vegans on request. Vegetarian pastas, seasonal salads are also available and amongst the desserts the Seasonal Fresh Fruit Selection, (a biggie) makes a fitting finale to the feast. Plenty of choices for omnivore dining partners too.

Every Sunday and Monday evening, Sarastro hosts an Opera Cabaret Dinner that includes performances from young talented opera singers at £23.50 and Sunday Matinées from 1.30pm at £17.50, children half price. Recommended is The Tenor Menu, two courses for a tenner and definitely something to sing about.

Sister Branch at: Papageno Restaurant & Bar, 29-31 Wellington Street, WC2; Tel: 020 7836 4444 (see advert on page 31 for further details).

Sarastro

Sofra Covent Garden
Turkish, Classic

Vegetarian ★★★
Taste ★★★
Price ££

🖃 36 Tavistock Street, WC2
☎ 020 7240 3773
🚇 Covent Garden LU (5 min walk)
🕐 Daily 12noon-12.30am (last orders 11pm)

See Özer, Oxford Circus for food review (page 44).

Thai Square The Strand
Thai, Classic

Vegetarian ★★★
Taste ★★
Price £££

🖃 148 Strand, WC2
☎ 020 7497 0904
🚇 Charing Cross LU & Rail (5 min walk)
🕐 Mon-Sat 12noon-3pm, 5.30pm-11.15pm

Good Thai vegetarian choices for pre- and post-theatre goers at this smaller version of the flagship restaurant in Trafalgar Square (for food review see Thai Square at Trafalgar Square below).

Thai Square Trafalgar Square
Thai, Classic

Vegetarian ★★★
Taste ★★
Price £££

🖃 21-24 Cockspur Street, SW1
☎ 020 7839 4000
🚇 Charing Cross LU (3 min walk)
🕐 Mon-Thur 12noon-3pm and 5.30pm-11.30pm,
Fri-Sat 12noon-3pm and 5.30pm-1am,
Sun 12noon-3pm and 5.30pm-10.30pm

A stone's throw from Nelson's Column, this vast Thai restaurant serves a short vegetarian menu together with a pre-theatre starter and main meal deal with coffee for just £12 (5.30pm-7.30pm).

Attractively decorated, the restaurant is on two floors, with the ground floor pretty full by 8pm and the upstairs half full by 10pm. At the back of the ground floor dining room tables are set up for larger parties.

Portions here are big and it may be quite adequate for two people to split a starter and order a main each and one portion of rice. A starter of Corn Cakes (Tod Mun Koaw Pod) is spicy, enjoyable and copious. The corn comes with curry paste and chopped lime leaves and a sweet tasty dipping sauce.

Mains, however, are disappointing and my advice is that if you find that there is hardly any soy sauce or ginger, mushroom and spring onions with the fried beancurd with ginger (Pad Khing Toa Hoo) then call the manager and ask for more and you'll find this meal pretty good. Similarly, if you can't find any vegetables amongst the glass noodles of the steamed vegetable dish (Woonsen Ob Mor Din) – that is served with even more fried bean curd – then call the manager as well. When the vegetables do come again they are quite crispy and tasty but like the vegetarians on the next table to me who had ordered the same, the mushrooms as described on the menu were nowhere to be found. On a happier note, the pineapple rice, served in a half of pineapple was well presented and of quite reasonable taste. Talking to the vegetarians on the next table, who had eaten here several times and been quite satisfied, led me to conclude that the food here is of variable quality. Service certainly is attentive but technically leaves something to be desired. Whilst white wines come suitably cold they weren't kept so and waiting staff were over eager to clear plates away. If the food could match the place's good looks it would be an even bigger hit.

The Thai Square club downstairs holds 200 and is a huge basement bar with dancing and gets very busy on Friday and Saturday nights from 11pm onward with a mainly Chinese and Japanese clientele. Admission is free for women and £10 for men although if you dine you will most certainly get in for nothing, space permitting.

Thai Square is a chain with restaurants at the Strand (page 29), Oxford Circus (page 63), Islington (page 107), South Kensington (page 160), Soho (page 61), Mansion House (page 81) and the Minories in the City (page 80).

Woodlands
South Indian, Classic

Vegetarian ★★★★★
Taste ★★★★
Price £££

🔲 *37 Panton Street, SW1*
☎ *020 7839 7258*
🚇 *Leicester Square LU, Piccadilly LU (5 min walk)*
🕐 *Daily 12noon-3pm and 6pm-11pm*
🌶 *Vegan options*

Situated just off the Haymarket, the Panton Street Woodlands is more of a quick service venue. See Woodlands Chiswick for full food review (page 179), other Woodlands are at 77 Marylebone Lane W1 (tel 020 7486 3862) and 402, High Street, Wembley, Middlesex (tel 020 8902 9869).

Sarastro Restaurant
The Show After the Show

Sarastro is located in the heart of theatreland, one of London's most spectacular restaurants, it is a treat for the palate but also for the eyes and ears. Feast upon a fine array of Mediterranean dishes in flamboyant operatic surroundings.

Live opera performances every Sunday matinee and Sunday and Monday evenings. Sarastro is ideal for pre and post-theatre dining with a menu available at £12.50. Also available for lunch every and all day.

Private function room for all occasions (for up to 300 guests) available.

126 Drury Lane, London. WC2
Tel. 020 7836 0101   Fax. 020 7379 4666
www.sarastro-restaurant.com   Email. reservations@sarastro-restaurant.com

Papageno RESTAURANT & BAR
'Where the show goes on for the theatre workers and goers'.

In the heart of Covent Garden's theatreland, Papageno is dedicated to pre and post-theatre dining. Open all day, every day. A la carte menu, or daytime and pre-theatre set menu at £12.50. Live performances from a String Quartet Sunday afternoon/evening Monday evenings; adhoc appearances happen often!

Available for private functions for 300+ guests, Papageno has one of London's most beautiful rooms with its own private entrance and bar.

"Seeing is believing"

29-31 Wellington Street, London. WC2
Tel. 020 7836 4444   Fax. 020 7836 0011
www.papagenorestaurant.com   Email. reservations@papagenorestaurant.com

World Food Café
International, Classic

    14 Neal's Yard, WC2
    020 7379 0298
    Covent Garden LU (5 min walk)
    Mon-Fri 11.30am-2.30pm, Sat 11.30am-5pm
    Vegan options
    Child friendly

Vegetarian ★★★★★
Taste ★★
Price ££

Vegetarian world food by the plate at this spacious upstairs eaterie over-looking Covent Garden's famous Neal's Yard. An open plan kitchen at the back isn't worth the look, whilst the pine tables with yellow plastic chairs at the front are merely okay – try to snag a window seat with a courtyard view.

On the blackboard are Turkish Mezze, Mexican and West African dishes, Egyptian falafels, Spicy Indian Vegetable Masala and Special Stirfry salad at £6.85 each. No table menus are provided.

Dishes change seasonally and recipes can later be tried at home from their own cookbook: World Food Café by Chris and Carolyn Caldicott (Frances Lincoln, £15).

World Food Café attracts a mixed stew of veggie new-age tourists, local shop and office folk. It has a pleasant enough atmosphere and when I went there recorded vibrant Brazilian music was being played.

The Mexican and Spicy Indian plates taste fine, but rely a bit too heavily on cheap staples such as tortilla crisps and naan rather than the main event ingredients. Likewise, Mango Cheesecake (£3.45) whilst tasting okay, was a small slice topped with foamed cream to make it look bigger. Regrettably, eating here is not great value for money overall, but then it is a great tourist vantage point.

World Food Café

MARYLEBONE, MAYFAIR & BAKER STREET

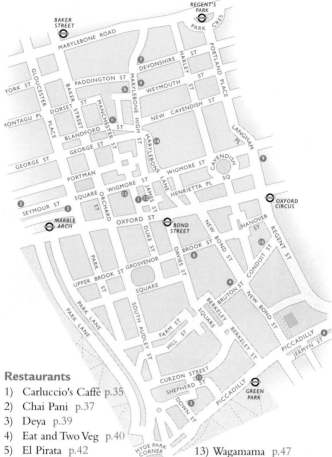

Restaurants

1) Carluccio's Caffè p.35
2) Chai Pani p.37
3) Deya p.39
4) Eat and Two Veg p.40
5) El Pirata p.42
6) Getti Jermyn St p.42
7) Getti Marylebone High St p.43
8) Gordon Ramsay at Claridges p.43
9) Özer Oxford Circus p.44
10) Sketch p.45
11) Sofra Mayfair p.46
12) Sofra Oxford Street p.46
13) Wagamama p.47
14) Woodlands p.47

Shops

a) Stella McCartney p.227
b) Total Organics p.227
c) Marylebone
   Farmers' Market p.275

This section covers some of the smartest shopping areas in London and includes equally smart restaurants such as Carluccio's Caffè and Gordon Ramsay at Claridges. If your budget is more modest there are plenty of alternatives including the great value Eat and Two Veg and Wagamama.

Carluccio's Caffè

Carluccio's Caffè
Italian, Classic

⌨ *St Christopher's Place, W1*
☎ *020 7935 5927*
🚇 *Bond Street LU (2 min walk)*
🕐 *Mon-Fri 8am-11pm, Sat 9-11pm, Sun 10am-10pm*
🥕 *Vegan options*
🍼 *Child friendly*
☀ *Outside seating*
i *Outside catering (tel 0207 629 0699), booking advised in evenings*

Vegetarian ★★★
Taste ★★★★
Price ££

This prime-positioned buzzy Italian restaurant café serves several well-crafted, value for money, vegetarian choices. It is the flagship of the popular chain of cafés conceived by superstar chef Antonio Carluccio and his wife Priscilla.

It's ideal for summertime outside eating, bar the occasional guest appearances from the local pigeon community. Inside the ground floor window tables give good views, downstairs offers eye candy at the bustling bar.

By 8pm it's crammed to the rafters with a 40 minute wait for non-reservations. Service is on the ball. Just mention that you're a vegetarian and the waiting staff will rattle off all the options and specials. The Caffè is popular with female diners (who tend to outnumber the guys by about three to one) and it's a great place for get togethers, with the highly gluggable Gavi di Gavi being the white wine of choice.

Antipasto di vendure, an Italian veggie starter is a sumptuous affair of roasted peppers, pesto, green beans, roasted tomatoes and olives. The savoury bread tin (£2.85) is best split between at least two. The Bruschetta is recommended with its delicious tomatoes with oregano and basil.

Egg Pappadelle with Wild Mushrooms as a main course is a perfect pasta/mushroom ensemble as expected from Carluccio, a world expert on mushroom dishes. I can vouch for the Calzone Imbottito, a fantastic deep fried pastry stuffed with peppers, spinach, aubergine and cheese. I loved it even without the recommended green salad. Pesche All'ammareto dessert is a fascinating big bright red peach half marinated in Dolcetto wine served with amaretti pureé with vanilla cream and a small amaretti biscuit. The ice cream is suitable for veggies, however the Panna Cotta contains gelatine and is not.

The caffè also serves wholesome basic breakfasts of muesli, yogurts, breads and eggs. The most expensive item on the menu is the Trasporti Piaggo Vespa (£1650), a fully automatic scooter imported from Italy!

Chai Pani

Rajasthani, Classic

🖃 *64 Seymour Street, W1*

☎ *020 7258 2000*

🚇 *Marble Arch LU (5 min walk)*

🕒 *Open daily: lunch 12noon-2.30pm, tea 3pm-5pm,*
dinner 6pm-10.30pm

🍴 *Child friendly*

Vegetarian ★★★★★
Taste ★★★★
Price £££££

Chai Pani

Point your camel to London's very own desert dining experience and take your tastebuds to India's 'Land of the Princes' at this luxurious North West Indian restaurant. Surrounded by Edgware Road's meaty Lebanese eateries this oasis of vegetarianism opened in September 2003 and is recommended. The cooking here is Maheshwari which shuns even garlic and onion foods in the belief that they excite the blood.

37

This themed restaurant has white walls representing the desert sand, camel shaped stools in the reception area, scenic Rajasthani pictures, puppets and a hookah pipe adorning the walls. Downstairs there's more dining space. Service is exceedingly gracious and attentive with serving staff decked out in spectacularly colourful Rajasthani regalia.

A set menu is posted outside the restaurant and changes daily. It's a banquet served at your table with as many replenishments as you like. No prices are printed inside the restaurant other than the drinks but budget for around £25 per head for food. On the table is a list of what you'll get but the staff can offer dietary alternatives if you telephone in advance. Everything is explained as it is served up. Dining is refined finger food-style although knives and forks are supplied. Peak time is 9.30pm when the restaurant fills with a mix of Indian, Brit and Euro foodies.

Traditionally, Rajasthanis don't drink alcohol with their meals but most diners here do. The wine list is international plus the usual Cobra lager but why not be adventurous and opt for the non-alcoholic options, a Rose Lassi perhaps or their delicious Rajasthani cocktail speciality, Sand Dune, thandai (milk with saffron, dried fruits and nuts) with amaretto.

A complementary Rose Sherbert arrives first, a smooth rose flowered syrup in water. The classic starter Dal Baati Churma of small hot bread rolls that you dip in dhal and then sugar is delicious and merits a couple of refills.

The main event is an array of small dishes presented Thali-style. Particularly good is the Potato with Pumpkin and the Urad Kahoori, a warm sweet pancake bread. The ginger mango chutney was intensely flavoured while the Sabu Dana Vada was a heavenly rice and lentil combination, accompanied by a cooling yogurty Lauki raita. The Guar Phali salad is strong tasting but small as are the spicy papadoms. The Malpua dessert is intensely sweet and also comes on the Thali along with everything else. Finish with the Masala Chai, a spicy milk tea or heavily fragranced Indian Coffee.

Deya Bar and Restaurant
Indian, Modern

Vegetarian ★★★★
Taste ★★★★★
Price *££££*

🖃 *34 Portman Square, W1*
☎ *020 7224 0028*
🚌 *Marble Arch LU (5 min walk)*
🕐 *Lunch served Mon-Fri 12noon-2.45pm, dinner served 6pm-11pm*
🍴 *Vegan options*

Quite simply the best Indian Vegetarian Tasting Menu in London. Deya opened in June 2004 and it's a classy affair as you would expect from Claudio Pulze, Raj Sharma and Sir Michael Caine. The service is excellent and the restaurant itself is located in a Grade II listed building with elegant decorative plastered ceiling and modern lighting sculptures. The busy bar is bright with painted Indian motifs and at back of house is a large party table with an impressive chandelier above. Diners come casually dressed and the restaurant is almost packed at 9pm.

The Vegetarian Tasting Menu by Head Chef, Sanjay Dwivedi of Zaika fame, is a five courser with three extra in-between treats. My meal began with mini-papadoms and four superb chutneys of mango, tomato, aubergine and hot spicy pickle. The next pre-meal treats were three different tasty Indian cheese hors d'hoeuves on a small bed of chutney. The first course was a tiny cup of Cauliflower Soup with fennel seeds with a side plate of minute Crispy Cauliflower fritters. Next, a clever Grilled Aubergine dish with cheese and bursting with flavours of chilli, ginger and red onions topped with a tomato chutney. The delicious Mixed Vegetable Dumpling came as two tiny almost mock sausages but 'Indian-style' with greens, cheese and smoked pine kernels with savoury sauce and rice. Then the best Vegetable Thali in London arrived and despite feeling almost full the exquisite display of flavours drove us through this platter of green beans, sugar snaps, exemplary black lentils, delicious cumin flavoured roast potato pieces, saffron rice, excellent raita and a mini-naan. The finale, Silky Chocolate and Caramelised Nuts, is a small delicately light chocolate mousse tower with a cluster of pine, cashew and pistachio nuts at its base accompanied by an intense mint ice cream.

The Tasting Menu is excellent value at £22 and a further £10 buys you four matched glasses of wine although unfortunately these are not vegetarian. The Head Chef's interest in healthy vegetarian cuisine informs the cooking at Deya, such as the way traditional ghee has been replaced by healthier monosaturate olive oils. The Tasting Menu is to be highly commended also for its sheer variety of flavours and careful matching of ingredients. A superb dining experience.

Eat and Two Veg
Mock Carnivore, American Diner-style

Organic ★★★★★
Vegetarian ★★★★★
Taste ★★★★
Price £L

🖂 *50 Marylebone High Street, W1*
☎ *020 7258 8599*
🚇 *Baker Street LU (4 min walk)*
🕐 *Mon-Fri 8am-11pm, Sat 9am-11pm and Sun 10am-10pm*
🌶 *Vegan options*
🍼 *Child friendly*
i *Booking advisable at weekends*

One of the hippest vegetarian and organic restaurants in London, this well-designed modern New York-diner style eaterie serves incredibly good soya burger sandwiches, classic English and Italian dishes. Run by Philipp Nagel and David Krantz of Racing Green and Blazer menswear fame, the joint is big, the atmosphere fast, the diners exuberant.

At the windowed front is a small bar with high stools and a few tables serving 13 pre-meal cocktails, four non-alcoholics and a choice of smoothies. Further inside, there's a tireless open kitchen, metal ceiling plumbing, exposed brickwork, good size tables and a row of red leather banquettes, the best seats in the house.

The menu is bold, well-explained, changes every 2 months and tries to use organic and GM free products across the board. The average cost per head is £25 with drinks and the service, courtesy of the t-shirted young waiting staff, is hyper-attentive.

No less than eight salads are on offer here and the Not Nicoise is recommended. In starter portion size it's still big and comes with marinated organic tofu, tiny pieces of avocado, leaves, green beans, potatoes, delicious capers and a free range organic hard boiled egg. Pan-fried Polenta is a very comfortable sized opener and is topped with button mushrooms and sun-blushed tomatoes in pesto red wine sauce with melted cheese. The EatV Burger is highly recommended and has the wow-factor, it looks just like a real chargrilled burger meal with a decent sesame bun, caramelised onions, tomatoes, lettuce and matchstick french fries – the best mock burger in London.

There are 10 main courses with English stalwarts such as Lancashire Hot Pot, Sausage and Mash and a Shepherd's Pie that's indistinguishable from the real thing and delicious.

The vegan Seasonal Fruit Crumble with berries, rhubarb and thin soya custard is unfortunately not so good but the Tiramisu, a biscuity dessert with coffee liqueur and Malibu cream cheese, arrives in a short sundae glass and slides down well.

Eat and two Veg has been voted one of the Best Five Breakfasts in London by Time Out so it's a no surprise that Sunday breakfasts here are busy with locals reading the Sunday papers. The front bar is quite good for anytime drinks and features four vegetarian wines while the Siete Sole white and red wines are vegan.

Located virtually opposite the restaurant is a Waitrose store for diners wishing to stock up on organic produce but for those who really can't get enough, plans are afoot to open another Eat and Two Veg in Canary Wharf and Westbourne Grove.

Eat and Two Veg

El Pirata
Spanish Tapas

Vegetarian ★★★
Taste ★★★★
Price ££

🖃 *5-6 Down Street, Mayfair, W1*
☎ *020 7491 3810*
🚇 *Hyde Park Corner LU (5 min walk)*
🕘 *Mon-Fri 12noon-11.30pm, Sat 6pm-11.30pm*
☀ *Outside seating*
i *Evening booking advisable*

El Pirate offers good value for money Spanish tapas up a backstreet in super expensive Mayfair. The place oozes relaxed joyful charm. The walls are patriotically festooned with Picasso and Miró prints and there's a good bar on the right hand side as you go in. The ground floor is the most popular although I like the modern basement with large tables for parties and secret alcoves for romantics. At mid afternoon, a vegetarian can drink and snack pleasantly cocooned in the Pirate's relaxed ambience, although at night the atmosphere can be manic.

The menu is well explained and there is a separate vegetarian section of 10 tapas. In addition there are veggie choices on the starter menu such as grilled wild asparagus or gazpacho soup. Six tapas choices between two people should be enough. There are four organic wines.

Enjoyable vegetarian dishes include Berenjena Jarniera (aubergine stuffed with veg and topped with cheese) and the chick peas, baby spinach and raisins. Tortilla here is excellent and the cous cous salad is also recommended.

The set lunch menu represents good value and comprises two tapas, bread with alioli and a glass of wine or soft drink for £8. This menu has six vegetarian choices.

Getti Jermyn Street
Italian, Modern

Vegetarian ★★★
Taste ★★★★
Price £££

🖃 *16/17 Jermyn Street, SW1*
☎ *020 7734 7334*
🚇 *Piccadilly LU (2 min walk)*
🕘 *Mon-Sat, lunch 12am-3pm, dinner 6pm-11pm*

Modern Italian restaurant well located for pre- and post-theatre meals and those wonderful Jermyn Street menswear shops. Friendly service is a feature here and the upstairs sports some good views over Jermyn Street. See Getti, Marylebone High Street for food review (page 43).

Getti Marylebone High Street
Italian, Modern

Vegetarian ★★★
Taste ★★★★
Price £££

🖃 *42 Marylebone High Street, W1*
☎ *020 7486 3753*
🚌 *Baker Street LU (10 min walk)*
🕒 *Mon-Sat 12noon-3pm, 6pm-11pm*
🥕 *Vegan options*
🍼 *Child friendly*
☀ *Outside seating*

With Sicilian and Sardinian influences, Getti serves a choice of simple but high quality classic Italian vegetarian dishes with modern twists in a chic upscale venue.

Inside, it's cruiseliner décor. White and blue walls with smart cherry wood tables and porthole windows want you to believe that you are sailing around Lake Como (from whence the owner's family, Fraqueli, come from). Downstairs are some alcoves perfect for a romantic evening for two. In the centre of the dining room there's ample room for big parties. On the ground level there's further seating and outside tables too.

There are four vegetarian antipasti of which the buffalo mozarella, roasted plum tomatoes with basil and olive oil is very good. Getti has a reputation for making good risotto and their Risotto with Wild Mushrooms and Chives will not disappoint. Penne pasta with tomato and mozzarella is of equally good quality.

If you're in the market for a bargain, Getti does a set menu meal deal: two courses £14.50, three courses £17.50 plus 12.5% optional gratuity. See also Getti, Jermyn Street (page 42).

Gordon Ramsay at Claridges
European, Modern

Vegetarian ★★★
Price £££££

🖃 *Claridges Hotel, Brook Street, W1*
☎ *020 7499 0090*
🚌 *Bond Street LU (5 min walk)*
🕒 *Mon-Fri 12noon-2.45pm & 5.45pm-11pm,*
   Sat 12noon-3pm & 5.45pm-11pm, Sun 12noon-3pm & 6pm-10pm
ℹ *Booking advised*

Some top notch vegetarian dishes are on the menu at TV celebrity chef Gordon Ramsay's opulent Art Deco restaurant in the world famous Claride's Hotel. The atmosphere here of an evening is pleasantly exuberant and as you walk through the elegant foyer you'll hear live piano music wafting over from the hotel lounge where guests linger over their afternoon tea or sip champagne. Towards the right of the lounge can be found the bar to Gordon Ramsay's restaurant, perfect for pre-meal drinks and canapés. Tell the maître d' that you are vegetarian and he'll give you the special vegetarian menu with a choice of three vegetarian starters, three main courses and a choice of desserts.

From the bar you enter an impressive spacious dining room hung with long lanterns. Starters may include a grilled asparagus salad with grated black truffle or white onion and garlic sauce with sautéed wild mushrooms. Mains tend to be Italian with dished like broad bean and onion risotto, chervil and mushroom tagliatelle pasta and a braised and roasted vegetable selection with tomato and herb vinaigrette.

Three courses in the evening cost £55 whilst the same at lunch will set you back a very reasonable £30.

Özer Oxford Circus
Turkish, Classic

Vegetarian ★★★
Taste ★★★
Price (buffet) £
(à la carte) ££

🖃 5 Langham Place, W1
☎ 020 7323 0505
🚌 Oxford Circus LU (4 min walk)
🕓 Open all year 12noon-12midnight
🥕 Vegan options
🍼 Child friendly
☀ Outside seating
i Booking advised

A buzzy upscale Turkish restaurant serving a bargain buffet with good vegetarian choices. The front of house bar area is a busy low-seated cushioned affair sprawled out with regulars, some from the BBC next door, and serves snacks, whilst the main tableclothed evening dining area is at the back. For a Turkish eaterie it's quite modern and spacious, dark and moody with a sophisticated sculptured ceiling.

The help yourself, eat-as-much-as-you-like buffet (£6, 12noon-7pm, £8 after 7pm) runs to a real three course blow-out and is excellent value for the West End.

The classic vegetarian hot and cold mezzes are right on the money particularly the Börek, a delicious feta cheese and spinach filled filo. Falafel, hummous and flat bread are also good. To finish there are three desserts such as fruit salad, Baklava and Sutlak, a rice pudding. Helpful staff are on hand if you are unsure which dishes are pure veggie. The buffet, however, is only available in the winter though the à la carte, served throughout the year, is still good value and offered at all sister branches of Özer and Sofra.

The à la carte is served till midnight with cold veggie mezzes such as Tabbouleh, Mutabel, Lentil Köfte (lentil balls with onion, olive oil and herbs) whilst the hot mezzes include Patlican Kizartma (fried aubergine and green pepper with a thick tomato sauce). Three vegetarian mains are on offer: Silk Route, a mediterranean mixed-veg stir fry with rice, Spinach and Leek, a dish of baby spinach and leek stewed with baby potatoes and a Vegetarian Moussaka. Özer, however, will convert their carnivore dishes to vegetarian if you ask. About 20% of their diners are vegetarian and they are used to serving big parties of diners where some are pure vegetarians.

Özer Oxford Circus is the flagship of the Sofra chain whose sister restaurants are Sofra Mayfair (page 46), Sofra Covent Garden (page 29), Sofra St Christopher's Place (page 46), Sofra Exmouth Market (page 91), and Sofra St John's Wood (page 148).

Sketch

European, Modern

Organic ★★★
Vegetarian ★★★
Price £££££

🖳 9 Conduit Street, W1
☎ 0870 777 4488
🚎 Oxford Circus LU (5 min walk)
🕐 Tue-Sat 12noon-2pm, 7pm-10.30pm
🥕 Vegan options
i Booking essential

Splash the cash with the Vegetarian Tasting Menu at London's most expensive and possibly most innovatively designed gastronomic destination. The lobby displays modern art pieces and the bathrooms are encrusted with crystals. The menu changes seasonally and has a good selection of vegetarian dishes.

The six course menu at £65 begins with fresh garden vegetables in a lemon balm jelly, a seasonal salad dressed in fine Sicilian olive oil and braised honey turnips followed by Paimpol Beans cooked in sage, served with a slice of roasted tomato and Romanesco cabbage. Organic produce is used where possible and sourced from suppliers in England, France and Peru. Portion sizes are fairly substantial throughout the menu but will leave you comfortable without feeling overfed. Dishes can be partnered by a selection of vegan wines from £24.50 per bottle.

Finish on a dessert of preserved red peppers in a lemon syrup, Scandinavian drink flavoured sorbet, raspberry coulis and dried black olives. Forget your bank account and savour the fabulousness of the Sketch experience.

Sofra Mayfair
Turkish, Classic

Vegetarian ★★★
Taste ★★★
Price ££

18 Shepherd Street, W1

020 7493 3320

Green Park LU (5 min walk)

Daily 12noon-12.30am (last orders 11pm)

See Özer Oxford Circus for food review (page 44).

Sofra Oxford Street
Turkish, Classic

Vegetarian ★★★
Taste ★★★★
Price £

1 St Christopher's Place, W1

020 7224 4480

Bond Street LU (2 min walk)

Daily 12noon-12.30am (last orders 11pm)

This branch has good outside seating on St Christopher's Place precinct. See Özer Oxford Circus for food review (page 44).

Sofra

Wagamama

Japanese, Modern

▭ *101a Wigmore Street, W1*
☎ *020 7409 0111*
🚌 *Marble Arch LU (5 min walk)*
◷ *Mon-Sat 12noon-11pm, Sun 12.30pm-10pm*
✦ *Vegan options*

Vegetarian ★★★★★
Taste ★★★★
Price £

Excellent value for money, modern, noodle eaterie. Located in a brightly lit basement. It's just a short stroll from swanky department store Selfridges and the upscale boutiques of St Christopher's Place.

Outside, queues of youthful dressed down urbanites wait to be assigned seating and it gets especially busy around the manic 7–8pm slot. Inside the décor is beige 'n' benches minimalist. The menu is informative with 12 vegetarian dishes. Waitpersons with hand-held computers radiosignal your orders to the kitchen and before you know it, your food's on the table.

A noodle or rice dish and a side order leaves you full which is just as well as there are no starters or desserts here. Moyashi Soba, a vegetable soup with noodles and courgettes; and stir fried tofu with ramen noodles and spring onions are both heartwarming and satisfying. Alternatively, try a Yasai Cha Han, an egg fried rice and tofu dish with snow peas, sweetcorn and mushrooms alongside a veggie miso soup. A side order of the Yasai Gyoza, grilled vegetable dumplings filled with cabbage, carrots and served with chilli garlic soy sauce is substantial and a great accompaniment to your meal.

Wagamama is a great concept – enjoyable Japanese noodle dishes at bargain prices. They've also a raw food juice selection for health foodies. For those venturing outside W1, there are branches in Bloomsbury (see page 15) and Camden (see page 121).

Woodlands

South Indian, Classic

▭ *77 Marylebone Lane, W1*
☎ *020 7486 3862*
🚌 *Marble Arch LU (5 min walk)*
◷ *Daily 12noon-3pm, 6pm-11pm*
✦ *Vegan options*

Vegetarian ★★★★★
Taste ★★★★
Price £££

There's fine vegetarian dining at this classic-style Indian restaurant, the first of the Woodlands chain to open in London. See the review for Woodlands, Chiswick (page 179) for the same menu.

SOHO

Restaurants

1) Beatroot p.49
2) Country Life p.51
3) Eateas p.52
4) Govinda's Vegetarian Restaurant p.55
5) Joi p.55
6) Leon p.56
7) Maoz p.56
8) Mildreds p.57
9) Pizza Express Dean St p.59
10) Plant p.59
11) Red Veg p.61
12) Soho Thai p.61
13) Tai Buffet, Chapel St p.63
14) Tai Buffet, Greek St p.63
15) Tai Buffet, Goodge St p.63
16) Thai Square p.63

Shops

a) Country Life p.228
b) Fresh & Wild p.228
c) Peppercorns p.229

Great eating places can be found in London's night-life area famed for its night-clubs, hip bars, music venues and red light strip joints. Daytime, check out the unique boutiques. Plant, Mildreds, and RedVeg are vegetarian trailblazers with great world-food at Beatroot, bargain Indian at Govinda's, falafels (and french fries!) at Maoz and takeaway salads at Eateas. In the evening, Pizza Express on Dean Street offers great veggie pizzas often accompanied with live jazz.

Beatroot
International

▦ *92 Berwick Street, W1*
☎ *020 7437 8591*
🚌 *Tottenham Court Road LU (10 min walk)*
🕐 *Mon-Sat 9am-9pm*
🌱 *Vegan options*
◊ *Child friendly*
☀ *Outside seating*
i *Counter service*

Organic ★★★
Vegetarian ★★★★★
Taste ★★★
Price £

It's vegetarian-to-go at this popular street-wise café bang in Soho's thriving Berwick Street fruit 'n' veg market. The meal-deal is a pick 'n' mix in a box based around a choice of ten hot dishes and nine cold salads and is good value at £3.15 (small), £4.15 (medium) and £5.15 (large). Food is laid out canteen style and servers are pretty helpful. Wised-up diners, however, first get the day's menu sheet by the till that explains all.

The love it or hate it interior is bright orange and green with some plants. Seating is mostly wooden bench-style more functional than comfortable so grab one of the regular tables instead if possible. Lunchtimes get crowded with a mix of local market traders, media types, and tourists.

Food is served in a cardboard box with plastic fork, fine for takeout but a bit mean for eating in. Nevertheless, lunchers munch delightedly despite the diverse dish choices running into each other in the box. Evening is more chilled except Fridays when post 6pm it revs up with out of towners mooching around for pre-night-on-the-town cheap eats. That said, I went past on a Monday night and it was packed.

The Dal Curry and Organic Rice has good flavour, the spicy Moroccan Veg Tagine is even better whilst falafels, veggie sausage and broccoli are fine. Whilst my medium-size world food box left me satis-fyingly stuffed, most people seemed to be grazing contentedly on the

Large. My lunch partner's Tofu Stir-fry was delicious as was the big splodge of a Spanish Omelette. Beatroot is to be applauded for their original recipes on a tight budget and is 30% organic. Homemade cakes, several vegan, are highly inviting.

Beatroot

Country Life
International

🖼 *3-4 Warwick Street, W1*

☎ *020 7434 2922*

🚇 *Piccadilly LU (5 min walk)*

🕐 *Sun-Thur 11.30am-4pm, Fri 11.30am-2.30pm,*
   Mon-Thur evenings 6pm-9.30pm

🖊 *Child friendly*

Organic ★★★★★
Vegetarian ★★★★★
Taste ★★
Price £

Pleasant basement vegan restaurant connected to the 7th Day Adventist movement. Expect to see thin anorak clad diners grazing on greens, devout Adventists (one family come every Thursday for their weekly dine-out treat), as well as veggie tourists doing the Regents Street/Piccadilly shopping drag and local office workers all with plates piled high with salad and hot buffet concoctions. Maurice, himself a vegetarian since 1987, manages the eaterie and gives out information leaflets to people after they pay the bill. "It's about a philosophy of lifestyle and a concept to educate people" explains an enthusiastic Maurice. "The food is about 50% organic but were it not for costs it would be 100%. The greens, cereal, rice, beans and soya are organic but not the tomatoes, carrots and broccoli because of the costs."

The place itself is canteen style with wooden chairs, floral prints on the walls and soft Andalusian pipe music.

Evenings feature an eat as much as you like buffet for £7 and diners pile their plates sky high. Not so at lunchtime, where one pays by weight (11p for 10g), the average plate coming out £3.50-£7. Desserts and drinks are extra as is the freshly baked organic bread. On the salad station, the fave salads include Quinoa Salad and the Bulghar Wheat Salad both quite good and a vegan Waldorf Salad (so-so). On the hot deck, Tofu and Pinto Bean Casserole with mixed herbs, cornflour, paprika, garlic and olive oil was passable, however, being a buffet some dishes such as the Stuffed Peppers filled with Couscous were not warm enough.

The speciality dessert is Banana Carobella a vegan dessert of banana, carob and vanilla granola (£1.80) although the Chocolate Cappuccino Cheesecake made from Tofutti and the fresh fruit salad also goes down well. Organic tea and canned drinks are available. Filtered water is free.

Country Life is a good place to meet other vegans and vegetarians although there are religious overtones to the place. At street level they have a well-stocked shop (see page 228).

Eateas

International, Classic

🖷 *173 Wardour Street, W1*
☎ *020 7434 0373*
🚇 *Tottenham Court Road LU (5 min walk)*
🕓 *Breakfast Mon-Fri 7.30am-11am, Buffet lunch 11am-4pm*
i *Eat in (buffet service) & Takeaway*

Vegetarian ★★★★
Taste ★★★
Price £

Bargain help-yourself salad bar and hot station where veggie Soho folk stuff as much as they can in a box for £2.75. Opened in September 2003 as Eatsies it has changed name several times and is now known as Eateas. Eatsies, began life as a omnivore takeout and did not do well, switching to vegetarian helped business to really pick up and the rest they say is history. Eateas still does some non-vegetarian fish salad options and some sandwiches but otherwise it's full steam ahead with 70 different veggie buffet.choices and the customers love it.

Eateas is a big bright modern takeout sitting on the corner of D'Arblay and Wardour Street and although breakfast kicks in at 9am, manic feeding time is between one and three. Customers are adept at filling their boxes in a structured way so as to have a few scoops of a salad starter, a small samosa perhaps, some hot main and enough room for fresh fruit salad dessert. The day I went they were also throwing in a free apple.

Half the selection is hot and those I had were reasonably warm. Vegetable Noodle, and the Mushroom Noodle in hoisin sauce is fairly good as is the Coconut Curry. There are some decent chunky flavour-some mushrooms here and the vegetable rice dishes are good. The warm Penne Pasta with Sundried Tomato is great value and tasty. The Cauliflower Bake with a veggie cheese sauce and broccoli is very reasonable. Bombay Aloo, a spicy potato dish is also worth a try.

Eateas aims to serve delicious vegetarian dishes at affordable prices and does so successfully. The salad bar's eclectic mix includes couscous, potato and vegetable salads, a veggie Waldorf and Mexican rices.

Eateas

Govindas

54

Govinda's Vegetarian Restaurant
Indian and International, Classic

Vegetarian ★★★★★
Taste ★
Price £

⌂ *9 Soho Street, W1*
☎ *020 7437 4928*
🚇 *Tottenham Court Road LU (5 min walk)*
🕐 *Mon-Sat, 12noon-8pm*
🌱 *Vegan options*
🍸 *Unlicensed*
i *Counter service*

Old-style 100% vegetarian cuisine in friendly but blandly decorated Hare Krishna canteen. A stone's throw from bustling Soho Square, this eaterie tends to be peopled by tranquil diners, meditatively grazing on their food. The jewel in Govinda's crown is its £4.99 Indian Buffet from 12noon to 7pm which drops to a mind-boggling £3.99 after 7pm. Typically, it's mixed veg, brown rice or white basmati rice, lentil soup, bean hot pot, fresh green salad accompanied by plain roll and papadom. The whole ensemble doesn't look very appetising but it has its followers who eat there regularly. For those wanting just a lite-bite, vegetable fritter, baked potato and the ubiquitous veggie burger feature on the main course list.

Govinda's offers a dozen desserts, mainly western style such as lemon or apple pie, cheesecake and flapjack although they do laddhu, a tasty Indian sweet chick-pea and butter fudge recipe or burfi, a creamy fudge. Coffee here is only decaff and quite unlikeable so it's probably better to opt for the herbal tea or the lassi (a traditional Indian yogurt drink).

Joi
Thai/Chinese

Vegetarian ★★★★★
Taste ★★★
Price £

⌂ *14 Percy Street, W1*
☎ *020 7323 0981*
🚇 *Goodge Street LU (5 min walk)*
🕐 *Daily 12noon-10pm*
🌱 *Vegan menu*
i *Eat in (buffet service) & Takeaway*

One of the bigger venues of this ever-growing fast food Thai chain offering bargain all-you-can-eat vegan cuisine for £5. The most popular dish here is the mock crispy duck, but for a full food review see Tai Buffet (Camden branch) page 120.

Leon
Mediterranean and English Fast Food

	Organic ★★★
	Vegetarian ★★★
	Price £

🖼 *35 Great Marlborough Street, W1*
☎ *020 7437 5280*
🚇 *Oxford Circus LU (5 min walk)*
🕐 *Mon-Fri 7.30am-11pm, Sat 9.30am-11pm, Sun 10.30am-6pm*
🌶 *Vegan options*
🍼 *Child friendly*
☀ *Outside seating*
i Eat in & Takeaway

Opened in July 2004 this natural fast food eaterie and takeaway has organic leanings with several vegetarian Mediterranean mezzes, salads, hot and cold vegetarian breakfasts, English fruit salad, smoothies and organic coffee.

The menu indicates V for vegetarian choices but confusingly ignores salmon, tuna and white fish dishes that also get the V-symbol. That said, Leon is a competent set up with dishes developed by Allegra McEvedy recipe writer on The Evening Standard and former chef at the Good Cook in Kensington. Leon is passionate about organic food and its principles. There are plans to include more organic items as pricing becomes more competitive.

Maoz
Vegetarian Falafel Café

	Vegetarian ★★★★★
	Taste ★★★
	Price £

🖼 *43 Old Compton Street, W1*
☎ *020 7851 1586*
🚇 *Tottenham Court Road LU (10 min walk)*
🕐 *Mon-Thur 11am-1am, Fri-Sat 11am-2am, Sun 11am-12midnight*
☀ *Outside seating*
i Eat in (counter service) & Takeaway

Soho's falafel hangout. It's a small nondescript place with a mixed bunch crowded at the tables and grazing folk standing around. New initiates get cheap kicks with the £2.50 falafels, moving on to big bowls of Belgian chips for sharing. I joined the chickpea mainliners with a £3.50 falafel with hummous in nutritious wholewheat pitta, a quality experience that left my tastebuds satisfied. It comes already part filled with veg and then it's over to you to top up and experiment from a varied salad station of cous cous, coleslaw, carrot, tomato, pickled cucumber, chillis and sauces.

Mildreds
European, Modern

Organic ★★
Vegetarian ★★★★★
Taste ★★★
Price ££

▭ *45 Lexington Street, W1*
☎ *020 7494 1634*
🚌 *Oxford Circus LU (10 min walk)*
🕐 *Mon-Sat, 12noon-11pm*
🥕 *Vegan and wheat-free options*
i *Lunchtime takeaway service*
  Credit cards not accepted

A busy, inexpensive restaurant with the best vegetarian private dining room in London. Originally set in the heart of Soho's filmland, Mildreds is aptly named after the waitress Mildred Pierce, the iconic character played by Joan Crawford in the film of the same name. Mildreds now resides at larger premises on Lexington Street but is as popular as ever. The no bookings policy means that by 7pm you're likely to be in for a twenty minute wait for a table. Front of house is a small nondescript bar serving well described organic wines suitable for vegetarians. Skip the so-so house red and plump for the more flavoursome and rewarding Merlot instead.

At the back, the dining room is bright and airy, with modern abstract photos on the walls, a few green plants and pleasant background music. The punters are a gossipy crowd of 20 and 30 something media types in smart-casual dress, who like to dine with wine.

Stir-fried Vegetables in sesame oil and teriyaki sauce are crispily cooked with garlic and ginger and come with tasty organic brown rice. The Masa Harina, a wrap of smoked cheddar cakes, maize and butternut squash with a hot harissa side sauce is also highly enjoyable. Vegeburgers are firm favourites here and there are usually other mock-carnivore dishes such as tofu bolognaise. A completely organic salad with goat's cheese or organic tofu is available.

Upstairs the gracious chandeliered private dining room with small old photos of naked women on the walls (well, it is Soho) makes a great venue for a party and Mildreds will also help plan your own special party menu. Well worth checking out.

Mildreds

Pizza Express Dean Street

Italian, Fast Food

  🖃 *10 Dean Street, W1*
  ☎ *020 7437 9595*
  🚌 *Tottenham Court Road LU (5 min walk)*
  🕒 *Daily 11.30am-Midnight*
  🥕 *Vegan options*
  🎵 *Live jazz music nightly*

Vegetarian ★★★
Taste ★★★
Price £

Very popular modern pizza venue in the bustling Soho district. The lunchtime atmosphere here is relaxed with an amiable mix of TV/film folk and West End shoppers. This branch of Pizza Express famously features a live Jazz club in the evenings and the Jazz Room is open 365 days a year. For bookings and information on their great jazz evenings telephone 020 7439 8722.

Part of a big pizza chain (see the High Street Chain chapter, page 273 for further details).

Plant

International, Modern

  🖃 *47 Poland Street, W1*
  ☎ *020 7734 7528*
  🚌 *Tottenham Court Road LU (5 min walk)*
  🕒 *Café: Mon-Thur 8am-11pm, Fri 8am-7pm, Sun 12noon-9pm*
    Restaurant: Lunch Mon-Fri 12noon-3.30pm;
    Dinner Mon-Thur 5.30pm-11pm, Sat 6pm-11pm
  🍸 *Alcohol-free zone*
  🥕 *Vegan and wheat-free options*
  i *Counter service in café & table service in restaurant*

Organic ★★★
Vegetarian ★★★★★
Taste ★★
Price ££

Veggie heaven at this crisp upscale restaurant, a runner up in the Vegetarian Society's awards for Best Restaurant and Café 2003. At front of house is a snazzy high-stooled café serving gourmet breakfasts including: organic scrambled eggs, toasted tomato bread and Plant's own seasoned baked beans. Amongst the lite bites, there's a notable mock chicken caesar sandwich, various wraps and four salad trays. The milk, eggs and tofu are all organic as are the fruit and veg on a where possible basis.

Situated at the back, the restaurant is serene, light and voluminous. Its likeable appearance is complemented by some really interesting vegetarian dishes. The starter of savoury Caribbean Fried Dumplings had a good firm texture and were delicious with a hot chilli sauce whilst the Asparagus Salad, usually a tasty safe bet anywhere, came served a little over-chilled. Other starters include grilled marinated tofu crostini and pitta dips that are popular with the regulars.

Seitan Stroganoff, an innovative and highly satisfying main course dish, is big on mushrooms, and also features an enjoyable herb cashew cream sauce, caramelised onions, red peppers and seitan, a processed type of wheat gluten and useful protein source that imparts a deliciously smoky flavour. East Meets West, a light fusion of Afro-Caribbean and Eastern influences is a delectable dish of okra and chickpeas in an intriguing spicy tomato and coriander sauce and comes with plantain and yam.

On the pudding front, the Vanilla Pancake is filled with a good soya ice cream topped with a warm carob and vanilla sauce. The pancake's spelt flour makes it a little tougher than a normal pancake to eat but nevertheless it's quite reasonable. The homemade Apple Crumble with soya ice cream is better and for vegans an organic pear and nut loaf is available.

Sticking to its guns on health, Plant is a not just a smoke-free zone it's alcohol-free too. Here, the house specialities are smoothies and the top slurp is the Classico, a banana and strawberry mix with a dash of ginger. Non-alcoholic wines seem a hit with the celebratory tables of birthday party crowds and couples. However, more discerning wine drinkers, will be totally unimpressed with the alcohol-free Rosé and Reisling and should go for the juices or organic sparkling drinks instead.

Red Veg

Red Veg
American, Modern Mock Carnivore

Organic ★★
Vegetarian ★★★★★
Taste ★★
Price £

🖃 *95 Dean Street, W1*
☎ *020 7437 3109*
🚌 *Tottenham Court Road LU (5-10 min walk)*
🕘 *Mon-Sat 12noon-10pm*
i *Counter service*

Modern veggie fast food take-out with micro eat-in space. With seating for just 12, Red Veg draws in some of the edgiest pierce-nosed, shaven headed young characters in Soho yet also gets a peppering of straight dressed local workers.

Burgery meal choices are postered on the wall alongside pics of Lenin, Marx and Che Guevara. But don't be deceived, Red Veg is the real deal... it's Veg Society certified, GM-free and strictly vegetarian cheese.

The menu is simple with six burgers from which to choose. The Red Vegburger can come with processed cheese whilst the Hickory Smoked Burger arrives with Monterey Jack cheese. Both efforts are big boys' portions filled with tomato, pickled cucumber and onion. The matchstick french fries, are very good and lunchers on the Noname Nugget boxes and organic falafels seemed content. Wash down with a can of organic raspberry lemonade, or cola – could this be the shape of global fast food veg to come? They've already opened in Brighton...

Soho Thai
Thai, Classic

Vegetarian ★★★
Taste ★★
Price £££

🖃 *27-28 St Anne's Court, W1*
☎ *020 7287 2000*
🚌 *Tottenham Court Road LU (5-10 min walk)*
🕘 *Mon-Sat 12noon-3pm, 6pm-11.30pm*

Ornate pre- and post-theatre Thai restaurant that's part of the Thai Square restaurant group. See food review for Thai Square Trafalgar Square (page 29).

Tai Buffet
Thai, Chinese

Vegetarian ★★★★★
Taste ★★★
Price £

🖳 *3 Chapel Street, W1*
☎ *020 7439 0383*
🚇 *Tottenham Court Road LU (5 min walk)*
🕐 *Daily 12noon-10pm*
🥕 *Vegan menu*
☀ *Outside seating*

For food review see Tai Buffet (Camden branch) page 120.

Tai Buffet
Thai, Chinese

Vegetarian ★★★★★
Taste ★★★
Price £

🖳 *10 Greek St, Soho, W1*
☎ *020 7287 3730*
🚇 *Tottenham Court Road LU (5 min walk)*
🕐 *Daily 12noon-10pm*
🥕 *Vegan menu*

For food review see Tai Buffet (Camden branch) page 120.

Tai Buffet
Thai, Chinese

Vegetarian ★★★★★
Taste ★★★
Price £

🖳 *32 Goodge Street, W1*
☎ *020 7637 4819*
🚇 *Goodge Street LU (2 min walk)*
🕐 *Mon-Thur 12noon-10pm, Fri & Sat 12noon-11pm,*
   Sun 12.30pm-10pm
🥕 *Vegan menu*

For food review see Tai Buffet (Camden branch) page 120. This buffet style eaterie opened early 2003 and offers a Takeout Box deal for £3 with one free beverage for students.

Thai Square
Thai, Classic

Vegetarian ★★★
Taste ★★
Price £££

🖳 *Hanover Square, 5 Princes Street, W1*
☎ *020 7499 3333*
🚇 *Oxford Street LU (1 min walk)*
🕐 *Mon-Sat 12noon-3pm, 6pm-11pm*

Busy in the evenings, quiet at lunchtime. See Thai Square Trafalgar Square for food review (page 29).

SOUTHWARK & WATERLOO

This district is home to Borough Market, London's finest gourmet food market with organic and vegetarian speciality foods and juices at Totally Organic, speciality falafels at Arabica, tarts, cakes and pastries at Artisan Foods, fab tomatoes at Isle of Wight Tomatoes and organic herbs and spices at Herbs from Heaven, Spices from Hell.

Restaurants

1) Borough Market p.64
2) Coopers p.66

Shops

a) Coopers p.229

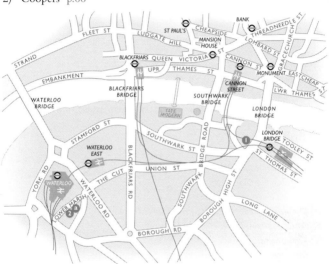

Borough Market

🖳 *8 Southwark Street, SE1*

🚉 *London Bridge LU &Rail (5 min walk)*

🕘 *Fri 12pm-6pm, Sat 9am-4pm*

This gourmet food market is well worth a visit as it offers high quality vegetarian and organic choices.

Total Organics, one of the largest operators in Borough Market, is all organic and vegetarian with as much produce as possible being UK sourced. At the front they sell an organic vegetarian salad box for £4. You point and they neatly fill it up for you. Mine was a bean and chickpeas salad with sliced cucumber in mint sauce, tomato, lettuce, rice and was quite filling, notably fresh but over chilled which diminished some of the flavour. Spanish omelettes are very tempting and they are £1.50 per slice. Further inside Total Organics is a juice bar that does a brisk trade in wheatgrass shots and has a few high stools for perching on. The deli counter has a scrummy array of hummous, pesto and vegetarian pâté and cheeses. There's also a colourful fruit and veg stand and at the far back shelves of pre-packaged food items. Owner Gary Greenland who also does Thursdays at Portobello Market says, "We opened up at Borough Market in 2000 when it was all foods for carnivores. We wanted to give a veggie option. We just started with a fruit and veg stall and it just grew and grew. The customers who come to us don't like supermarkets, they want to come and see what they are eating." Total Organics is a family run business (all vegetarians) and they have recently opened a shop on Marylebone High Street (page 227).

Herbs from Heaven, Spices from Hell, a busy stall is within the Total Organics concession and sells 100% organic certified packeted herbs and spices as well as plants, teas and herbal infusions. Dark Sugars is a vegetarian cake stall with some tempting creations although it is not organic. They also sell at Notting Hill Market on Sundays. Isle of Wight Tomatoes is a specialist fruit stall with organic plum and aranca tomatoes. They are going through a conversion process to get all their tomatoes organically certified.

Borough Market

Amazing looking tarts and quiches, 90% of which are vegetarian, can be found at Artisan Foods. Neal's Yard Dairy have a shop near the market and stock good selections of top notch cheese suitable for vegetarians. Those unsuitable are clearly labelled as having animal rennet. Arabica serves organic falafels and gets very busy with takeaways. Also, in Borough Market is biodynamic vegetable specialist Fern Verrow Vegetables which is certified biodynamic and organic and is run by a family with a smallholding on the Wales-Herefordshire border.

Coopers

Café, International

Vegetarian ★★★★★
Taste ★★
Price £

🖃 *17 Lower Marsh, SE1*
☎ *020 7261 9314*
🚆 , *Lambeth North (5 min walk), Waterloo LU &Rail (5 min walk)*
🕒 *Mon-Fri 8.30am-17.30pm*
🥕 *Vegan options*
i *Eat in (counter service) & Takeaway*

This friendly, family-run neighbourhood snack café has been serving pure veggie wholesome food at Lower Marsh Market for over twenty years. Nowadays the market itself is not up to much and most customers are lunchtime Waterloo Station commuters and office workers although market folk are always frequenting the place.

Coopers offers three different quiches as well as three kinds of savoury tart, all served with salad for £4.25 and soups for only £2.40. Make sure you get there before 3pm after which time most of the best food is gone. Vegan celery and lentil soup is quite reasonable and filling. The pre-packed choices such as the warmed up Vegetarian Spring Roll (hardly any veg inside) are worth a miss whilst the Vegetable and bean wrap is just passable. Instead, make a dive for the attractive, freshly made Organic Tomato and Feta Focaccia with veggie ham and free range egg or the Organic White Baguette with mozzarella, tomato, pesto and basil. Coffee, too, is organic and they do Lavender Orange cake, croissants and notably good scones,

Tip for drivers: car drivers can park after 4pm in the market traders' places for free. For a review of the shop see page 229.

Borough Market

HYDE PARK CORNER, VICTORIA & PIMLICO

With cash to splash in the heart of Central London, Roussillon, Nahm and The Lanesborough are three of the best restaurants in the capital. Next door to the Lanesborough, there's Pizza on the Park for veggie pizzas with a jazz accompaniment. Another excellent veggie culinary experience can be found at City Inn Hotel, home to the City Café where there's veggie gastronomic art on a plate, well it is only a few yards from Tate Britain!

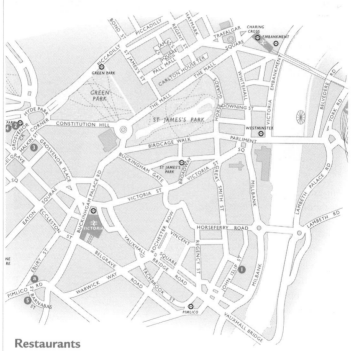

Restaurants

1) City Café p.69
2) The Lanesborough p.71
3) Nahm p.73
4) Pizza on the Park p.74
5) Roussillon p.74

Shops

a) Pimlico Farmers' Market p.276

City Café

International, Modern

🖼 *City Inn Westminster, 30 John Islip Street, SW1*

☎ *020 7932 4600*

🚇 *Pimlico or Westminster LU (10 min walk)*

🕐 *Breakfast Mon-Fri 6.45am-9.30am, Sat 7am-11am, Sun 7am-11am;*
Lunch Mon-Fri 12noon-3pm, Sat-Sun 12.30pm-3pm;
Dinner Mon-Sun 6pm-11.30pm

◊ *Child friendly*

☀ *Outside seating*

Vegetarian ★★★★★
Taste ★★★★
Price *£££*

Ultramodern hotel with slick cool restaurant serving a completely vegetarian menu and well worth popping into after the Tate. Opened in September 2003, it's located on a street off the Embankment at the back of Tate Britain. Art lovers come in along the special 'Side Street' into the restaurant or from the main hotel entrance on John Islip Street.

Al fresco diners spill out onto 'Side Street', the capital's first ever street conceived as a work of art. Created by one of Britain's most acclaimed artists, Susanna Heron, Side Street is 80 metres long and seven metres high and features monumental five metre-high slate engravings, the result of 12 month's carving in Heron's studio. A vast textured mirrored-glass wall reflects light and provides views around the corner and back into the street.

The restaurant is big and the seating area partitioned off for different groups. At 11pm the place is still buzzy and well populated when many other hotel restaurants are thinning out.

The Garden Menu conceived by Bank executive chef Peter Lyons consists of five starters, five mains and seven desserts with top quality complimentary breads to start. Crunchy Asian Salad is a wonderful appetiser and perfect as a midday main for ladies-that-lunch. Its crispy carrots, red and yellow peppers, green beans and mushrooms, mixed with chopped roasted cashews and peanuts in a delicious soy dressing. Several people were picking at that old classic Globe Artichoke, which here comes with a Gribiche dressing of egg, caper and mild vinaigrette and makes a fine light starter.

A most interesting main is the delicious North African Aubergine Ragout with Tomato and Date Chutney. Gnocchi with Wild Mushrooms is of a good standard and comes with garden peas, broad beans, rocket pesto and parmesan shavings. The wine list carries a French Red Syrache organic wine and the water is Llanllyr Source, a spring water drawn from beneath organic fields in South Wales.

Desserts are prepared by Amanda Whittaker formerly of Marco Pierre White's Criterion and include Blackberry Doughnuts with Vanilla Pod Ice Cream topped with a fascinating Apple Compote. The Hot Chocolate Fondant was fantastic – a finale of satanic majesty.

For breakfast, there's soya based vegetable sausages, organic baked beans and free range eggs produced by Bank Farm in accordance with the RSPCA Freedom Food scheme. If you fancy something sweeter to start the day then sample the various cereals, fresh fruit bowls, nuts and seeds or organic maple syrup waffles.

The hotel itself looks like a cross between the latest airport Travelodges and the Malmaison in the Barbican – cool and relaxed post-millennium modern.

Veg out
in City Café

City Café's Garden Menu
dedicated to vegetarian cuisine.

Sample dishes include:
- Grilled Artichoke Heart with French Beans, Capers and Tarragon Dressing
- Tibetan Buckwheat and Spinach Roast with Grilled Asparagus and Haloumi Cheese

www.citycafe.co.uk
westminster.citycafe@cityinn.com

tel 020 7932 4600

30 John Islip Street
London, SW1P 4DD

CITY CAFé
restaurant · bar · terrace

The Lanesborough

European, Mediterranean

🔲 *1 Lanesborough Place, Hyde Park Corner, SW1*

☎ *020 7259 5599*

🚌 *Hyde Park Corner LU (30 sec walk)*

🕐 *Daily 12noon-12midnight*

🥕 *Vegan options*

☀ *Booking recommended*

Organic ★★★
Vegetarian ★★★★
Taste ★★★★★
Price *££££*

One of the classiest and most romantic settings in London, serving exceptional gourmet vegetarian food. Arrive by car at this five star hotel's entrance and let the head porter valet park it for you. Inside, an opulent hallway leads to the Conservatory, a mouthwatering art deco candle-lit chinoiserie restaurant, with several hideaway dining sections for more private dining. On Friday and Saturday, it's the setting for highly enjoyable dinner dances to live popular jazz. Dress code is formal/informal, certainly no jeans but not necessarily evening wear either although for a special occasion black tie would not be out of place.

Paul Gayler's Vegetarian Menu is short and exquisite with a choice of three starters, three mains and seven desserts. There are a few other vegetarian choices on the carnivore menu too or why not go American and request something off-menu (but do preferably give 24 hours notice).

Complimentary breads include brown bread with raisins and focaccia with sundried tomato and are delicious. An amuse bouche of mushroom and celeriac soup arrives in a tiny coffee cup to whet the appetite. The Goat's Cheese pastilla with grilled vegetable and olive vinaigrette is a triumph, generous in portion and scintillating of taste whilst the Jerusalem Artichoke Soup with truffle oil and parmesan is memorable. The Gnocchi main with cepes, chestnuts and salsify is excellent whilst Oriental ravioli with braised pumpkin, coconut and Asian Pesto is a symphony of flavour. Before the desserts, there's a second dainty amuse bouche – a liqueur glass filled with lime mousse and lychee jelly. The recommended dessert is Iced White Chocolate Mandarin Turban which bursts with flavour. Topped with a mandarin sorbet and served with Chocolate Beignets it is sensational. Cannelloni of Pineapple with Lime and Ginger Ice cream is quite superb too.

All the vegetables are organic but not the wines. However, vegetarian and organic wines can be pre-ordered with 24 hours notice as can gluten-free or special dietary dishes. The service is chic and amiable. A world class vegetarian venue.

Breakfast at the Conservatory
☺ *Daily 7am-11.30am*

The Lanesborough Hotel is notable for providing vegetarians a top class service 24/7 and its breakfast and room service menu deserve special mention confirming that this is also an excellent venue for the discerning vegetarian traveller.

Breakfast is served in the Conservatory with attentive service at a relaxed and leisurely pace. Dress is casual or businesslike.

Freshly squeezed passion juice is very good and unlimitedly refilled as is the exceptionally good Columbian coffee. The Conservatory Vegetarian Breakfast is carefully made with two small mild flavoured lentil cookies that look somewhat like slices of veggie sausage, grilled tomatoes, a couple of eggs, small mushrooms and a wonderfully flavoured large hash brown. It's pleasantly filling without leaving one uncomfortably full and one of the best vegetarian breakfasts in London. Lemon ricotta pancakes with seasonal berries is also a great choice and is delicately cheesy with good lemon vibes and a dazzling berry coulis and warmed mixed berries. For those with larger appetites, the bakery basket has ultra fresh homemade brioche, a notable apricot Danish, muffins, breakfast rolls, toast and top notch marmalade and honey. Budget for about £22.50 per person, service included and it is good value bearing in mind the beautiful location and the quality of the food. Other options include a variety of juices, homemade compotes, fresh fruit salad, cereals, yoghurts and eggs any way you like.

The 24-hour room service menu is available to hotel guests and apart from including all the breakfast options, also features a Vegetarian Club Sandwich, Vegetarian Spring Rolls, a Middle Eastern veggie mezze menu with options such as hummous and pitta bread. In addition, they will do off-menu options for those on the most pinickity diets as one would expect in a hotel of this calibre. For a review of the hotel rooms, see page 296.

Nahm
Thai, Modern

🖼 *The Halkin Hotel, Halkin Street, SW1*
☎ *020 7333 1234*
🚇 *Hyde Park Corner LU (10 min walk)*
🕐 *Lunch Mon-Fri 12noon-2.30pm;*
   Dinner Mon-Sat 7pm-11pm, Sun 7pm-10pm
🥕 *Vegan options*

Organic ★★★
Vegetarian ★★★★
Taste ★★★★★
Price £££££

The Halkin is one of London's leading boutique hotels and Nahm, its top class Thai restaurant, offers exemplary vegetarian dining. Forget notions of a traditional Thai dining room lavished with gilded buddhas and artefacts, at Nahm, the look is classy modern chic with gleaming gold and russet walls, gold columns and teak tables. Overall, the place exudes style – even the staff wear Armani.

Opened in 2001, Nahm was the first Thai restaurant in Europe to get a Michelin Star Award. Australian chef David Thompson, prepares all the dishes freshly so let them know that you are vegetarian or vegan and the staff will put together a fantastic meal according to your preferences of diet, spicyness and appetite. Although there are a only a few vegetarian choices on the menu, all the dishes can be converted to vegetarian. At lunchtime, there's a set menu at £22.50 with a tasting menu at £47 in the evenings. Vegetarian breakfasts of a high standard are available although these are prepared in the Halkin Hotel itself.

The meal begins with four superb pineapple and mandarin canapés topped with sugar beet and coriander. Next, a well-presented tray of wafers with a green curry sauce and lychees wrapped with ginger. All this was a prelude to the main event of a fantastic Smokey Red Curry, rich in complex flavours of galangal, mace and tofu giving the dish a 'meaty' consistency. Served simultaneously is a cucumber and coriander salad, that works well with the curry. The starfruit, red chilli and red onion salad is absolutely excellent and stirfry of cornichons, spring onion and asparagus was very good too. The Spicy Coconut Soup flavoured with lemongrass, coconut slices, mushroom and green chilli was a great accompaniment to the main meal. The meal ends with banana dessert grilled with sticky rice and a small bowl of lychees.

Much of the food is sourced directly from Thailand being delivered in one and half days from Bangkok. According to David Thompson "about 40% of the menu is organic, but they are striving to increase the use of organic ingredients. At the moment there are three Californian organic wines and one biodynamic."

Pizza on the Park
Fast Food, Italian

Vegetarian ★★★
Taste ★★★★
Price ££

🖃 *11 Knightsbridge, SW1*
☎ *020 7235 5273*
🚇 *Hyde Park Corner LU (5 min walk)*
🕐 *Daily 9am-12midnight (restaurant)*
🎵 *Live jazz music (Larry's Room) 7.30pm-midnight*

Celebrated jazz pizza venue so smokey you can sometimes cut the atmosphere with a knife – although this may change with new legislation on the way. Larry's Room, downstairs, is their music venue with good sized round tables so punters can watch the sets and eat pizza, pasta and salads. Booking is essential and entrance costs about £10-£12 evenings and Sunday lunchtimes.

At ground level entrance is free to the large eating area. In addition to a classic pizza menu there's vegetarian lasagne, chilli senza carne (a vegetarian dish from Arizona), jacket potatoes and a good choice of salads. Pizzas here are good and they will cater for special requests such as the cheeseless vegan pizza that a friend of mine asked for.

Roussillon
French, Modern

Vegetarian ★★★★
Taste ★★★★★
Price £££££

🖃 *16 St Barnabas Street, SW1*
☎ *020 7730 5550*
🚇 *Sloane Square LU (5 min walk)*
🕐 *Wed-Fri lunch 12noon-2.30pm;*
   Mon-Sat dinner 6.30pm-10.30pm
👶 *Child friendly*

Amazing vegetarian tasting menu from chef Alexis Gautier who used to work with Alain Ducasse in Monte Carlo. Alexis has Michelin star cred and creates dazzlingly inventive dishes. Set in suave Pimlico, down a short residential side-turning, its premises are in fact, a small converted pub although you would never guess it once inside. Two adjoining rooms on ground level are cool and crisp and delight the eye with spaciously arranged tables, smart Hiram Wild cutlery, immaculate white tablecloths, elegant abstract paintings and lush flower arrangements. Around the tables are wealthy food-savvy Americans, neighbourhood regulars from Chelsea, Fulham and Pimlico politicos such as a former chancellor of the Exchequer, an indication that your credit card is essential. Downstairs is a private dining room with its own bar and lounge for parties of up to 26.

The Garden Menu is seven courses long with a lacto-ovo vegetarian focus easily adaptable for non-egg eaters and all discriminating vegetarians. It begins with complimentary warm Chick Pea Beignets Canapés and throughout the meal fabulous breads are offered of which the Olive Bread is highly recommended. Cauliflower Soup to start might sound a tad boring but this lightly creamed dish is a real treat. The small bright Green Swiss Chard Risotto is a smooth operator and a great prelude to the attractive and delicious Roasted Long Carrots with spices and honey. At the menu's half-way point comes the perfect Fried Welsh Duck Egg, somewhat larger than a chicken egg and stronger in flavour and ideal for dunking in warm buttered soldiers. The alternative, the Winter Vegetables cooked with black truffle and balsamic vinegar is exquisite.

At lunchtimes, some time-poor diners belt through the courses in a single hour. Don't! Pace yourself and take time to leisurely pause before the next course and aim for a quintessential 2-3 hour banquet. Whilst there is a cheese course none unfortunately is vegetarian. The first dessert course is Lemon Three Ways, three servings of curd, marmalade and sorbet which you can sample in different combinations for different flavours. This was followed by a Chestnut Soufflé that leaves you satisfied but still comfortable. The meal at £50 (plus 12.5% service) is expensive but bearing in mind the intensive labour and skill involved it is good value.

As its name suggests, Roussillon is big on wine. A wine tasting menu picked by the talented sommelier, Roberto Della Pieta is fabulous. Eight small glasses, from the 400 bin selection, match each course and offer a veritable olfactory adventure. Of particular note was the 2002 Sauvignon Blanc, Côtes du Duras – a stunning organic wine from South West France. Regrettably there are no veggie wines but there are several organic champagnes, wines and a few biodynamics as well. The wine tasting menu is £35 and highly recommended although wines can also be bought individually by the glass.

Of note for Chelsea Flower Show in May is the Special Flower Menu. Warm Fuschia and tofu sandwich, lovage and tomato dressing are just a few examples. Definitely a place to revisit time and again.

CITY OF LONDON

The most historical setting in London for a vegetarian eatery and hugely popular with city workers is The Place Below in a real Norman Crypt! Maybe they should build a small monument for Futures! The pure vegetarian takeout food here deserves some sort of accolade. The newest addition to this part of town is a beautifully designed Thai Square at Mansion House with lots of veggie choices.

City of London

City of London
Restaurants

Hoxton & Shoreditch
Restaurants

Shops

Smithfield, Barbican, Farringdon & Exmouth Market
Restaurants

Shops

CTB
Thai, Chinese, Classic

Vegetarian ★★★★★
Taste ★★★
Price £

🖃 *88 Leather Lane, EC2*
☎ *020 7628 3666*
🚇 *Chancery Lane LU or Farringdon LU & Rail (8 min walk)*
🕒 *Mon-Sat 12noon-10pm*
🌶 *Vegan menu*

Bargain £5 all you can eat vegan Thai/Chinese cuisine. For food review see Tai Buffet (Camden branch) page 120.

Futures!
International, Classic

Vegetarian ★★★★★
Taste ★★★★
Price £

🖃 *8 Botolph Alley, Eastcheap, EC3*
☎ *020 7623 4529*
🚇 *Monument LU (1 min walk)*
🕒 *Breakfast Mon-Fri 7.30am-10am, lunch served 11.30am-3pm*
🌶 *Vegan options*
i *Takeaway only (catering service available, see page 278)*

The tiniest takeout in town for pure vegetarian and considering what you pay the food served here is remarkable. Found down a City back alley, the 1pm lunch-rush manifests itself as a queue of twenty office workers eager to order from Futures! excellent all-vegetarian take-out menu that changes daily. By 1.30pm it's a lot quieter although it's not long before the queue starts up again. Tourists visiting the nearby Monument be advised: factor in a lunchtime or breakfast visit here.

The daily choice format is soup, hot pot, bake, savoury, quiche/pizza, four salads and desserts. Chilli Mexcaine, a vegetable chilli bake topped with tortilla crisps is a sheer delight, substantial in size with lots of cauliflower, beans and other veg – a meal on its own and a bargain. Sweet and Sour Vegetables is delicious with plenty of chunky peppers, courgettes, mushrooms, green beans and pineapple on a bed of rice. Both these mains came in sturdy cartons with the food at the perfect temperature. Apple and Blueberry Crumble sells well here, although there's also a healthy looking fresh fruit salad. Delivery is free for orders over £15.

Best on the Breakfast Menu is the toast (three different breads are made on the premises) and Futures! own blend Muesli. Service is slick and fast.

The Place Below
International, Classic

Vegetarian ★★★★★
Taste ★★★
Price £

🖼 *St Mary-le-Bow Church, Cheapside, EC2*
☎ *020 7329 0789*
🚇 *St Pauls LU (3 min walk)*
🕐 *Mon-Fri 7.30am-3.30pm, lunch served 11.30am-2.30pm*
☀ *Outside seating*
🍸 *BYO (no corkage charged)*
i *Eat in (counter service) & Takeaway*
   Vegetarian catering service available (see page 278)

The Place Below

London's most historic venue for vegetarian food is deep down in a voluminous Norman crypt. This is a Christopher Wren church with beautiful stained glass windows and it's almost surreal to see smart city guys in shirts and ties eating their meals off serving trays in this most unusual of city eateries. Going since 1990, The Place Below is run by Crypt Restaurants, a private firm that supports some of the church's projects.

79

It's a friendly, well-run sort of place with the staff knowing many customers by name. At lunchtime the place is thronged with queuing diners. First timers should take the main church entrance and stairs downwards otherwise you'll be walking around the church perimeter forever (you can tell I've done it!)

Once in, on the right is a coffee and cake counter serving sandwiches and focaccia Brie de Meaux, Neal's Yard Mature Cheddar, Roast Aubergine with red pepper salad, croissants and smoothies. At the far end is the main serving station with the selection written up on the menu noticeboard. Indonesian casserole of couscous, brocolli and roasted peanuts in a mildly spicy sauce is fine and includes courgettes, carrot, onion and babycorn. The Healthy Bowl, a very filling wholegrain rice salad of puy lentils, mushroom, courgettes, tomato, green bean, carrot garnished with coriander was even better. Fruit salad dessert here is good as is the warm Apple and Blackberry Crumble with clotted cream or Greek yogurt. Other choices may include a potato, watercress and orange soup, whilst on mains there may be a large potato or, quiche salad.

The best place to eat to get the real crypt feel is the large dining room. In the middle is a large communal table with other smaller tables dotted about. On the tables are large jugs of water and you can bring your own wine (no charge for corkage), although few do. The recipes here are devised by director and owner Bill Sewell and on sale are his two veggie cooking books Food from the Place Below (Bill Sewell with Ian Burleigh and Frances Tomlinson) and Feasts from the Place Below (Bill Sewell).

In the mornings, you can smell the tantalising waft of freshly baked bread that's made on the premises and see The Place Below busy with porridge eaters reading the morning newspapers.

Thai Square City
Thai, Classic

Vegetarian ★★★
Taste ★★
Price £££

⌨ 136, The Minories, EC3
☎ 020 7680 1111
🚇 Aldgate or Tower Hill LU
🕐 Mon-Thur 12noon-10pm, Fri 12noon-11.30pm

Part of the Thai Square chain of restaurants this follows their traditional extravagantly ornate Thai design format with seating for 250 and a license for a further 240 people in their basement bar until 2am. Popular for business lunches or after work chow downs. See Thai Square, Trafalgar Square for review, page 29.

Thai Square Mansion House
Thai, Classic

🖼 *1-7 Great St Thomas Apostle, EC4*

☎ *020 7329 0001*

🚇 *Mansion House LU (30 seconds walk)*

🕐 *Mon-Fri 12noon-3.30pm and 5.30pm-10.30pm*

Vegetarian ★★★
Taste ★★
Price £££

Opened August 2004, this is the latest and one of the smallest of the restaurants in the Thai Square chain. See Thai Square, Trafalgar Square for review, page 29.

FUTURES !

Top quality savouries, salads & desserts prepared fresh every weekday
see our review on page 78

8 Botolph Alley, Eastcheap, EC3
020 7623 4529
Mon-Fri 7.30am-10am, lunch served 11.30am-3pm

HOXTON & SHOREDITCH

Cay Tre
Vietnamese, Classic

Vegetarian ★★★
Taste ★★★
Price £

🖂 *301 Old Street, EC1*
☎ *020 7729 8662*
🚇 *Old Street LU (5 min walk)*
🕐 *Mon-Thur 12noon-3pm & 5.30pm-11pm,*
  Fri-Sat 12noon-3.30pm & 5.30pm-11pm, Sun 12noon-10.30pm
🥕 *Vegan options*
👶 *Child friendly*
i *Eat in (table service) & Takeaway; Booking advised at the weekends*

Possibly the best Vietnamese eaterie in London to offer a good range of yummy vegetarian choices at bargain prices. The Sunday lunchtime I visited it was initially busy with Vietnamese giving way to a local brit-neighbourhood crowd of mixed ages. Night-wise, it's Hoxtonite club-bers, weekdays it's city slickers slurping down a swift soup meal.

Vietnamese family-run, service here is pretty good. Do let them know you are vegetarian as your waitperson will reveal a lot more options than the six choices on the vegetarian section of the menu. Furthermore, they will also convert several omnivore dishes to veggie on request.

Vietnamese Pizza is one such conversion, a traditional warm pancake starter dish where you cut a slice, add some fresh Vietnamese watercress, marjoram, dipping sauce, wrap it in lettuce and let the wonderful medley of flavours melt in your mouth – delicious! Crispy Vietnamese Spring Rolls are big and chunky, more gluttinous and tastier than their typical Chinese counterparts and come with soya sauce (really good). The veggie version of Canh chua, a popular aromatic soup containing pieces of fresh tomato, pineapple chunks, tofu strips, celery slices and accented with basil, produces a delightful mix of flavours and is recommended. Vegetarian Cay Tre Salad is definitely not to be missed.

Other tempting choices include crispy seaweed starter, veggie Special Pho and the Braised Aubergine in black bean sauce. All the desserts are vegetarian although most people are too full and don't get around to eating them. Fresh pineapple juice is good quality with a large glass (£1.20) representing good value.

Eating at Cay Tre (that incidentally means bamboo) is an enjoyable experience and for the budget conscious the best veggie bet in Hoxton/Shoreditch. Go for it!

Fifteen

Italian, Mediterranean, Modern

🖂 *15 Westland Place, N1*

☎ *020 7251 1515*

🚌 *Old Street LU & Rail (5 min walk)*

🕙 *Trattoria restaurant: Mon-Sat 8.30am-11pm, Sunday 12noon-5pm*
Fifteen restaurant (booking essential): Daily lunch 12noon-4.30pm,
dinner 6.30pm-11.30pm

☀ *Vegan options*

◊ *Child friendly*

This place made famous by the TV series 'Jamie's Kitchen', is a magnet for fans of TV chef Jamie Oliver. The food is great and mostly organic, and there are now two eateries to choose from, one with a complete vegetarian tasting menu that changes daily. Granted, it comes at a pukka price but remember profits go to Cheeky Chops, a charity that trains 30 unemployed youngsters a year to become the next new wave of chefs.

The actual place is a dreary walk from Old Street Tube and the venue is a dull looking warehouse surrounded by equally boring office blocks and more grim warehouses. However, one could say it's just a New York style restaurant, crap on the outside but everything you could wish for on the inside.

Once in, you're into Jamie's world. There's a small bar area packed with punters waiting with a drink for their table. Expect a fifteen minute wait unless you arrive early. On the ground level is the Trattoria, in the basement, Fifteen. The Trattoria offers more menu flexibility for vegetarians and it's cheaper but Fifteen is spunkier in design and the atmosphere more electric.

Most people venturing here are making a one-off visit to have the 'Jamie Oliver Experience'. Expect cameras flashing and videos recording as dads capture the family on safari in the Trattoria and frenzied friends taking party pics on their mobiles down in Fifteen.

Most of the food is organic. However, one ingredient in a dish may not be – so there's no mention of organic on the menu. Organic and biodynamic wines are here but you will need to quiz the sommelier to find out what's what. Similarly, double check the menu with a waiter for what is vegetarian. One waitperson thought that a seafood risotto was vegetarian.

Fifteen Trattoria

Organic ★★★★
Vegetarian ★★
Taste ★★★★★
Price £££

The décor here is striking, featuring lots of good quality dark woods, comfortable seating spread well apart, chandelier lighting and shocking pink graffiti scrawled on the back wall.

The food too is well presented and the complimentary breads with olive oil are superb and not to be missed. Tortellini with three cheese, figs and orange gremolata, is excellent, although the portion size is more starter than main. Spinach and Ricotta Gnocchi comes in a light buttery sauce and avoids being gummy; it's delicious without being mind blowing although it too is on the small side. Small portion sizes are great news for young kids and dieters but guys will need a full monty of three courses. On other days choices may include a pasta and bean soup, salads, ravioli of artichoke, penne pasta or hand-cut tagliatelle, chilli, purple figs and goat's curd.

Half the reservations are bookable, the other half of the space is kept for those without reservations.

The Restaurant at Fifteen

Organic ★★★★
Vegetarian ★★★★
Price £££££

Downstairs is so rich in personality you'll want to buy it by the pound. The open kitchen, the shocking pink banquettes, black columns and funky pink artwork burst with vitality. At lunch it's fab with a swanky dressed crowd who want to be 'seen'. For more privacy and romance book a booth. Book well in advance as this restaurant is red hot.

The lunchtime à la carte choices may include starter of Mozzarella with Peaches, Basil, Mint and Rocket followed by main of Gnocchi with Chanterelles or one of Jamie O's speciality risottos.

In the evening everything turns set menu downstairs. The eight course Vegetarian Tasting Menu is a whopping £55 per person with a special wine package to match the courses for another forty quid. As vegetarian tasting menus go the choices are not as exciting as Roussillon, and Morgan M but the ambience of the place will certainly make it a night to remember.

Rivington Grill
British, modern

Vegetarian ★★★
Price £££

- 28-30 Rivington Street, EC2
- 020 7729 7073
- Old Street LU (5 min walk)
- Daily 12noon-3pm, 6.30pm-10.30pm

Tuck into modern Brit comfort food at this smart, buzzy and bright eaterie in the heart of the Hoxton and Shoreditch warehouse district. Grungy clubbers, leave your smelly jeans and trainers at home – this place exudes well-heeled nouveau riche neighbourhood residents, city wide boys and chic professional women. Immaculate white walls, wooden floorboards, comfy large lounge leather sofas, good size tables with crisp white tablecloths define a look far superior to most gastropubs leaving one with the expectation of high quality food.

A new short vegetarian menu of three starters, three mains and seven desserts was initiated in August 2004 following a surge in demand from local vegetarians. For starters there's Steamed Globe Artichoke (hot or cold) or Watercress Salad of Goats' Cheese and Cob Nuts. The most tempting main is a modern veggie version of the traditional English dish, Bubble and Squeak accompanied by fried egg and wild mushrooms. Other mains are Eggs Florentine and Beetroot salad with cob nuts. A further six veggie side dishes – Champ, Purple Sprouting broccoli, Greens with Garlic butter and Roasted Pumpkin and Squash – add versatility to this somewhat limited menu. Desserts, however, make a strong showing with Banana Custard, Plum Crumble and an intriguingly named Chocolate soggy belly pudding with Jersey Cream among the choices.

With bags of personality and some unique menu choices, Rivington Grill is a likeable and fashionable eaterie.

SMITHFIELD, BARBICAN & FARRINGDON

Veggie lunchtime food is to be had at The Greenery in Farringdon and Wheatley Vegetarian Café near the Angel. For a more fashionable eating environment live it up in West Smithfield at The Bar and Grill, a hip bar and restaurant serving vegetarian food. Nearby you can enjoy fine Italian cuisine in a relaxed environment at Carluccio's. Further north, Sofra have opened a new restaurant in Exmouth Market offering excellent Turkish cuisine with plenty of veggie options. For distinctly well-prepared Mediterannean cuisine in the Old Street area there's Carnevale.

The Bar and Grill
International

Vegetarian ★★★
Taste ★★★★
Price ££

- 🖾 *2-3 West Smithfield, EC1*
- ☎ *0870 4422541*
- 🚇 *Farringdon & Barbican LU (2 min walk)*
- 🕑 *Mon-Thur 12noon-12midnight, Fri 12noon-1am, Sat 11am-2am, closed Sun*
- ◌ *Child friendly*
- ♫ *Music (DJ)*

Formerly the Living Room (West Smithfield), in September 2004 this venue switched from being a neighbourhood eaterie to become a slick destination grill and pizza venue offering some modern veggie takes on 70's diner classics. At 8pm the bar is thronged with dressed-down city suits and office chicks ready to hit nearby hot spot Fabric. Live DJ sessions are held Wednesdays-Saturdays with smooth R&B the night I went. It's dead at high noon but packed 12.30pm-2.30pm with suits.

Totally refurbished, the bar and restaurant now exudes more sophistication with cream coloured walls, columns and high back chairs contrasted with black leather banquettes, black wooden tables and some large leafy plants. The Living Room's family pictures have been replaced by mirrors and an exposed bare brick walled section at the back gives the place an understated urban sensibility.

The menu too is new and features three vegetarian stone baked pizzas, seven veggie starters and three other veggie mains. Selectionwise, it's top heavy on Stilton, mushrooms and rocket. However, they will be introducing a corn on the cob starter and veggie grill main special and will adapt omnivore items if you request. If all else fails, they will always rustle up an off the menu omelette and fruit salad for you.

Staff here are friendly, proactively efficient and vegetarian savvy.

Red Onion, Pesto and Stilton Tart starter is tasty, substantial and well-presented whilst the Blue Cheese (Stilton again) and Poached Pear Salad is good too. The Grilled Vegetarian Skewer main arrives on a wooden slab, looks appealing with yellow and red peppers, lemon and courgettes, and is delicious. Veggie burger fans may be disappointed when they discover that the Portobello Mushroom Burger is simply two halves of a smallish bun housing several large garlicky mushrooms. This is no conventional mushroom and soya mix mock burger. That said the chips are quite good as is the fresh tomato relish. Those worried about fibre-overload are best advised to opt for the Vegetarian Sausage and Mash that slides down a treat.

Desserts are all vegetarian and the Apple Crumble with custard is quite reasonable, whilst Banoffi Pie topped with sliced banana deserves to be more enterprising. Having seen the Hot Chocolate Fudge Cake on another table, next time that's what I'll be going for.

The Children's Menu features stone baked plum tomato and mozzarella pizza, veggie sausage and mash, omelette, and apple crumble with custard. There's also a choice of organic baby foods for main course and desserts.

Carluccio's Caffé
Italian, Classic

Vegetarian ★★★
Taste ★★★★
Price ££

🖼 *12 West Smithfield, EC1*
☎ *020 7329 5904*
🚌 *Farringdon LU & Rail (5 min walk)*
🕐 *Mon-Fri 8am-11pm, Sat 9am-11pm, Sun 10am-10pm*
🥕 *Vegan options*
👶 *Child friendly*
☀ *Outside seating*
i *Booking advised in evenings, (outside catering tel 020 7629 0699)*

Another well designed Carluccio eaterie this one with attractive outdoor seating. The clientele is a mix of city business folk and fashionable Clerkenwell designers. The place is busy during the day, but also buzzing until its close at 11pm. For food review see Carluccio's, St Christopher's Place page 35.

Carnevale
Mediterranean, Modern

Organic ★★
Vegetarian ★★★★★
Taste ★★★★
Price ££

- 135 Whitecross Street, Barbican, EC1
- 020 7250 3452
- admin@carnevalerestaurant.co.uk
- www.carnevalerestaurant.co.uk
- Old Street/Barbican LU (5 min walk)
- Mon-Fri 10am-10.30pm, Sat 5.30pm-10.30pm
- Vegan options
- Child friendly
- i Eat in (counter and table service) & Takeaway

Carnevale

Opened in 1994, this small pure vegetarian restaurant serves well conceived Mediterranean dishes using fresh seasonal ingredients, many organic. The black painted entrance opens into an enticing deli-counter selling good takeaway sandwiches and tempting jars of gourmet produce. The main event, however, is further inside with restaurant tables and a small conservatory out back housing a few more. The atmosphere is relaxed and casual with evenings candlelit.

The set menu is an absolute steal at £13.50 and offers three courses or two with a glass of wine or non-alcoholic drink, 12noon-3pm and 5.30pm-7pm. The short à la carte menu has six starters, five mains and four desserts and is quite inviting with Carnevale happily catering for vegans and those with special nutritional needs. For example, there's a gluten-free bread option and every course has at least one vegan recipe.

Roasted Red Pepper with Basil Soup comes up thick, rustic and flavoursome and is served with a delicious walnut bread. Preserved Lemon and Goats' Cheese Tart with Roasted Aubergines in Harissa, one of the best mains here is a tasty tangy treat that marries well with a side order of Lemon and Rosemary Roast Potatoes. Tuscan Bean & Vegetable Casserole with Saffron is hearty and substantial enough not to need a side dish – although do try the roast potatoes if you can.

Summer Pudding Terrine is a noteably good dessert and comes tanked up with fruitiness and a pleasant texture of walnuts – having been made with walnut bread. Raspberry Crème Brûlée is cool, thick and creamy and of high quality.

At £20 a head, the à la carte menu, is good value for what you get. Most ingredients come from a local Surrey farm and the menu changes every six weeks to take advantage of seasonal availability. There's a small but carefully chosen selection of organic wines at £13-£22, and organic champagne at £27 a pop. Most of these are vegetarian or vegan.

Much of Carnevale's trade comes from its takeout lunch counter where freshly prepared sandwiches and salads are sold to local work people. The deli-counter is rich with selections of upscale prepacked foods from Sicilian capers to delicacies like Belgian fruit spread. The Mediterranean Hampers are very popular – particularly at Christmas – and start from £20.

The Greenery
International, Classic

Organic	★★
Vegetarian	★★★★★
Taste	★★★★★
Price	£

🏠 *5 Cowcross Street, EC1*
☎ *020 020 7490 4870*
🚌 *Old Street LU & Rail, Barbican LU (3 min walk)*
🕐 *Mon-Fri 7am-5pm*
☀ *Outside seating*
i *Eat in (counter service) & Takeaway*

There's a queue right down the street at lunchtimes for the impressive food at this inexpensive, efficiently run city eaterie. Runner-up in the Vegetarian Society's Best Vegetarian Restaurant Awards 2003, the Greenery has been going strong since 1989 and before that was a Cranks restaurant franchisee. The only remaining connection now is the Cranks organic bread that they sell.

Inside, there are high stools and window countertops to eat at. Eating outside there's much officespeak about web page design, e-mails and job changing from dressed-down city types. Check out the dinky photocopied menu sheet for the regular dishes and also the blackboard for the day's special. Salad choices look appetising, portions are generous and there's an inviting selection of pies, pizza, pastas, quiche, pasties, jacket potatoes, soup, sarnies and baps.

Vegetable Lasagne with mixed salad is substantial and tasty. The Homity Pie of potato, onion, cheese, herbs and garlic is good and contrasts well with flavoursome chickpeas, yellow, green and red peppers, onion and courgette.

Although there are no organic dishes, about 25% of ingredients are organic on a where possible basis. There's a good juice bar selection of which the faves are the Greenery Cleanser of carrot, apple, lemon, pineapple and ginger and the Beetroot Blast of carrot, beetroot, apple and ginger both powerpacked with natural antioxidants. None are organic but I did have bottled pressed organic juice that was fine.

The Greenery delivers free to local offices for orders over £10 providing orders are phone/faxed/emailed by 11am. The Greenery is also a popular place for breakfast with favourites such as scrambled eggs on toast and a selection of mueslis.

Rye Wholefoods
Café & Organic Shop

Organic ★★★★
Vegetarian ★★★★★
Taste ★★
Price £

- ⌖ *35a Myddleton Street, EC1*
- ☎ *020 7278 5878*
- 🚌 *Angel LU (10 min walk)*
- 🕐 *Mon-Fri 9am-5pm, Sat 1pm-5pm*
- 🥕 *Vegan options*

Small 80's-style vegetarian and vegan, organic provisions shop with a couple of tables for eating in although the place is geared up more for takeaway. The food is as much organic as it can be. See page 231 for shop review.

Sofra Exmouth Market
Turkish, Classic

Vegetarian ★★★
Taste ★★★
Price ££

- ⌖ *21 Exmouth Market, EC1*
- ☎ *020 7883 1111*
- 🚌 *Farringdon LU & Rail*
- 🕐 *Mon-Sat 12noon-11pm, Sun 12noon-10.30pm*

See Özer Oxford Circus for food review (page 44).

Wheatley Vegetarian Café
Café, European

▫ 33/34 Myddleton Street, EC1
☎ 020 7278 6662
🚌 Angel LU (10 min walk)
🕐 Mon-Fri 8am-4pm
🌱 Vegan options
i   Eat in (counter service) & Takeaway

Excellent informal lunchtime al fresco eaterie with food that has bags of wholesome personality. With no credible veggie eats on Exmouth Market apart from Sofra, Wheatley is but a five minute stroll away and sits on a small parade of shops and is well worth a visit.

Its bright, spacious, no-thrills interior seats 20 with large tables for sharing, whilst outside the back garden gets packed in the summer. Trainee barristers, students and workers from the Guardian newspaper and Amnesty International sip tasty thick homemade lentil, carrot and coriander soup accompanied by chunky sunflower seed bread that in itself is a filling meal.

The blackboard menu changes daily and there's a choice of mock carnivore standards such as an interesting Veggie Bacon Sandwich with spinach, tomato chutney and mayo. It's a doorstop but the bacon tastes more like salami. There are also veggie burgers and lasagne made with aubergine, peppers and courgette. The Spinach Wrap crammed with hot roasted root vegetables, curried chick pea and feta cheese salad comes as a huge portion and is quite excellent. Most of the customers are women and the three home-made salads to choose from seem to go down particularly well with them. There's also some low fat organic cakes and 90% of the food is vegan.

NORTH LONDON

North

Mandola Café

ISLINGTON

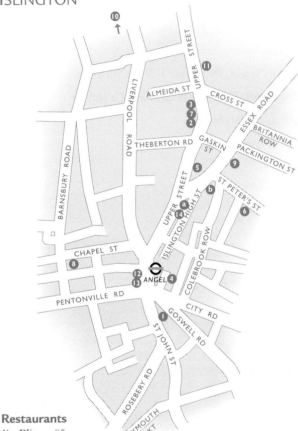

Restaurants

Shops

Islington has been transformed in the last twenty years from a modest local neighbourhood into a major shopping and eating area with numerous restaurants along Upper Street. Among the super-bargain veggie places to eat are the Indian Veg Bhel-Poori House and Tai Buffet. For great value Turkish food there are several Gallipoli restaurants and the buzzing Italian, Carluccio's Caffè on Upper Street. The area also has exemplary French vegetarian haut cuisine at Morgan M and the best organic pub in London, The Duke of Cambridge. For vegetarian food in a unique atmosphere, Candid Café is a great alternative to more mainstream eateries. Just the other side of the junction is Bliss – which is a firm favourite with the locals.

Bliss
French, Modern

Vegetarian ★★★★★
Taste ★★★
Price £

▭ *428 St John Street, EC1*
☏ *020 7837 3720*
🚌 *Angel LU (5 min walk)*
🕑 *Mon-Sat 8am-6pm, Sun 9am-4pm*

There was something fishy going on the day we visited this vegetarian patisserie and boulangerie that's been open since '89. A tuna mayonnaise baguette on the menu. "Well, business hasn't been so good at the moment... but we only sell maybe 6 a day and they're not even on the menu most days." Moral of the story, the tuna here isn't mock omnivore... it's real. Everything else, however, is vegetarian and the pastries are made with vegetable fat on the premises downstairs. The strawberry and raspberry flan tastes rather good but the warmed up plum frangipane was a tad dull as was the coffee and décor. Quiches and pizzas look attractive but the real star of the show is the almond croissant.

Café Gallipoli
Turkish

Vegetarian ★★★
Taste ★★★★
Price ££

- 🖾 *102 Upper Street, N1*
- ☎ *020 7359 0630*
- 🚇 *Angel LU (5 min walk)*
- 🕐 *Sun-Thur 10.30am-11.00pm, Fri-Sat 10.30am-12midnight*
- ☀ *Outside seating*
- *i* *Booking advisable*

Party-on at this good value traditional Turkish café. Situated on Upper Street, cheap eats central for North London, Gallipoli gets crammed to the rafters in the evenings with the out-for-a-good-time 20-40 year old crowd. Friendly and obliging waiters always manage to find you a table no matter how full they are.

Rickety old tables, wobbly chairs, lively Turkish music, pictures and ornaments recreate a noisy informal bazaar atmosphere. Front of house is suitable for bigger birthday parties who dance on the chairs whilst the back room is only slightly quieter.

The choice of seven main vegetarian dishes includes Vegetarian Moussaka, Imam Bayildi – fried aubergines stuffed with an onion mushroom mix – and very filling falafels. For the full works we opted for the delicious Set Meal that included a big veg mezze selection, any main dish off the menu, coffee, tea and a light milk pudding with apricots. The wine is reasonably priced and there are meat and fish dishes on the menu to keep your non-veggie friends happy.

A sister café, Café Gallipoli Again, 120 Upper Street offers the same menu (see below) and there's also Gallipoli Bazaar, 107 Upper Street (see page 100).

Café Gallipoli Again
Turkish

Vegetarian ★★★
Taste ★★★★
Price ££

- 🖾 *120 Upper Street, N1*
- ☎ *020 7359 1578*
- 🚇 *Highbury Islington LU & Rail or Angel LU (5 min walk)*
- 🕐 *Sun-Thur 10.30am-11pm, Fri-Sat 10.30am-12pm*
- ☀ *Outside seating*

Sister café to Café Gallipoli, 102 Upper Street with which it shares the same menu. Here though, the place is smaller and less frenzied.

Candid Café

International, Classic

  🖃 *3 Torrens Street, EC1*
  ☎ *020 7278 9368*
  🚌 *Angel LU (5 min walk)*
  🕐 *Mon-Sat 12noon-10pm, Sun 12noon-5pm*
  🥕 *Vegan options*
  ☀ *Outside seating*
  i   *Banqueting suite for 30 people*

Vegetarian ★★★
Taste ★★
Price £

A popular haunt for arty young vegetarians. Located in the Candid Arts Trust building, the café is just minutes away from the main Islington dining strip and identifiable by the half horse statue sticking out of its front wall. Various contemporary art and design exhibitions and fairs are held here as well as life drawing classes.

Once up the old council flat-style stairs, order at the counter and crash out on one of the comfy green velvety sofas, now in a mild state of disrepair. The Sunday afternoon I visited, the spacious renaissance-style main dining room was packed. Around the big communal wooden dining tables in the centre, diners ate and chatted cheerfully. On the perimeter, young couples sipped coffee at small tables with gilded banquet room chairs. At night, the place is romantically candlelit. I really liked the genuine friendliness of the people here who were up for relaxed conversation with anyone in the room.

On the blackboard menu, there's always a vegan organic soup such as carrot and coriander or pumpkin, crusty brown bread and butter and a selection of sandwiches.

Of the three veggie main courses Stilton Broccoli Quiche, whilst arriving nicely warm, is rather dull in taste and comes with a sad lettuce and tomato side salad. Roasted Red Pepper stuffed with wild rice, courgette, mushroom and more chopped red pepper was reasonable, but variable in temperature and accompanied by another sorry looking side salad. A Greek salad is also available. None of the cakes are vegetarian and a disappointed couple sharing a table with me had left most of theirs because it was stale. Perhaps the kitchen was having a bad day – if the food was as good as the atmosphere they would be onto a winner.

Carluccio's Caffè

Carluccio's Caffé
Italian, Classic

⊞ *305–307 Upper Street, N1*
☎ *020 7359 8167*
🚇 *Angel LU (5 min walk)*
🕐 *Mon-Sat 8am-11pm, Sun 9am-10pm*
☀ *Outside seating*
i *Booking advisable in evenings*

Vegetarian ★★★
Taste ★★★★
Price ££

Although it's one of the smaller eateries of the ever expanding Carluccio Caffé chain, every time I visit it's always packed with delighted diners and it's busy even on a Sunday evening. It's a place where you can go for just a cup of coffee or a substantial three course meal.

For a quick hearty bite I can recommend the nourishing Pasta E Fagioli soup, a thick bean and veg soup that you can almost stand your spoon up in. They drizzle it with olive oil and it comes with a chunky square of foccacia. Ice-creams here are really intense and good.

For a fuller review see the entry for Carluccio's, St Christopher's Place, W1 (page 35).

Duke Of Cambridge
Organic, British, Mediterranean, Modern

⊞ *30 St Peter's Street, N1*
☎ *020 7359 3066*
🚇 *Angel LU (5-10 min walk)*
🕐 *Lunch Tue-Fri 12.30pm-3pm, Sat & Sun 12.30pm-3.30pm;*
  Dinner Mon-Sat 6.30pm-10.30pm, Sun 6.30pm-10.00pm
🍼 *Child friendly*

Organic ★★★★★
Vegetarian ★★★★
Taste ★★★★
Price ££

The mother of organic gastropubs with a knock-out list of organic wines and draught beers. A capacious corner pub, it's just a short stroll down a gentrified street away from Islington's manic main dining strip. Large old wooden tables with non-matching chairs and stripped wooden flooring informalise the setting. At the back, a candlelit conservatory dining room exudes a New Age vibe. Weekday evenings attract eco-conscious affluents, weekends are more family centred. Booking is advisable especially on Sunday.

The short blackboard menu changes daily. Food here is as organic as can be as are the drinks except whiskey, tequila and rum. There are four organic real ales, Pitfield Brewery's Eco Warrior, Shoreditch Organic Stout, St Peter's Organic ale and Singhboulton (named after the pub owners) and all are well worth a try.

The complimentary warm crusty bread is very good and comes with olive oil. Baked bruschetta, with roast celery, cherry tomato, courgette and mozzarella is tasty and substantial. Spaghetti with herb pesto, garlic and olives with a vibrant tang of lemon breadcrumbs made a delicious vegetarian main course. There are appealing good organic choices for carnivore friends too.

A very reasonable £6.50 lunch deal of a main course plus a half pint of draught Freedom beer, ale, fruit juice or wine is available Mon-Fri. The Duke's sister gastropub is The Crown (Victoria Park, Hackney, see page 211).

Gallipoli Bazaar
Turkish

Vegetarian ★★★
Taste ★★★★
Price ££

107 Upper Street, N1
020 7226 5333
Highbury Islington LU & Rail or Angel LU (5 min walk)
Sun-Thur 12noon-11.30pm, Fri-Sat 12noon-12midnight

The latest edition to the Gallipoli empire, featuring the same menu as Gallipoli (see page 96) plus a few Moroccan specials. Set on two floors, the ground floor being a souk sofa chillout zone, Islington's answer to Momo on Heddon Street. Serves cocktails and is about 10% pricier than the other Gallipoli's.

Indian Veg Bhel-Poori House
Indian

Vegetarian ★★★★★
Taste ★★
Price £

📧 *92/93 Chapel Market, N1*
☎ *020 7837 4607*
🚌 *Angel LU (5 min walk)*
🕐 *Daily 12noon-11.30pm*
🍴 *Vegan menu*
🍸 *Alcohol-free zone*

Bargain-priced, pulse-based restaurant that proudly wears its veggie heart on its sleeve, promoting cruelty-free food, world hunger issues and vegetarian health benefits. Based on Islington's competitively price-driven street market dining strip, the jewel in the crown is the eat-as-much-as-you-like lunch and dinner buffet at £2.95 attracting stallholders and local office types at lunchtime, voraciously hungry but well-mannered 18-25's and budget-conscious eco-aware neighbourhood locals at evening time.

The atmosphere is friendly, chatty and without music. Décor is old-style Indian restaurant with mint coloured walls, worn carpets, small chandeliers and assorted self-promoting posters and cuttings. Good tablecloths, decent plates, knives and forks and dignified service are pleasant features at this incredibly cheap restaurant.

The self-service buffet changes weekly. Most diners don't have a clue what they are eating as there are no dish descriptions, yet delight in refilling and piling their plates high. On offer are two okay tasting vegetable curries and two good rices (one organic). The deep fried onion, cauliflower and potato were disappointing with more fry than veg, and the wheatflour puri was not warm and the papadom came as small broken bits rather than whole. Some of the dishes looked bland and unappetising and were not as hot as they should be, a problem frequently encountered with buffet-dining in general.

On the salad station, the choice is a bit limited but there's a decent shredded cabbage with mango chutney, two onion salads and three reasonable sauces of mango, mint and spiced tomato ketchup. All the food is vegan, except on occasions when they put panir (cheese) in the curry

There are lots of of soft drinks including five non-dairy lassis, (traditional sweet or savoury yoghurt drinks). The Soya Mango Lassi is to be recommended although it doubles the price of the meal! There's also a good selection of organic canned drinks although the hard up here just drink tap water. It's the cheapest veggie eaterie in town.

The Living Room

International

Vegetarian ★★★★
Taste ★★★★
Price ££

🖃 *18-26 Essex Road, N1*

☎ *0870 44 22 712*

🚌 *Angel LU (5 min walk)*

🕐 *Mon-Wed 12noon-11.30pm, Thur 12noon-12midnight,*
Fri 12noon-2am, Sat 11am-2am, Sun 11am-11.30pm

◻ *Child friendly*

♫ *Live music nightly*

This is where vegetarians have a tipple, hang out and party. An upmarket bar and restaurant it opened in 2002 and has never looked back. The restaurant is done out living room style with banquettes and a few large canvasses on the wall. The menu is long with five veggie starters, three salads, two or three mains and always one veggie special. Soup of the day was tomato and carrot.

The Living Room does a good choice of alcoholic concoctions and a Chauffeur's Choice of alcohol-free cocktails, where the hot sellers are 'Virgins Kiss' and 'Sea Biscuit'.

It's more an evening than a lunchtime destination and the Friday evening I went with my wife, there was live piano and guitar music in the bar with some very decent 70's renditions being played. Jazz and soul singers also do live gigs on Thursday, Friday and Saturday nights whilst at Sunday Brunch there's live piano. In the summer the place opens out onto the pavement.

We kicked off with one of the three bread openers – a fine ciabatta with onion, balsamic vinegar and olive oil. Starters are sensibly small and the Roasted Garlic Field Mushrooms with Dolcelatte cheese, wild roquette and tomato compote was quite good but could have done with a bit more cheese. Better was the Goats' Cheese, Asparagus, Red Pepper and Sweet Onion Tart. Vegetarian Bangers and Mash were an excellent main course, three chunky sausages nicely crisp on the outside and a delicious gravy – an admirable attempt at the real thing. Mains arrive in massive dishes and the Wild Mushroom Risotto was no exception, although the actual portion was not overly generous. The risotto temperature was variable and the taste average. However, the Belgian Waffles were superb, warm in a succulent sweet maple syrup and served with ice cream. Also delicious was the The Lemon Meringue that came as an individual pie with a good firm pastry and surrounded by a raspberry coulis. The ambience of The Living Room is lively and fun with several groups enjoying a private party and couples wining and dining.

The Children's Menu has three veggie starters, one veggie main, a pasta with roast veg and tomato sauce and a choice of desserts. Of note is the selection of organic baby foods for main course and desserts.

Some of the staff are vegetarian and are adept at handling dietary questions. Artificial coloured and flavoured products are avoided as much as possible and data sheets are available. Service is very attentive and our waiter, Thiago, was very helpful in making menu suggestions.

Further branches of the Living Room are due to open in Heddon Street (April 2005) and the City (May 2005) with other openings scheduled for Oxford and Cambridge. Living Rooms can also be found in Manchester, York, Birmingham, Edinburgh and several other major northern cities.

Morgan M
French, Modern

▦ *489 Liverpool Road, N7*

☎ *020 7609 3560*

🚆 *Highbury and Islington LU & Rail (5-10 min walk)*

🕐 *Lunch Wed-Fri & Sun 12noon-3pm;*
   Dinner Tue-Sat 7pm-12.30am (last orders 10pm)

i *Booking required*

Organic	★★★
Vegetarian	★★★★
Taste	★★★★★
Price	*£££££*

Vegetarian haute cuisine five course set menu with food that's amongst the best in London. The formal dark green exterior speaks serious dining and inside, it's all cool white walls with modern paintings, gracious high backed chairs and spaciously arranged tables laid with Robert Welch cutlery. The service is elegant, the atmosphere refined, the clientele discerning foodies from Canonbury, Hampstead and Highgate. Evenings are busy, lunchtimes much quieter.

The 'From the Garden' menu costs £27 and changes seasonally and four different delicious wines by the glass are suggested to match the courses at £18. I would recommend this, although an extensive wine list is available. An amuse bouche of warm Cream of Cauliflower sauce with parsnip shavings in a tiny espresso cup begins what is a series of small dishes, each sparkling with different and delightful tastes. A starter of Cream of Pumpkin soup with beignet of Wild Mushroom was good, whilst the Légumes à la Greque was excellent. A tasty Gnocchi Ragout with exquisite cherry tomatoes was followed by a sumptuous Ricotta Cannelloni with wild mushrooms. The Pineapple Soufflé was exemplary although the Chocolate Moelleux was quite incredible too. Allow two and half hours to enjoy this wonderful dining experience that will leave you satisfyingly full. A meat and fish set menu is available for fellow omnivores.

Ottolenghi
Mediterranean, Classic, Modern

  🖼 *287 Upper Street, N1*
  ☎ *020 7288 1454*
  🚌 *Angel LU (7 min walk)*
  🕐 *Mon-Sat 8am-11pm, Sun 9am-7pm*
  🥕 *Vegan options*
  🍼 *Child friendly*
  ☀ *Outside seating*
  i   *Eat in (table service) & Takeaway*

Organic ★★★★
Vegetarian ★★★★
Taste ★★★★
Price Lunch *££*
Dinner *£££*

Ultra cool minimalist dining room serving high quality well-crafted dishes just across the road from the Almeida Theatre. Islington foodies are forever peering in through the window at the fabulous pastries, tempting breads and the two long dining tables which are seductively candlelit in the evenings. These are the only tables in the place, a major plus for socialisers, movers and shakers, a minus for diners who prefer a bit of privacy. Personally, I liked it.

The Friday night I dropped in the place was half full of sophisticated diners who knew what they were in for – a unique dinner party with chance encounters with strangers who like themselves are ever intrigued by new gastronomic experiences.

The short Dinner Menu changes daily with three veggie starters, two-four veggie mains and four desserts and is mostly organic. Allow £21.50 per head for three courses without drinks. However, if you don't want starters (£4.50 per person) you need to let the waiter know as soon as possible as they automatically come up when you are seated. To be sure of eating at the time you want, booking is advised for the evening meal on one of the long tables. The other table is unbookable and is for walk-ins on a first-come first-serve basis.

At lunch there are ten veggie salads (see Ottolenghi Notting Hill on page 169 for food review) and vegetarian patisserie is available day and night.

Opened in July 2004, Ottolenghi is a most welcome addition to the Islington scene and offers a refreshingly different approach to informal dining.

Tai Buffet

Thai, Chinese, classic

Vegetarian ★★★★★
Taste ★★★
Price £

- 🖃 13 Islington High St, N1
- ☎ 020 7837 7767
- 🚃 Angel LU (1 min walk)
- 🕒 Daily 11am-12midnight
- 🥕 Vegan menu
- ☀ Outside seating
- i Buffet Service

Tai Buffet is one of the very many bargain Thai, takeout box eateries that continue to sprout up all over London. For food review see Tai Buffet (Camden branch) on page 120. What makes this one different is the aggressive, street canvassers distributing leaflets to pull the punters in. It seems to work. At lunchtimes, there are queues into the street and inside it's manic. Sample menu is Pa Tai Noodle, Tai Curry Rice, Sweet and Sour veggie balls, Tai salad. The £5 buffet, £6 after 5pm deal is unbelievably good value.

Tai Noodle Bar

Chinese, classic

Vegetarian ★★★★★
Taste ★★★
Price £

- 🖃 11 Islington High Street, N1
- ☎ 020 7833 9399
- 🚃 Angel LU (2 min walk)
- 🕒 Daily 12noon-10.30pm
- 🥕 Vegan options
- i Eat in (table service) & Takeaway

Despite the name, this is a Chinese style noodle eaterie. Tai means great and is not a misspelling of Thai as most people would think. It was opened in September 2004 by the same friendly folk who brought us Tai Buffet a few doors away.

The Tai Noodle Bar menu is an entirely different gastro-quest, more distinct dishes and a décor in accord with a menu that should be twice the price. That said the look somehow doesn't quite work. A fusion of old meets new – modern Shoreditch-style flooring mixes uncomfortably with bamboo stalls, semi-circular wooden tables against the wall and square antique ones for bigger dining parties. Still the overall effect is impressive for a budget eaterie offering a starter and main course for only £8.

The short well explained menu gives some idea of the significance of vegetarian cuisine in Chinese culture. Starters are only £2.50 and the Zha da Xia is a remarkable substitute for Japanese tempura. The Mock Crispy Aromatic Duck starter is of good texture and reasonable taste; whilst Tai Noodle's signature dish – boiled dumplings (£5.50) – is substantial enough for two. The menu considerately advises to take care with the chilli based dipping sauce that may be too hot for some people. I tried it – hot sauce fanatics should find it a breeze.

On mains, the minced bean noodle dish, Zha jiang mian, arrives in a massive bowl of hand-made noodles with bean paste that's said to be the forerunner of spaghetti bolognese. Whatever your opinion on spag bol's ancestry this mock mince dish is well worth a whirl. Broad noodle soup endowed with sliced mock pork, noodles, and various vegetable is a tasty whole meal on its own at £5.50.

Thai Square Angel
Thai, Classic

    Vegetarian ★★★
    Taste ★★
    Price £££

🖃 *347-349 Upper Street, N1*
☎ *020 7704 2000*
🚌 *Angel LU (5 min walk)*
🕓 *Mon-Fri lunch 12noon-3pm, dinner 6pm-11pm;*
   Sat 12noon-11.30pm; Sun 12noon-10.30pm
🥕 *Vegan options*
i *Eat in (table service) & Takeaway*

With 18 vegetarian Thai dishes to choose from and one of the most beautifully designed restaurants in Islington, Thai Square is developing into a big Islington favourite especially in the evenings. Its basement bar can hold 100 and is licensed to 2am. See Thai Square, Trafalgar Square for meal review (page 29).

CAMDEN TOWN, PRIMROSE HILL & CHALK FARM

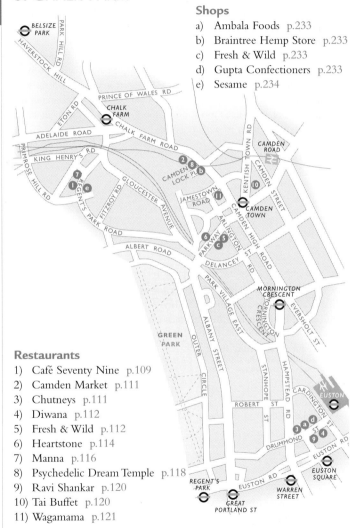

Shops

a) Ambala Foods p.233
b) Braintree Hemp Store p.233
c) Fresh & Wild p.233
d) Gupta Confectioners p.233
e) Sesame p.234

Restaurants

1) Café Seventy Nine p.109
2) Camden Market p.111
3) Chutneys p.111
4) Diwana p.112
5) Fresh & Wild p.112
6) Heartstone p.114
7) Manna p.116
8) Psychedelic Dream Temple p.118
9) Ravi Shankar p.120
10) Tai Buffet p.120
11) Wagamama p.121

This area of London is one of the most vibrant, dominated as it is by Camden Market which has a vast selection of veggie food to choose from including the truly original Psychedelic Dream Temple. Just south of the market is Heartstone which offers top notch organic and veggie café cuisine. Further north, Café Seventy Nine in Primrose Hill has a much more relaxed atmosphere and Manna is a great innovative organic vegetarian restaurant in the same neck of the woods. If you fancy something spicy there are great value Indian restaurants on Drummond Street, the best of which are reviewed below. Also of interest, Liz Heavenstone's Guest House – somewhere to stay that has organic breakfasts (see accommodation section on p.297)

Café Seventy Nine
Mediterranean, International, Modern

🖭 *79 Regent's Park Road, NW3*	Organic ★★★★
☎ *020 7586 8012*	Vegetarian ★★★★★
🚎 *Chalk Farm LU (5 min walk)*	Taste ★★★
🕐 *Mon-Sat 8.30am-6pm, Sun 9am-6pm*	Price £
✐ *Vegan options*	
🍼 *Child friendly*	
☀ *Outside seating*	

Despite the des-res surrounds, the menu prices are very reasonable. There's a delightful ambience where diners can enjoy all-day veggie breakfasts, and caffeine up with cafetière coffees and espressos. The place is a favourite neighbourhood eaterie with an interesting mix of artists and locals among its patrons.

All day breakfasts are the thing here and the special is particularly recommended. Scrambled eggs, mushrooms and toast with two home-made veggie sausages quite heavy on mustard and well worth a whirl. The home-made Veggie burger ensemble with salad and mayo unfortunately doesn't really work with wholemeal pitta bread used instead of the traditional bun. However, it is a popular light option compared to the heavier Bagel Burger served with vegetarian Cheddar and deep fried new potatoes. Miranda, who cooks, uses organic, free range eggs from Tim Norris's farm at Sarratt in Hertfordshire and eight of the cakes and puds are made in their own kitchen.

Café Seventy Nine is not an in your face vegetarian eaterie and there's no mention of its veggie credentials outside or even on the menu. Yet, this is one of the best veggie café's in London. A swell place to visit when around Primrose Hill.

Fresh & Wild

Camden Market
International, Classic

🖼 *Camden Town*

🚇 *Camden Town LU or Chalk Farm LU (5 min walk)*

🕐 *Saturday- Sunday 9am-5pm*

If you've worked up an appetite haggling over clothes purchases at London's most in-your-face market, then the food stalls of The Stables (a subdivision of the main market) is the place to set your sights. Expect no-frills street food with many national variations represented: English, Indian, Chinese, Japanese and Thai. It's cheap and cheerful take-away food but there are also some old outdoor benches if you want to take a more leisurely approach to your food.

Chutneys
Indian, Classic

Vegetarian ★★★★★
Price ££

124 Drummond Street, NW1

☎ *020 7388 0604*

🚇 *Euston LU & Rail (3 min walk)*

🕐 *Mon-Sat 12noon-10.30pm (daily lunch buffet 12noon-2.45pm);*
   Sunday all day buffet 12noon-10.30pm

🌱 *Vegan options*

The first Indian buffet in London, this is now the most up-to-date and biggest of the three Indian restaurants on Drummond Street and makes a big thing of advertising itself as a vegetarian restaurant.

During the week its clientele is mainly European and it is popular with German and Swiss vegetarian tourists. On Fridays, Saturdays and Sundays there's more of a mix with Asian families. With background Bollywood music and a relaxed, sophisticated atmosphere, it's the most upscale of the Drummond Street restaurants.

The most popular choice is the Chutney's Deluxe Thali, a complete three course meal although the Kerala Set Menu at £12.95 is worth a try. Thalis here tend to be bigger than at Diwana and Ravi Shankar. The eat-as-much-as-you-like Sunday Buffet is a selection of over 40 dishes and is good value at £5.95.

Diwana

Indian, Classic

🏠 *121-123 Drummond Street, NW1*
☎ *020 7387 5556*
🚇 *Euston LU & Rail (1 min walk)*
🕐 *Mon-Sat 12noon-11.30pm, Sun 12noon-10.30pm*
🥕 *Vegan options*
🍽 *BYO (no corkage charged)*

Organic ★★
Vegetarian ★★★★★
Taste ★★★
Price £

Diwana is the oldest Indian vegetarian restaurant in the UK and has been going strong since 1970 with a classic Bhel Poori House menu and good value lunchtime buffet at £6.50.

The décor consists of bright wooden varnished tables, chairs and a few Indian artifacts; it's a big place with non-smoking and smoking areas and upstairs there's seating for a further 40 people. At 6.15pm the smoke-free zone gets packed with lively chatty office workers and a few veggie tourists. Most go for juices but some bring their own wine.

The menu is fairly extensive and well explained. Rava Deluxe Dosa is a huge flavoursome lacy, semolina based dosa with seasoned vegetables and comes with a good coconut chutney and passable sambar. The Gujarati Thali, comes with a quite spicy potato and pea curry with reasonable rice, dal and veg. Both these mains are quite sufficient but diners with bigger appetites could opt for starters and savouries as well. The lunchtime buffet (12noon-2.30pm) is popular and can attract 100 people per day.

Fresh & Wild

Organic Vegetarian, International

🏠 *49 Parkway, NW1*
☎ *020 7428 7575*
🚇 *Camden Town LU (2 min walk)*
🕐 *Mon-Fri 8am-9pm, Sat 9.30am-9pm, Sun 11am-8pm*
☀ *Outside seating*
i *Eat in (counter service) & Takeaway*

Organic ★★★★★
Vegetarian ★★★★
Taste ★★★
Price £

A great place to fill up on organic goodies when visiting Camden Market. Has buffet/deli counter so you can eat in or out. See Fresh & Wild Notting Hill for food review (page 168) and shop review (page 248).

Fresh & Wild

Heartstone
Organic, International

|📺| 106 Parkway, NW1

☎ 020 7485 7744

🚌 Camden Town LU (3 min walk)

🕐 Tue-Sat 8.30am-9pm, Sunday 10am-4pm
   (breakfast served 8.30am-12noon and all day Sunday)

✏ Vegan options

🍼 Child friendly

i Eat in (table service) & Takeaway, (outside catering available)

Organic ★★★★★
Vegetarian ★★★★
Taste ★★★★
Price £££

The quintessential organic neighbourhood café and chillout zone. The outside is purposely designed to be discreet – so much so that it took me three attempts to find it – but once you know it's close to Bairstow Eves at the Regent's Park end of Parkway, there's no problem.

Heartstone draws a money's-no-object high-maintenance, health and eco-conscious set. On Sunday by 2pm it's full of affluent brunchers, a heady mix of North West London intellectuals, musicians, actors, twenty-something socialites and some older couples. The service, too, is top end and the staff committed – Michaela the waitress serving me told me she's been an organic vegetarian herself for some years on health grounds.

Once inside, there's a takeaway food and juice bar and further along is the laid-back café area, chicly decorated with black wooden tables and chairs, a white and lilac colour scheme and a flickering light sculpture. At the far end is an open kitchen and above, a skylight with pink and yellow panes. A shelving unit houses luxury organic provisions such as tea, coffee, incense sticks, New Age books and magazines so you can continue the Heartstone experience at home.

Recommended is the Vegetarian Breakfast (£9.50) comprising a slender, grilled tofu vegetarian sausage, mushrooms, cherry tomatoes, scrambled egg, and excellent sour dough bread. There is also a gluten-free bread option and sweet snacks such as chocolate pecan brownie made with organic Green and Black's chocolate.

Porridge comes in a big bowl with raisins, pumpkin seed, sunflower seed and sliced almonds. My wife asked for no almonds as she is allergic – but it still turned up with them although they did immediately make a fresh nut-free one. It's a timely reminder that those with allergies should always double check ingredients even in eateries such as Heartstone's that specialise in gluten-free, dairy-free and vegan. Incidentally, the porridge tasted very good as did the Monmouth Street

Heartstone

Coffee, although it did arrive in a measly sized cup in relation to its hefty £2.50 price tag.

Smoothies are very well made here and the 'Vanilla', a mix of apple juice, banana, Madagascan vanilla, flaxseed oil, lecithin and vitamin E is the most popular. Others I saw going down well were the green 'Revolution' juice of spinach, celery, fennel, apple and lime and also the 'Wizard', a red concoction of carrot, beetroot, lime and ginger. All the juices are loaded with marvellously healthy nutrients but they are pricey at £5.50 reg/£6.50 large.

At Heartstone, the coffee, milk and wines are all certified organic. The wine and beer list includes Holmes Brothers Sauvignon Blanc and a biodyanamic Fleury Champagne. All food and juices are freshly prepared to order, with ingredients sourced from certified producers where possible. Heartstones will appeal to raw food enthusiasts as they are strong on salads and adept at catering for gluten-free, dairy-free and vegan dietary requirements. Carnivore options are also available.

In the evenings the ambience mellows considerably with candles and incense. Budget watchers should note that a 12.5% service charge is added in line with most good restaurants and the 'filtered water' arrives in a jug and costs £1 per head!

Manna

Mediterranean, International, Modern

Organic ★★★★
Vegetarian ★★★★★
Taste ★★★★
Price £££

- 🖼 *4 Erskine Road, Primrose Hill, NW3*
- ☎ *020 7722 8028*
- 🚌 *Chalk Farm LU (3 min walk)*
- 🕐 *Daily 6.30pm-11pm (last orders 10.00pm),*
  lunch Sundays 12.30pm-3.00pm
- 🥕 *Vegan options*
- 👶 *Child friendly*
- ☀ *Outside seating*
- i *Booking required; Catering service available see page 278)*

Opened in 1966, Manna is the oldest Veggie restaurant in London and continues to push the boundaries, winning the Vegetarian Society's 'Best Vegetarian Restaurant' Award in 2003.

Located on a side turning off the main Regent's Park Road/Primrose Hill restaurant drag it's a popular destination, offering informal dining and strong on organic choices. Madonna, Paul McCartney, Kate Moss and Woody Harrelson have vegged out here and Manna has done outside catering for Radiohead and Coldplay.

Celebrities aside, Manna attracts an affluent, casual-dressed twenty to fortysomething crowd and has a friendly atmosphere with a gentle background soundtrack of jazz music, and 70'/80's progressive music.

The organic drinks range is marvellous. There's an exemplary organic aperitif selection which includes the Juniper Green Gin and Tonic and also the Utkins Organic Vodka and Cranberry Cocktail (both recommended). There are twenty organic wines with the Sicilian Dry White making a very decent house choice and three organic beers and organic cider. To finish is a selection of eight organic liqueurs.

The short menu is inviting and changes every two months with different specials each day. The Butternut Squash and Coconut Soup is to die for and comes with an organic bread selection of which a red and green pepper encrusted white bread is excellent. Organic Ravioli filled with herbed ricotta served on walnut pesto, parmesan and rocket leaves is enjoyably light and subtle whilst the Tofu Triangles look tantalisingly attractive. The organic Fennel Schnitzel is a big boy's portion as are all the mains at Manna. Arriving on a bed of crushed potatoes, a wad of kale with tarragon and pinky-white peppercorn sauce, it works rather well. The Wild Mushroom and Flageolet Bean Ragout, is also good and comes on a root vegetable square with caramelised baby onions and baby leeks.

Save room for the desserts. Of the five organic choices, the Organic Fruit Crumble with either dairy or soya cream is recommended. Vegans might like to try the Organic Orange & Amaretto Tiramisu which, although it doesn't taste of traditional Italian Tiramisu, is a landmark recipe in its own right.

Matthew Kay, Manna's owner and Executive Chef and his team have served ground breaking dishes for years and continue to innovate. The service is attentive and staff have an extensive knowledge of vegan, gluten-free and wheat-free cuisine. Given 24 hours notice Manna can knock something up for even the most pinickity vegetarian with food allergy.

Bargain tip: Manna serves an early bird special of two courses for £13.25, Sunday to Thursday 6.30pm-7.30pm.

The Psychedelic Dream Temple

Organic Café, Juice Bar, International

Organic ★★★★
Vegetarian ★★★★★
Taste ★★★
Price £

    Unit 21/22 Stables Market, NW1
☎ *020 7267 8528*
🚇 *Chalk Farm LU (3 min walk)*
🕐 *Daily 11am-6.30pm,*
Ø *Live DJ events Fri, Sat & Sun 9pm-2am (£3 admission)*
🌶 *Vegan options*
i   *Counter service; Parties catered for (see page 279)*

This trippy-hippy upstairs café serves organic vegan food, coffee, juices and smoothies. Located in the middle of the Stables Market in Camden, it can be hard to find but if you can't pin point it immediately just ask one of the stall holders for directions.

The ground floor of the Dream Temple sells CDs and vinyl and is a shrine to trance, lounge, ambient, world fusion and all those hard to come by psycho-grooves.

Upstairs is home to the café, as well as a specialist mind, body and spirit bookshop. The fantasy-styled café has a Buddha, a resident flying fairy, a cosmic ceiling and intriguingly painted walls that convey the impression you are sitting in a Moroccan castle. The café is popular with a self-consciously alternative crowd, guys with pony tails and girls with pierced noses lying back on the cushioned sofas contemplating the enigma of the universe.

Two young guys were sucking smoke on an ornamental sheesh (£5). "It's apple flavour and I get a triple nicotine rush from it without the throaty effect you get with cigarette tar," explained one. Asked if I would like a smoke I declined preferring my enjoyable organic vegan pizza and a huge cup of organic latte.

Food is only served on Saturdays and Sundays when it can get quite hectic and comprises vegan pizzas or interesting vegetable soups such as Spinach and Peanut. The rest of the time there are usually light bites like organic chocolate brownie or mango and apple coconut slice to keep the hunger at bay.

At weekends, £5 buys you two scrummy pizza slices with goat's cheese, broccoli, tomato, pesto sauce and a decent salad of pasta shells, carrot, sliced cucumber, tomato and tahini that is quite filling enough for one or as a light snack for two. Not all the pizza ingredients are organic due to availability and the desire to keep prices down. The pizza itself has a good flavour but on the small plate filled with salad it's all too cramped to eat comfortably.

The Psychedelic Dream Temple

Coffees and herbal teas are all organic but their freshly made apple juice whilst delicious is not totally organic. Mahni Dare, the chef, is a vegetarian with a keen interest in organic who used to be a cook at Caravan Dream, a veggie eaterie in New York. She would like to make it completely organic when prices fall rather than outprice her current customers.

Whilst one of the specialities here is the organic hemp milk, many opt for the smoothies to which they can add organic supplements or one of the Arabic teas served in a traditional metal tea pot. The orange fragranced Alambra Dream is not bad at all.

The Dream Temple Café is the most 'far out' place in veggie organic London and a recommended experience for those seeking an alternative experience away from the mainstream.

Ravi Shankar

Indian, Classic

Organic ★★
Vegetarian ★★★★★
Taste ★★★
Price £

🖃 133-135 Drummond Street, NW1
☎ 020 7388 6458
🚊 Euston LU & Rail (2 min walk)
🕓 Daily 12noon-10.30pm
🌶 Vegan options

Ravi Shankar shares the same ownership as the two other Drummond Street Indian restaurants Diwana and Chutney and the food is indeed very similar. Ravi Shankar, like Chutney's, doesn't allow you to bring your own booze but they stock three French organic wines suitable for vegetarians and vegans.

A popular Indian eaterie, it's decked out with sandy dessert coloured walls and dark wooden furniture with seats on the ground floor and upstairs. The house special is the Shanka Thali, a substantial three-course meal. Lots go for the lovely looking Paper Dosa – a paper thin pancake with a veggie filling.

Tai Buffet

Thai/Chinese, Classic

Vegetarian ★★★★★
Taste ★★★
Price £

🖃 6 Kentish Town Road, NW1
☎ 020 7284 4004
🚊 Camden Town LU (30 sec walk)
🕓 Daily 12noon-10.30pm
🌶 Vegan menu
🍼 Child friendly
i Eat in (buffet service) & Takeaway

Bargain £5 all you can eat vegan cuisine that goes up by just a quid more after 5pm and on Sundays. Opened in September 2003, the place boasts a modern café interior and serves twenty, regularly replenished, options at its buffet table.

It's about 80% eat in, 20% takeaway despite the amazing £3 takeaway box offer. I piled a respectable mountain of soya mock beef, soya lamb, sweet and sour soya chicken, soft Singapore noodles, veg chow mein and tofu into my plastic box that was delicious and satisfyingly filling. They've a good spread of salad dishes too and I spotted a rock musician luncher filling his carton with a couple of dozen spring rolls for the band to nosh back at a nearby recording studio. When you taste them you'll know why! This is a great mucho cheapo pitstop.

Some food is organic, the policy being that if the buy-in price is a little higher than non-organic they will purchase. Thai Buffet is related to a whole stream of similar outfits that used to be run in conjunction with a Buddhist group. The situation is that they have become less meditative and more commercial and are planning rapid expansion. The meal deals are great and essentially the same at all these restaurants. Ken Chow, the head honcho, also runs free vegan cookery classes.

Wagamama
Japanese, Modern

🖵 *11 Jamestown Road, NW1*
☎ *020 7428 0800*
🚃 *Camden Town LU (5 min walk)*
🕐 *Mon-Sat 12noon-11pm, Sun 12noon-10pm*
🍴 *Child friendly*

Vegetarian ★★★
Taste ★★★★
Price £

Wagamama is a superb chain of thirteen noodle bars all with the same menus serving very good inexpensive Japanese vegetarian choices. What makes this one different is that it's the only Wagamama with a street level view. For more details about the food see the review of Wagamama, Wigmore Street (page 47).

Tai Buffet

Organic13
International, classic

⌧ *13 Brecknock Road, N7*
☎ *020 7419 1234*
✍ *www.organic13.com*
🚌 *Tufnell Park LU (10 min walk),*
   253 or 29 buses run nearby
🕐 *Mon-Sat 9am-6pm, Sun 9am-5pm*
🥕 *Vegan options*
◊ *Children-friendly*
i *Eat in & Takeaway*

Organic ★★★★★
Vegetarian ★★★★★
Taste ★★★
Price £

Organic vegetarian gourmet café deli and juice bar that's strong on social and environmental issues and Soil Association and Vegetarian Society certified. Opened in August 2004, in the local alternative community in Brecknock, Organic13 is bright white, modern and airy with pinewood floors and aluminium and wooden chairs and tables. Upstairs is the food counter, a few high stalls and maybe you'll see Peter McCaig, editor of Green Events magazine (see page 286) whose office is in the same building, taking time off to sip a glass of 'imploded reverse osmosis filtered drinking water'.

Most people, eat in the spacious basement to the sounds of ambient music. It's very popular with young mothers with high chairs, bumbos, a baby changing zone, play area, organic cotton bibs, buggy parking, bottle and baby food warming and children's menu.

Organic13 runs a vegan kitchen and has a short blackboard menu that changes regularly. Minestrone soup (£2.99) comes up good and hearty, slightly spicy with several slices of chunky wholemeal bread. Thai Green Coconut Curry with quinoa and kumquat salad (£6.95) delivers yummy tastes and comes with sprout salad of chickpeas aduki beans, mung beans, lemon juice and beansprouts together with a root salad of beetroot, apple and red onion. Available also are fast foods such as organic vegeburger, paninis and a good selection of salads for raw foodists – hummus and guacamole too. Overall, food here is not cheap but good quality and good value for money. There are different sized bowls and takeout boxes to suit all appetites and wallets.

See Eco13 on the same premises (page 240), also Bumble Bee and Natural Remedies (page 239) a stone's throw away.

HAMPSTEAD, FINCHLEY & GOLDERS GREEN

Golder's Green, the vegetarian 'falafel mile' is fab for snacks, light bites and bakeries with veggie choices. Amongst the best of the fast food Jewish joints are Taboon and Tasti Pizza, with Milk and Honey offering comfortable seating and a varied menu. VitaOrganic, on Finchley Road has its faithful raw foodist followers and offers an imaginative international menu. The much loved Rani in Finchley Central reigns supreme with it's upscale Indian buffet, perhaps the best in London.

FINCHLEY & GOLDERS GREEN

CTV
Thai and Chinese, Classic

Vegetarian ★★★★★
Taste ★★★
Price £

  ▦ *22 Golders Green Rd, Golders Green, NW11*
  ☎ *020 8201 8001*
  🚇 *Golders Green LU*
  🕐 *12noon-10pm*
  🥕 *Vegan menu*

Bargain £5 all you can eat vegan. For food review see Tai Buffet (Camden branch) page 120.

Milk 'n' Honey
International, Classic, Kosher

Vegetarian ★★★
Taste ★★★★
Price £££

  ▦ *124 Golders Green Road, NW11*
  ☎ *020 8455 0664*
  🚇 *Golders Greens LU (5 min walk)*
  🕐 *Sun-Thur 10.30am-11pm, Fri 10.30am-3pm,*
     Sat 8pm-11.30pm
  🥕 *Vegan options*
  i *Eat in (counter service) & Takeaway*

An eclectic mix of kosher Italian, Israeli and Oriental dishes in a big informal dining room. I started the extensive menu at the 'Appetiser – Let the fun begin' section with Vegetable Samosa with mint sauce and garnish. They weren't joking about the fun – the samosa arrived with tomato sauce. That said the samosas were okay but what was really nice was the side salad of pickled cucumbers and tomato. Main courses are generous and of note are the Vegeburger and fries, Stir Fry of noodles with peppers, courgettes and mushrooms with soy sauce and the big selection of vegetarian pastas and pizzas. To finish there's a healthy Fresh Fruit Salad or decadent pastries the size of doorsteps and a list of sorbets and sundaes as long as your arm.

Milk 'n' Honey draws a garrulous clientele of Golders Green grannies–who–lunch, local Jewish ladies and young men.

Paradise Bakery
International, Kosher

Vegetarian ★★★★★
Taste ★★★
Price £

▫ 109 Golders Green Road, NW11
☎ 020 8201 9694
🚇 Golders Green LU (5 min walk)
🕐 Sun-Fri, 6.30am-10.30pm or one hour before sabbath on Fridays
🌱 Vegan options
i Eat in (counter service) & Takeaway

Pastries, cakes, chollahs, bagels suitable for vegetarians. Also, to take away, mini bourakis, pizzas and rolls.

**"OPTIMUM NUTRITIOUS
& DELICIOUS WHOLEFOOD
FOR CLEANSING & REJUVENATION!"**

★ ★ ★ ★ ★
Commuter Magazine

"Excellent restaurant, the food is wonderful and there is a very good atmosphere"
www.veganlondon.co.uk

"a must for everyone... a delight"
Optimum Nutrition Magazine

**VITAORGANIC RESTAURANT
ALTERNATIVE CAFE & JUICE BAR**
279c Finchley Road, London, NW3 6LT
Tel: 020 7435 2188   WWW.VITAORGANIC.CO.UK

Rani

Indian, Gujurati

Vegetarian ★★★★★
Taste ★★★★
Price £ £

⌨ *7 Long Lane, Finchley Central, N3*

☎ *020 8349 4386*

🚌 *Finchley Central LU (6 min walk)*

🕐 *Daily evening buffet 7pm-9pm (buffet closes 10pm);*
Sunday lunch Buffet 1pm-2.30pm (buffet closes 3.30pm);
Business lunch buffet (Mon-Fri 12.30pm-2pm (buffet closes 3pm)

✒ *Vegan options (more than 50%)*

◊ *Child friendly*

i *Eat in (table and buffet service) & Takeaway*

Lifelong vegetarian Jyotindra Pattni, a portly gentleman in a dark suit, stands proudly and contentedly at the reception desk having checked in a full house of evening diners. He and his wife (who is the chef) offer one of the best and most reasonably priced buffets in London. The dishes are excellently presented, well labelled and all are at the correct temperature. Hygiene standards are of the highest. An attentive waiter stands at the buffet area to assist and check that no used plates are brought into the area so that there is no cross contamination of food.

Rani has been running for 20 years and whilst the service is quite formal the waitering staff are friendly. Less than half the clientele are Finchley locals, with vegetarians trekking in from Islington, Camden, St Albans, Harrow and Wembley. Rani serves 100% vegetarian home-style Gujarati the way Jyotindra and his wife had back home.

The restaurant is large and comfortable, with 70's Indian style mango and red décor and green tablecloths. The eat-as-much-as-you-like buffet offers a big choice, and this is what most people go for although there is an extensive à la carte menu which works out more expensive. The buffet choices change weekly so that regulars never get bored.

At the Cold Starter station, there is Dhai Vada, Aloo Papri Chat and Bhel Poori (all good) with an excellent selection of 18 accompaniments – the lime/chilli chutney, apple chutney and the mango chutney are particularly recommended. Of the hot starters I had Palak Bhaji (very good) and Rani Mogo (good). For mains, I enjoyed tasty Methi Poori and Banana Methi, pitch perfect Pilau Rice, Gurati Dal and Liloti Sak. On the dessert front, the Meth Sev is fine whilst the Fruit Shrikand is very good indeed.

The à la carte menu is most informative and wheat, nut and dairy dishes are clearly marked for those people with special dietary needs.

Taboon

Jewish, Classic, Kosher

🖃 *17 Russell Parade, Golders Green Rd, NW11*
☎ *020 8455 7451*
🚇 *Brent Cross LU (10 min walk)*
🕐 *Sun-Thur 9am-12midnight, Fri 9am-4pm, Sat 8pm-1am*
🥢 *Vegan options*
i *Eat in (counter service) & Takeaway*

Vegetarian ★★★★★
Taste ★★
Price £

Kosher falafel filled pittas meet pizza slices and chips in this popular small neighbourhood nosh bar decked out with high stalls and zero décor. Inside, it's a mix of observant N.W. London Jewish adults and school-kids with a few non-Jewish local workman.

Your unsmiling server diligently crams falafels into the pitta pocket leaving you to top it up from the self-service salad station with coleslaw, chopped salad, hummous, green chilli, and various sauces. Shame – you can't get much extra in! Still, it tastes okay while the pizza slices look just about alright. It's fine for a cheap pit-stop and they do latkas and burekas, a Yemenite speciality in cheese, potato, spinach and mushroom flavours. Drinks are canned and the Israeli Strawberry and Banana Spring Water is good.

Taboon also have a branch in Edgware (tel 020 8058 5557).

Tasti Pizza

Jewish, Modern, Kosher

🖃 *252 Golders Green Road, NW11*
☎ *020 8209 0023*
🚇 *Brent Cross LU (10 min walk)*
🕐 *Sun-Thur 12noon-10.30pm, Fri 12noon-4pm (in summer),*
  Sat after sabbath till late
🥢 *Vegan options*
☀ *Outside seating in summer*
i *Eat in (counter service) & Takeaway*

Vegetarian ★★★★
Taste ★★
Price £

Kosher mostly-vegetarian menu in schlochy fast food eaterie that looks more like an old Wimpy Bar than a nosh bar. Lunchtime, it's jammed with Jewish guys, other times it's 50% mums and kids. Like Taboon, a few doors down it serves pizza, chips, latkes and falafel but here they also do jacket potato and blintzes.

See also Tasti Pizza in Stamford Hill, N16 (tel 020 8802 0018).

VitaOrganic
International, Classic, Organic

🖃 *279c Finchley Road, NW3*
☏ *020 7435 2188*
🚌 *Finchley Road LU (4 min walk)*
Finchley Road & Frognal Rail (4 min walk)
🕒 *Daily 12noon-3pm, 6pm-10.30pm*
🥕 *Vegan menu*
◌ *Child friendly*
i *Eat in & Takeaway*

Organic ★★★★★
Vegetarian ★★★★★
Taste ★★★
Price ££

Vitaorganic opened in Autumn 2001 and is a health-orientated Asian vegan restaurant, café and juice bar. Outside, it is unremarkable but inside there are waterfalls, coloured lanterns and bamboo seating, which provides a great atmosphere in the evenings when the place is candlelit.

There's enough choice for anyone who eats 100% raw. Eight raw soups are available including gazpacho, miso soup, tom yum Malaysian spicy soup and Russian borsht clear soup. Some can be ordered warm as well.

The buffet meal allows you to fill your plate to the brim with a wide selection of hot and cold dishes for £6.90. I had a very pleasant mixed plate of Black Bean Stew, Orange Masala Dal (a mixture of pumpkin, sprouted lentils, carrots, green leaves) and something called a Transitional Sweet and Sour, a speciality that is very enjoyable. VitaOrganic has placed a great emphasis upon healthy eating and Mr Phong the manager is on hand to give plenty of good advice about the menu. Some of the meals are prepared with particular dietary requirements in mind, but if you're looking for more flavour try the 'Speciality Selection' of seven dishes that are more flavourful. The temperature of dishes is variable but intentionally so. VitaOrganic cooks to keep the food proteins intact and to minimise the destruction of vital vitamins and essential fatty acids.

The restaurant is 98% organic and is in the process of going through Soil Association Certification. Non-organic items are marked on the menu. The juices are without added sugar and cost £3.50-£4.90. There are 15 additional choices to customise smoothies such as Aloe Vera, Ginseng, Flax and Mix seed cream at 90p extra. There is also a great choice of herbal, fruit and green teas and chocolate alternatives like a soya carob latte.

HAMPSTEAD

Good Earth Express
Chinese, Classic

🖃 335 West End Lane, NW6
☎ 020 7433 3111
🚋 West Hampstead LU & Rail
🕒 Daily 5.30pm-11.30pm
i Takeaway and delivery service only

Vegetarian ★★★★
Taste ★★★★★
Price £££

See Good Earth Knightsbridge for food review (page 155).

Hugo's
International, Modern

🖃 25 Lonsdale Road, NW6
☎ 020 7372 1232
🚋 Queen's Park LU (2 min walk)
🕒 Daily 9am-11pm (booking required)
◊ Child friendly
♫ Live music Tuesday, Wednesday and Sunday
☀ Outside seating

Organic ★★★★
Vegetarian ★★★
Taste ★★★★
Price £££

Sister restaurant to Hugo's in Kensington with essentially the same menu (see page 156 for food review). The décor at this organic café is brown rustic and at this branch there's live music on Tuesday and Wednesday with jazz on Sunday.

Hugo's

Mulan

Chinese, Classic

🔲 *91 Haverstock Hill, NW3*

☎ *020 7586 1257*

🚌 *Belsize Park/Chalk Farm LU (5 min walk)*

🕐 *Lunch Mon-Sat 12noon-2.30pm, Sun 12.30pm-2.45pm;*
   Dinner Mon-Sat 6pm-11.30pm, Sun 6pm-10.30pm

🖋 *Vegan choices*

Vegetarian ★★★★
Taste ★★★★
Price £&

A high quality restaurant offering Beijing vegetarian choices and set menu. Situated on the former Vegetarian Cottage site, Mulan, is a three-room restaurant decorated in a traditional Chinese style and run by the amicable Joseph Chan – previously of the Good Earth restaurant group. The menu is more adventurous than the décor with Asian influences and delectable mock carnivore choices. Recommended is the Aromatic Crispy Mock Duck starter that you wrap in pancakes with cucumber and hoisin sauce. Their Chinese-style samosas filled with chopped veg and sweet chilli side sauce make a refreshing change from the ubiquitous Indian versions.

Tofu dishes here are tops. There's a hot spicy peppercorned tofu deep fried starter and the sweet and sour main course is succulent and delicious. Two notable dishes are the Dried Shredded Aubergine that arrives in a hot spicy sauce and the crunchy "Three-in-One" – a dish with ginger, mushroom and cashew nut in a Szechuan sauce.

Evenings are much busier than lunchtime – partly due to the severe resident parking restrictions that operate during the daytime and are lifted in the evening. Omnivore options are available.

HIGHBURY & ARCHWAY

The Peking Palace
Chinese, Classic

🖻 *669 Holloway Road, N19*
☎ *020 7281 8989*
🚌 *Archway LU (1 min walk)*
🕐 *Mon-Sat lunchtime buffet 12noon-3pm, dinner 6pm-11pm;*
   Sun dinner 6pm-11pm
🥕 *Vegan menu*
◗ *Child friendly*
🍸 *BYO (£1 corkage charged)*
i *Eat in (table service) & Takeaway*

Vegetarian ★★★★★
Taste ★★★★
Price ££

A wholly vegetarian Chinese restaurant whose speciality mock-carni-vore dishes will leave you pleasantly full, taste buds intrigued and your concepts of soya-driven cuisine changed forever. Peking Palace has the longest vegetarian menu in London with over a hundred dishes, all of which are vegan. The Set Dinners represent good value at £12.50-£18.50 per person. The works is Set Dinner C, voluminous enough to satisfy a Sumo wrestler. Set A or B will suit most appetites. Swop dishes from the other Set Dinners if you fancy.

Complimentary cassava crackers compare well with prawn crackers in taste and texture. Don't eat too many – you'll need room for your starters! Set Dinner C begins gently with traditional appetisers of mini Vegetable Spring Rolls, Sesame on Toast, Crispy Seaweed (shredded green cabbage) and Grilled Dumplings with sweet 'n sour sauce and a ginger and onion sauce. Nothing too special here until you get to the yummy Satay Veggie Chicken, mock-chicken pieces with pepper chunks and onion pieces on skewers. The second act is a very reason-able Crispy Aromatic Veggie Duck appearing as strips covered with a 'veggie batter'.

The best showings are in Act 3 with the Veggie Beef Steak Peking style arriving as big succulent slices, an enormously satisfying Veggie Chicken with Cashew Nuts in Yellow Bean Sauce, Stir-fried Broccoli with Mangetout in Veggie Oyster Sauce and a good Thai Fragrant Steamed Rice. The big star undoubtedly is the Veggie Fish in Black Bean sauce that I swapped with the Veggie Prawn on the set menu. The best mock-fish dish in London, it has a smoked haddock flavour and texture and comes in three pieces rimmed in seaweed. Dessert choices are limited although the fried banana with sesame and vegan Swedish Glace ice cream slides down well.

Evenings are busy by 8.30pm with a casually dressed North West London crowd. Some bring their own wine and pay the £1 corkage, others opt for virtually alcohol-free lager, Schloer White Grape drink or a pot of tangy traditional Organic Kukicha Roasted Bancha Twig Tea.

Service here is attentive with knowledgeable and helpful staff. If any criticism can be made, it's the décor which is completely forget-table. However, this will in no way detract from what will be a very enjoyable vegetarian meal.

HIGHGATE & MUSWELL HILL

This part of London has two great cafés, Oshobasho and the Queen's Wood Weekend Café, both of which offer great food in the midst of lush woodland. The Cue Organic Garden gets a special review, just because it is such a great resource for those wanting to garden organically in the capital.

Oshobasho Café

Mediterranean and English, Classic

    Vegetarian ★★★★★
    Taste ★★★
    Price £

🖾 *Highgate Wood, Muswell Hill Road, N10*
🚌 *Highgate LU (5 min walk)*
🕐 *Open all year including Bank Holidays (except Christmas)*
   Mon 10.30am-3pm, Tue-Sun 8.30am till 30 min before gates close
🍴 *Vegan options*
🍼 *Child friendly*
☀ *Outside seating*
i *Eat in (counter service) & Takeaway*

Pleasant outdoor garden for veggie lunches, snacks and a great place to bring kids. Set in the heart of an ancient wood, it's best approached from Gypsy Gate on Muswell Hill Road, although I had to ask several times for directions before I found it. Fortunately, there's a Wildlife Information Unit near the café, with brochures and a map for next time!

On an idyllic lazy summer's afternoon the place is joyously packed with families, couples and kids sipping, slurping and grazing in the big dining area (reportedly enough for 200). The tables in the shade are particularly popular, presenting an enjoyable view of the colourful roses and fragrant wisteria that surround the enclosure.

If possible avoid the afternoon tea-time rush as there can be a queue 20 long with a ten minute wait. Behind me some Italians were grouching about the wait-time and complaining that the staff didn't know how to make good cappuccino. They were right, the coffee was not good and I wished I'd opted for a herbal tea or barley cup, however, the chocolate and vanilla cheese cake was spot on and as good as anywhere else I know. The cakes do look good here with the carrot cake apparently the all time bestseller. There are some mini vegan cakes too.

For hungrier souls there's more substantial fare including Broccoli and Potato Soup with bread, Greek Salad, Spanish Omelette, Hummous Salad and Penne Pasta with tomato sauce. Alternatively there's ciabatta bread with a choice of two fillings which come delivered to your table. Veggie cooked breakfasts and cereals are also available.

There's further seating inside the café, which is nice to know if it pours down. The café is opposite the wood's sports ground with its cricket and football pitches. Nearby is an award winning children's playground and there is a small car park for disabled drivers and a disabled toilet next to the café.

Oshobasho Café

Queen's Wood Weekend Café & Organic Garden

Mediterranean, English, Classic

Organic ★★★
Vegetarian ★★★★★
Taste ★★★
Price £

▭ *42 Muswell Hill Road, Highgate Wood, N10*
☎ *020 8444 2604*
🚌 *Highgate LU (5 min walk)*
🕐 *Weekends only 10am-6pm (Summer), 10am-5pm (Winter)*
🖊 *Vegan options*
◊ *Child friendly*
☀ *Outside seating*
i *Eat in (counter service) & Takeaway*

A woodland haven with a community-run veggie organic café complete with its own organic garden (see next page). A short walk from Muswell Hill Road, this former derelict building now has a charming forest cabin exterior whilst inside the look is cosy-grot with an old sofa, a couple of tatty armchairs, some folding chairs and chocolate coloured tablecloths.

At 4pm it's packed with all ages sipping organic tea and coffee and woofing down organic cake. The food here is pure vegetarian and the café is committed to organic on a 'where-possible' basis. There are about eight main meals including Spicy Burrito served with fresh mixed salad and salsa and a very respectable range of toasted ciabatta sandwiches with combinations of mozzarella, roast veg, chargrilled aubergine, avocado and tomato.

The vegetable soup with beans and rice served with a big chunk of bread and butter is a popular choice and the organic cakes are freshly made, delicious and enough for two. The Lemon Polenta is moist and yummy while the goodlooking Fruiti De Bosco (fruits of the forest pie) is what I'll try next time.

Goblin-themed children's parties, treasure hunts and private functions are held here that also utilise the nearby woodlands. You could almost imagine a performance of A Midsummer's Night Dream being performed here. After 6pm sometimes there are wedding parties. What an enchanting idea!

During the week, the Friends of Queens Wood use the building for a variety of local community projects.

Cue Organic Garden

This garden attached to the Queens Wood Café is a must see for anyone interested in urban organic gardening. A working garden, it might not look much aesthetically but is extremely informative and educational with useful printed notices explaining practices like crop rotation and mulching.

There's a good example of Square-Foot Gardening showing how London urbanites can grow a wide variety of organic plants in a very small area usually comprising 16 tiny units. This system is ideal for children and beginners and on show the day I visited were onions, tomatoes and lettuce that were used in the cafe's salad. There's also a greenhouse to look around as well as a section on Organic Container Gardening where containers are hung up, stood on the ground or in a window box, ideal for gardenless Londoners. Amongst the foods grown that are used in the café are carrot, courgette, tomato, lettuce and potato.

The Cue Organic Garden experiment forms part of a project giving urban solutions to eco-problems. No matter where you live in London there's advice on sustainable development, solar energy and the principles of growing fresh organic fruit and veg.

The Garden runs regular volunteer workdays, an Organic Gardening Course and occasional education and local community workshops as well as continuing research into environmental problems.

Organic gardening volunteer work varies from delicate plant tending to labour intensive compost heap turning on Thursdays 10am-4pm. Travel expenses and free lunch are provided.

Tai Buffet
Thai/Chinese

Vegetarian ★★★★★
Taste ★★★
Price £

🖼 *271 Muswell Hill Broadway, N10*
☎ *020 8442 0558*
🚇 *Highgate LU*
🕐 *Daily 12noon-10pm*
🌿 *Vegan menu*

Bargain £5 all you can eat vegan cuisine. For food review see Tai Buffet (Camden branch) page 120.

Tai Buffet

STOKE NEWINGTON

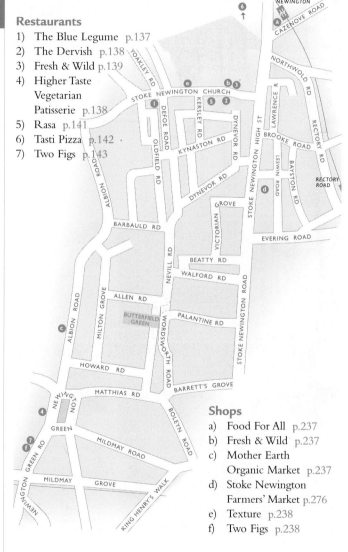

Restaurants

1) The Blue Legume p.137
2) The Dervish p.138
3) Fresh & Wild p.139
4) Higher Taste Vegetarian Patisserie p.138
5) Rasa p.141
6) Tasti Pizza p.142
7) Two Figs p.143

Shops

a) Food For All p.237
b) Fresh & Wild p.237
c) Mother Earth Organic Market p.237
d) Stoke Newington Farmers' Market p.276
e) Texture p.238
f) Two Figs p.238

S toke Newington is a diverse area with a varied social and racial mix making up its inhabitants. The restaurants of the area are largely concentrated around Church Street with The Blue Legume and Rasa both proving long established favourites. We have cast our net more widely to include both Newington Green and the great Tasti Pizza further north on Amhurst Parade. The arrival of a smart branch of Fresh & Wild is a great addition to the shops of Church Street and further indicates the increasing gentrification of the area.

The Blue Legume
English, Classic
101 Stoke Newington Church Street, N16
☎ *020 7923 1303*
🚌 *Stoke Newington Rail (10 min walk),*
Highbury and Islington LU & Rail (20 min walk)
🕐 *Daily 9.30am-6.30pm, Tapas Bar Wed-Sat 7pm-11pm*
i *Counter service*

Organic ★★
Vegetarian ★★★★
Taste ★★★
Price £

The Blue Legume

Relaxed chillout zone serving good value vegetarian breakfasts, snacks and lunches attracting TV media types, psychologists and laid-back intellectuals. To blend in perfectly bring a newspaper, book, friend or kid and wear bohemian black, grey or beige. Paintings by local artists spice up the walls and there's a totem pole of Punch sitting on a frog (maybe that's why they get so many psychologists). Look up and you'll see a kitsch mock-Sistine Chapel ceiling complete with a New Age sun.

The breakfast of vegetarian sausage, peppery pan fried mushrooms, baked beans, poached egg, grilled tomato and fresh wholemeal toast is tastily satisfying at £5.75. Mushrooms on toast with crème fraîche is another delicious option or you could perhaps try the popular organic honey waffles with fresh fruit, yogurt and maple syrup. Organic ginger cordial and lemonade are available.

The blackboard changes daily and among the vegetarian choices there are five salads, quiches, chickpea and tahini burger or leek and gruyère tart. Evening-wise, things go Spanish with 5 vegetarian tapas including garlic mushrooms with sherry and a vegetarian paella.

The Dervish
Turkish, Classic

Vegetarian ★★★
Taste ★★★★
Price ££

🖳 15 Stoke Newington Church Street, N16
☎ 020 7923 9999
🚌 Stoke Newington Rail (10 min walk)
🕓 Daily 9.00am-10.30pm

Although it has the same menu as Gallipoli Again (see page 96) and is decorated better, the Dervish hasn't reached the same level of popularity yet and is somewhat quieter.

Fresh & Wild

Organic Vegetarian, International

Organic ★★★★★
Vegetarian ★★★★
Taste ★★★
Price £

🖼 *32-40 Stoke Newington Church Street, N16*

☎ *020 7254 2332*

🚌 *Stoke Newington Rail (10 min walk), 73 bus*

🕒 *Mon–Fri 9am-9pm, Sat 9am-8.30pm, Sun 10am-8pm*

Very popular Stoke Newington organic supermarket and eaterie. See Notting Hill branch for eats review (page 168) and organic shop review (page 248).

Higher Taste Vegetarian Patisserie
Turkish

Vegetarian ★★★★★
Taste ★★★
Price £

47 Newington Green, N16

☎ *020 7359 2338*

🚌 *Canonbury Rail (5 min walk), 73 bus passes by*

🕒 *Mon-Sat 7am-8pm, Sun 9am-6pm*

🥕 *Vegan options*

🍼 *Child friendly (but no high chairs)*

i *Eat in (counter service) & Takeaway*

A gem in Newington Green's 'Little Istanbul' dining area. At the back is a small vegetarian bakery making birthday and wedding cakes (£20-£25), cheese and potato pastries, spinach and cheese pancakes, cheese buns and a vast array of traditional Turkish biscuits and sweets. The rest of the place is a narrow greenish strip of a café, seating 15 with a counter serving hummous and hot snacks to hungry local Turks and Brits.

The vegetarian Baklava, topped with pistachio nuts and filled with a honeyless syrup is of good quality and pleasantly soft, whilst also worth a try is Sutlu Bogrek, a pastry filled with custard, and Seker Pare, small liquid filled sweets. The butterless Shortcake is quite novel and the coffee surprisingly good.

Rasa

Rasa
South Indian

Vegetarian ★★★★★
Taste ★★★★
Price £££

🖃 *55 Stoke Newington Church Street, N16*
☎ *020 7249 0344*
🚌 *Stoke Newington Rail (10 min walk)*
🕐 *Lunch served Sat & Sun 12noon-3pm;*
  Dinner served Sun-Thu 6pm-10.45pm, Fri & Sat 6pm-11.45pm
🥕 *Vegan options*
i *Eat in (table service) & Takeaway, booking essential in evenings*

This is the one everyone talks about. With its totally vegetarian Keralan cuisine and authentic atmosphere Rasa has become a hot destination in town. The relaxing rose-pink décor, pictures of tropical South West Indian village scenes and taped Keralan music creates a comfortable ambience in which casually-dressed, Stokey twenty-fortysomething intellectuals chat the night away.

Rasa's menu gives helpful introductory info on the region's cuisine as well as lucid dish explanations. Friendly, knowledgeable staff dressed in regional apparel explain what's what when they serve up. The 'Kerala Feast' is recommended and represents excellent value at £15.50 per head for pre-meal snacks, starters, side dishes, curry selection, rice, breads and sweet. The à la carte is an extensive menu offering 10 starters, 10 regional curries and 8 sweets.

Mango lassi and sweet lassi are enjoyable traditional yogurt drinks that most diners go for, although Rasa's own Bombay imported lager is popular too. Pre-meal snacks consist of pickles and chutneys, papadoms, crunchy sticks and achappam. The Mysore Bonda starter of gingery potato balls dipped in coconut chutney is tasty as is the Banana Boli. The fried aubergine Kathrikka served with tomato chutney is however too bland.

The curries here are right on the money. Particularly likeable is the aubergine main, Bagar Baingan, in a roasted nutty paste whilst the Moru Kachiathu, Rasa Kayu and Stir Fried Savoy Cabbage dishes went well with tangy lemon rice and were mopped up with a good paratha bread and appam. Pal paysam, a rice pudding with raisins and cashew nuts, slides down well.

Rasa means 'taste' and lives up to all expectations of its name. It's popular and by 9pm the two dining rooms are full with some customers waiting at front of house for their tables. Let's hope owner, Das Sreedharan, who has written two books on Indian Food, opens more pure vegetarian eateries like this.

Currently, the other Rasa's are veg/non-veg combinations and can be found at: Rasa, 6 Dering Street W1(veg & meat), Rasa Samudra, 5 Charlotte Street W1 (veg & seafood), Rasa Travancore, 56 Stoke Newington Church St N16 (mixed). Rasa Express, 5 Rathbone Sreet near Oxford Street (tel 020 7637 0222) and Rasa Express, 327 Euston Road offer a lunch time only snack and takeaway service.

Tasti Pizza
Mediterranean, Kosher

Vegetarian ★★★★
Taste ★★
Price £

🖃 *23 Amhurst Parade, Amhurst Park, N16*
☎ *020 8802 0018*
🚌 *Seven Sisters LU then bus to Stamford Hill*
🕘 *Sun-Thur 11am-10pm*
🍼 *Child friendly*
i *Eat in (counter service) & Takeaway*

Small kosher vegetarian pizza parlour with traditional Jewish/mediterranean snacks and soft drinks repertoire. Opened in 1994, inside it looks, well, just like a place that makes pizzas, and is mainly takeout although there is seating for up to eleven eat-ins. I took out, drove off and gobbled down my attractive cheese and tomato, topped with mushroom pizza at nearby Clapton Common. The pizza base was crispy but a bit burnt and overall just about satisfactory tastewise (even restaurant writers have bad days). Latkes here are, however, good and they also do hummous, tahini, falafel, jacket potato and chips. Options are available for fish eating dining companions. The Tasti Pizza in Golders Green (see page 126) uses the same pizza bases but with some differences in recipes and sourcing.

Two Figs
International, Café and Shop

Vegetarian ★★★★★
Taste ★★★
Price £

🖼 *101 Newington Green, N1*
☎ *020 7690 6811*
🚆 *Canonbury Rail (3 min walk), 73 bus passes by*
🕐 *Mon-Thur 8.30am-7pm, Fri-Sat 9am-5pm*
🥕 *Vegan options*
🍼 *Child friendly but no high chairs*
☀ *Outside seating*
i *Eat in (counter service) & Takeaway*

One of the friendliest (and smallest) vegetarian neighbourhood cafés in London with a good shop stock of wholefoods and organics (for shop review see page 238). With seating of three tables two inside and a couple of tables outside, this petite veggie café is frequented by local artists, writers and chatty mums. The Two Figs are Andrea and Christine, the owners who have created a 'small is beautiful' response to the proliferation of big supermarket chains throughout London.

They cook their own food and it's good. There's soup, salads, quiche, pasta bake, filled rolls, sandwiches, cake, coffee and juices. Favourites include Homity pie and Potato and Lentil pie. On Tuesdays there are speciality vegan choices whilst on Saturdays they do home-made Scotch Pancakes. The Golden Yellow Split Pea Soup is satisfyingly filling, the Ricotta Cheese and Spinach Quiche is very good, whilst the mixed salad of feta cheese, cucumber, tomato, beetroot and green leaves is tasty. Lemon Drizzle Cake here is delicious.

The deli counter is rich in some rarer British cheeses, organic olives, sun-dried tomato and salads. Freezer items include vegemince, ice-creams and ice-lollies. A great little place.

FINSBURY

Expressorganic
International, Classic

Organic ★★★★★
Vegetarian ★★★
Price £

🖼 *Platform 5&6, Finsbury Park Station, N4*
☎ *020 7281 8983*
🚌 *Finsbury Park Rail*
🕐 *Mon-Fri 7am-8.30pm, Sat 11.30am-7pm*
🥕 *Vegan options*
i *Takeaway*

Omnivorous train station kiosk specialising in organic takeout food, snack and drinks for discerning commuters and eco-warrior Arsenal supporters.

Opened in July 2003, it's located on the northbound overground platform of Finsbury Park Station. This is snack attack central serving vegetarian wraps and sarnies and three types of vegetarian quiches. Drinks include organic coffee, organic milk and soya milk, organic bioyoghurt, while hunger busting snacks include vegetarian Bombay Mix and vegetarian organic cakes of which the carrot cake is recommended. Prices are reasonably competitive and a further unit is planned for the southbound platform.

Expressorganic stays open late for football matches and other big local events. Some people eat seated on the platform benches others take their food on the train. "We tried salads and pastas but these didn't go down too well" says Amanda Fletcher of Expressorganic. "What we have now is highly manageable foods for a busy train".

Jai Krishna Vegetarian Restaurant

Indian, Classic

Vegetarian ★★★★★

Taste ★★★

Price £

- 🖼 *161 Stroud Green Road, N4*
- ☎ *020 7272 1680*
- 🚌 *Finsbury Park LU 10 min walk or two bus stops on the 210 or W7, Crouch Hill Rail (2 min walk)*
- 🕐 *Lunch 12noon-2pm, dinner 5.30pm-11pm*
- 🥕 *Vegan options*
- 🍶 *Child friendly but no high chairs*
- 🍽 *BYO*
- *i* *Eat in & Takeaway*

Popular budget-priced neighbourhood all-vegetarian Indian restaurant serving an extensive range of North and South Indian food. Situated close to Tesco's along the Stroud Green Road dining strip, from the outside it looks like one those Turkish men's clubs with its half net curtain to stop you from looking in. If only Jai Krishna took these down passersby would see that at 8.30pm it's packed even on Mondays. This is not surprising because it's inexpensive for what you get and the bring your own wine policy with only £1.25 corkage per bottle or 30p per can of beer also keeps the prices down. Most of the youthful t-shirted diners are wine drinkers and bring in bottles from Jack's Off Licence opposite.

There are, however, two odd things about Jai Krishna. First, at the table you get a menu and a pen and paper to write down what you want to order. Then you have to take it to the counter and they then deliver the plates to your table. The other oddity is if you want to go to the lavatory you actually have to leave the restaurant, turn right and go down an unattractive covered side alley to the back of the restaurant where the toilets are located. Not so great when the weather is inclement.

The menu features all the Gujarati signature dishes among which the Patra, their speciality of Advi leaves with a tamarind sauce, stands out as an enjoyable starter. Looking around the tables, the dosas, samosas and Indian pizzas were going down a treat. The atmosphere was buzzy, chatty and some tables were celebratory. The curry dish list is long and mains of Okra Curry, Mixed Vegetable Curry and Brown Rice with vegetables come packed with flavour and quality ingredients and are big enough for two. Most people, however, whilst seemingly knowledgeable about ordering veggie Indian food order twice the volume they can eat. If you want low-priced value for money veggie in the Finsbury Park, Crouch End areas this is the restaurant of choice. Lunchtimes are, however, quiet.

NEW SOUTHGATE

Jaaneman Vegetarian Restaurant
Vegetarian Indian, Classic

Vegetarian ★★★★★
Taste ★★★
Price £

- 170 Bowes Road, N11
- ☎ 020 8888 1226
- Arnos Grove or Bounds Green LU (5 min walk)
- Open Fri, Sat & Sun 6pm-10pm
- Vegan options
- Child friendly
- BYO (no corkage charged)

Small, informal neighbourhood Gujarati/South Indian pure veggie eaterie bang on the North Circular with bags of free offstreet parking space. The menu offers a good selection of popular starters and main dishes with a real strength in the sweet department (it has its very own sweet centre next door, see page 243 for more details).

The Special Thali comes highly recommended and consists of two curries, four purées or three chapattis, dal, boiled rice, a deep fried savoury potato and onion ball, one papadom and one sweet as well as salad and pickle. Very tasty sweets are the Three In One Barfi, Mango Barfi and the Carrot Halwa.

HENDON

Carluccio's Caffé
Italian, Classic

Vegetarian ★★★
Taste ★★★★
Price ££

- Fenwick, Brent Cross, NW4
- ☎ 020 8203 6844
- Brent Cross LU
- Mon-Fri 10am-8pm, Sat 9.30am-6.30pm, Sun 11am-5pm
- Vegan options
- Child friendly

The place to go when braving Brent Cross shopping centre. For review, see Carluccio's Caffé, St Christopher's Place, W1 (page 35).

Isola Bella
Kosher, Thai, Italian

🖂 *63 Brent Street, NW3*

☎ *020 8203 2000*

🚌 *Hendon Central LU (5 min walk)*

🕐 *Sun-Thur 8am-midnight, Fri 8am-4pm,*

Closed Sat (summer), open Sat evenings (winter)

🥕 *Vegan options*

◌ *Child friendly*

☀ *Outside seating*

🍷 *BYO Kosher Wine (they supply glasses)*

i *Eat in (table service, booking required) & Takeaway*

This cheerfully noisy, predominantly Jewish family-style neighbourhood restaurant serves a huge number of Thai and Italian vegetarian choices. Spacious, rich in personality, Isola Bella is a bit like the TV series 'Cheers', if you go there long enough it's a place where everyone knows your name.

Set along a Hendon shopping parade, outside it looks just like a typical modern café. Inside, there's an incessant din of chat, gossip and birthday party celebrations with the odd indoor firework going off. The front of house is the main socialising zone for orthodox Jewish clientele and although most men's heads are covered, it's not mandatory. Staff are friendly and efficient with a good sense of humour.

The large menu is 80% veggie and the portions are enough for two or even three. We skipped the starters and dived straight for the mains. Sida Loui Fay is a superb Thai crunchy medley of mushroom, cauliflower, broccoli, green bean, carrot, onion, potato and cornichons, stirfried in soya sauce and garnished with cashew nuts. The Salsa Baby Potato, a house speciality topped with salsa and béchamel sauce, was delicious, but far too large for my petite companion to finish. Other dishes I saw being enjoyed at other tables included noodles, soup, casseroles, omelettes, pizzas and pastas and all looked appetising.

Of the Oriental desserts, Wimala is reasonably good, a thick crêpe filled with banana and maple syrup and served with ice cream and whipped cream. However, the pièce de resistance is the Israeli-imported Chocolate Trio of three layers of meringues and dark, milk and white chocolate. Simply divine!

As I left Isola Bella, Alni, the owner said "Come again, Russell". "I think I will," I replied. He already knew my name.

MILL HILL

Good Earth
Chinese, Classic

Vegetarian ★★★★
Taste ★★★★★
Price £££

🖼 *141 The Broadway, NW7*
☎ *020 8959 7011*
🚌 *Mill Hill Rail (5-10 min walk)*
🕐 *Lunch served Mon-Sat 12noon-2pm, Sun 12.30-2.30pm;*
   Dinner served Mon-Sun 6pm-11pm
i *Eat in & Takeaway; Booking required*

Restaurant running along the same lines as Good Earth, Knightsbridge although at Mill Hill the vegetarian choice is somewhat smaller but nevertheless still good. For food review see Good Earth, Knightsbridge (page 155).

ST JOHN'S WOOD

Sofra St John's Wood
Turkish, Classic

Vegetarian ★★★
Taste ★★★
Price ££

🖼 *11 Circus Road, NW8*
☎ *020 7586 9889*
🚌 *St John's Wood LU*
🕐 *Daily 12noon-11pm*

See Özer Oxford Circus for food review (page 44).

WILLESDEN

Sabras
Indian, Classic

Organic ★★★
Vegetarian ★★★★★
Taste ★★★★
Price £££

🖼 *263 High Road, NW10*
☎ *020 8459 0340*
🚌 *Dollis Hill LU (7 min walk)*
🕐 *Tue-Sun 6.30pm-11.30pm (last orders 10.30pm)*
☀ *Vegan options*
i *Eat in (booking recommended) & Takeaway*

Opened in 1973 this sophisticated destination upscale Indian Surati vegetarian restaurant uses organic spices and an array of organic fruits and vegetables to great effect. Sabras oozes quality and has been the recipient of numerous Best Indian Restaurant awards (as evidenced by the many citations displayed throughout the place, inside and out).

The walls are painted a pleasant light mint and although the restaurant is somewhat bijou, the tables are well spaced apart, making dining comfortable if not luxurious. Most diners have learned about the place through word of mouth. Some are international vegetarians who have travelled far judging by the visitors signing book given at the end of the meal.

The menu is long, informative and only changes every couple of years. The starter of Banana-Methi Gota comes as seven small unripe banana balls mashed with spices and fenugreek leaves and fried. It is tasty and quite spicy and comes with an excellent apple and onion chutney together with a minty sauce. The Kasmiri Kofta main consists of mixed steamed veg with sesame and poppy seeds and is very good. Another main is Ravaiya, a slow cooked baby aubergine, potato and banana ensemble, filled with gram flour, coconut, garlic and herbs. It is fairly mild and goes down well. For two people a starter and two mains is enough together with a good sized portion of Lemon Bhat rice and a couple of chapati. Three of the accompanying chutneys are fiery so do ask what's what.

Sabras makes well crafted food using completely GM-free ingredients with a strong emphasis on high quality flavoursome, organic produce. The food here is also suitable for Jains (a diet without garlic, onion and root vegetables) and Hindus (Sabras don't allow or use eggs, meat, fish or lard in their kitchen).

Service is okay but of no particular note. There's a cover charge of 60p per person and a discretionary service charge of 12.5%. Overall the food here is of a high standard but it doesn't come cheap, although The Sabras Club gives discounts to regulars. Membership is £15 a year and members and their guests don't have to pay the service charge. Members also get 10% discount on takeaway orders.

Sabras is a delight for vegetarian foodies and well worth a visit.

Saravanas

Indian, Classic

Vegetarian ★★★★★
Price £L

🖼 77-81 Dudden Hill Lane, NW10
☎ 020 8459 2400
🚇 Dollis Hill LU (2 min walk)
🕐 Tue-Sun 12noon-10.30pm
🥕 Vegan options
i Eat in (table service) & Takeaway

Popular South Indian vegetarian restaurant and busy bar serving all the Indian faves. The bar, a separate affair from the restaurant, is dark, laid-back and serves Indian snacks and alcohol. The restaurant, in contrast, is a no frills alcohol-free canteen with wooden carvings on the wall and offers a full-on menu of 121 choices. On a Sunday evening, this too gets fairly busy. Regulars here often start with Methu Vadai, two fried urid dhall doughnuts and the Chilli Panneer, home-made cottage cheese fried with spices. Portions here are mega and those with a penchant for conspicuous consumption should opt for the Masala Dosai, a gigantic pancake packed with spicy potatoes. Of the three thalis on offer the Bombay Thali – pilau rice, chapati, vadai, four veggie curries, raita, rasam, papadom, butter chilli and dessert – represents good value at only £6.95.

WEMBLEY, MIDDLESEX

Woodlands

South Indian, Classic

Vegetarian ★★★★★
Taste ★★★★
Price £LL

🖼 402a High Road, Wembley, HA9 6AL
☎ 020 8902 9869
🚇 Wembley Central LU
🕐 Daily 12noon-3pm, 6pm-11pm
🥕 Vegan options

For food review see Woodlands, Chiswick (page 179). The Wembley Woodlands however is more of a quick service venue like that of Panton street (page 30).

WEST

West

KNIGHTSBRIDGE, KENSINGTON & CHELSEA

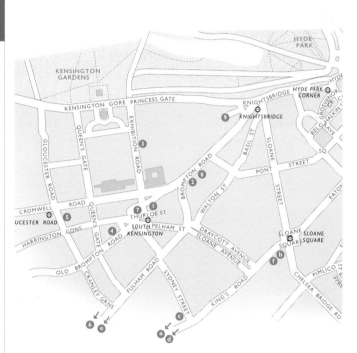

Restaurants

1) Daquise p.153
2) Good Earth p.155
3) Hugo's p.156
4) Pizza Organic p.158
5) Pizza Organic p.158
6) Planet Organic p.159
7) Thai Square p.160
8) Yao Thai p.160
9) Zuma p.161

Shops

a) Chelsea Health Store p.244
b) Fushi p.244
c) Here p.244
d) The Organic Pharmacy p.245
e) Planet Organic p.246
f) Space NK p.246

Cash to splash? Head for hip-mod Japanese at Zuma, or maybe try great mock carnivore Chinese at the remarkable Good Earth. Eco-conscious South Kensington has some great organic eateries: Hugo's, two Pizza Organics and something quite different, Polish vegetarian dishes at Daquise. Load up with organic food at Here in Chelsea Farmer's Market or Planet Organic in Fulham. This is also a great area for organic cosmetics with Space NK and The Organic Pharmacy among the outlets (see the Shopping section for further details).

Daquise

Polish, Classic

Vegetarian ★★★
Taste ★★★★
Price ££

🖼 *20 Thurloe Street, South Kensington, SW7*
☎ *020 7589 6117*
🚌 *South Kensington LU (2 min walk)*
🕐 *Daily 11.30am-11.00pm*
🥕 *Vegan options*
i *Evening bookings recommended*

Daquise

Step back to Poland c.1947 at this historic restaurant which serves some very enjoyable classic Polish vegetarian dishes. Located on a busy South Ken street corner, it somehow exudes an air of mystery from a bygone age and indeed it has been said that cold war spies secretly rendezvoused here. Today, it's a popular haunt for Polish writers, artists and sculptors, and lanky East European models grazing away from the catwalks of London Fashion week but alas no sinister secret agents in long raincoats and sunglasses.

At 7pm it's quite busy with a mix of young couples, single diners drinking Polish lager or one of the speciality vodkas or a carafe of the quite acceptable house wine. Daquise is on two levels and diners are advised to opt for the more lively groundfloor with its large Elizabeth II Coronation mural, a military painting by Fabian and some figurines rather than the downstairs bar which is more of an overflow or venue for private parties.

I must have been the customer from hell going into a Polish omnivore restaurant wanting vegetarian food and hating beetroot, the country's most celebrated ingredient. For starters there are three beetroot soups. Flummoxed at first, the waitress suggested the house speciality main of warm Crispy Potato Cakes served with sour cream and apple sauce and indeed they were delicious. To re-inforce my beetroot phobia I tasted the Barszcz with Ushka, a clear beetroot soup with mini mushroom ravioli. To my horror, it was fabulous and next time I'll definitely order it.

The vegetarian Polish Platter is an appetising selection of Mushroom Golabki (cabbage leaves stuffed with mushroom and rice), Pierogi (pasta shells stuffed with cabbage and mushroom), Potato Pancake, and cooked cabbage (sauerkraut). Vegetable Stoganoff is a big plate of courgettes, aubergine, peppers, mushrooms and onions, all mildly spiced and served with a small mountain of rice and cream. It was substantial and quite tasty.

Pancake à la Daquise is enough for two and is a delicious hot pancake folded around ice cream topped with a refreshing orange caramel sauce and sprinkled with almond flakes.

Good Earth
Chinese, Classic

Vegetarian ★★★★
Taste ★★★★★
Price £££

🖃 *233 Brompton Road, Knightsbridge, SW3*
☎ *020 7584 3658*
🚌 *Knightsbridge LU (5 min walk)*
🕓 *Mon-Sat 12noon-11.15pm, Sun 12.30pm-10.45pm*
🌶 *Vegan options*

Classy Chinese restaurant serving a superb selection of vegetarian dishes. If it's atmosphere you're after ask to be seated in the voluminous basement which has a more animated ambience and flamboyant Chinese décor. The street level dining room does, however, house a busy pre-meal drinks bar.

The dining here is upscale, service precise and formal, with the chances of a waitperson breaking into a smile 100-1. Good Earth attracts a monied European and Indian clientele smartly dressed in jacket and tie or open necked shirts and women in designer clothes.

The Vegetarian Menu is highly inviting with a generous choice of six starters, four soups and a dozen or so mains. The tofu and mock-meat dishes made from soya are the big speciality here and the Vegetarian 'Chicken' Szechuan that comes in a delicious hot sweet sauce is particularly enjoyable and well presented. Egg Noodles with Beansprouts is top notch and went well with Monks Casserole, a mega serving of mixed vegetables in a clay pot that seemed to keep hot indefinitely. These three dishes are sufficient for two. However, most diners order twice as much which is not surprising as the food here looks salivatingly good.

There are Good Earth branches at 143-145 The Broadway, Mill Hill NW7 (tel 020 8959 7011) and 14-18 High Street, Esher, Surrey (tel 01372 462489).

Express Good Earths are takeaway only and can be found at:

🖃 *Wimbledon,*
   81 Ridgeway, SW19
☎ *020 8994 8883*

🖃 *West Hampstead,*
   335 West End Lane, NW6
☎ *020 7433 3111*

🖃 *Richmond,*
   6 Friars Road, Surrey
☎ *020 8948 3399*

🖃 *Wandsworth,*
   116 St Johns Hill, SW11
☎ *020 7228 3140*

Hugo's

International, Modern, Organic

- 🖾 *51 Prince's Gate, (Exhibition Road), Kensington, SW7*
- ☎ *020 7596 4006*
- 🚌 *South Kensington LU (5 min walk)*
- ◔ *Mon-Sat 9.30am-11pm, Sun 9.30am-7pm*
- 🍼 *Child friendly*
- ☼ *Outside seating*
- *i* *Eat in (table service) & Takeaway*

Organic ★★★★
Vegetarian ★★★
Taste ★★★★
Price *£££*

Hugo's

Buzzy, family-run organic restaurant, café and bar serving quality recipes created by Carol Charlton, author of the Organic Café Cookbook. Often around, Carol's delighted to indulge in mealtime conversation about organic food happenings, sustainable farming and fairtrade issues whilst husband Bryn, a former chairman of Greenpeace, is equally happy for a chat.

Students are the predominant clientele (Imperial College is nearby and Hugo's shares a building with the Goethe-Institut) but Hugo's is also popular with pre- and post-concert Albert Hall goers and South Ken locals.

Hugo's wears it organic heart on its sleeve and its menu comes complete with a mission statement supporting organic farming and fair-trade practices as well as their list of organic ingredients. Knowledgeable waiting staff have a black belt in answering any organic queries you might have and provide a good service.

Organic Eggs Florentine (eggs with spinach) is a popular dish on the brunch menu, served until 5pm. Although largely an omnivore menu, vegetarian choices are marked and the meal gets off to a good start with complimentary green and black olives. Organic Celeriac and Chive Soup is a delicious recipe with a good spicy taste and comes with olive bread with dashes of olive oil. The Vegetarian Tart of spinach, broccoli and asparagus was pepped up with added pine nuts and a mixed leaf salad with cherry tomatoes, balsamic vinegar and parmesan shavings and was well above average. Of the three main vegetarian choices the Mushroom Feuilletée with Stroganoff Sauce on fragrant rice is to be recommended and features both fresh wild and domestic mushrooms. The Pasta of the Day, tasted fine but regrettably was no more special than a supermarket convenience meal. The organic Chocolate Tart Dessert was devilishly delicious. A non-organic creme brûlée with a raspberry side sauce was also enjoyable.

The house organic wine, Domine Millas, made with chardonnay and grenache grapes, is refreshing but Hugo's really scores with its list of organic beers and ciders that include Bücher Pilsner, Golden Promise Ale, and Weston's Strong Cider. Coffees and teas are organic and fairtrade.

Hugo's makes an excellent port of call when around Kensington and is made even better by it's enthusiasm for organic food. Their sister restaurant is Hugo's in Queens Park (tel 020 7372 1232), see page 128 for review.

Pizza Organic
Italian, Fast Food

🖃	*20 Old Brompton Road, SW7*
☎	*020 7589 9613*
🚇	*South Kensington LU (2 min walk)*
🕐	*Lunch served Tue-Fri 12.30pm-3pm, Sat & Sun 12.30pm-3.30pm;*
	Dinner served Mon-Sat 6.30pm-10.30pm, Sun 6.30pm-10pm
🍴	*Child friendly*

Organic ★★★★★
Vegetarian ★★★★
Taste ★★★★
Price £

Organic fast food heaven at Britain's first organic pizzeria. Located on the busy Old Brompton Road. The restaurant boasts a stylish décor with a deep burgundy splashed with red and grey colour scheme with some well designed modern chairs. The front of house is spacious while the back room is smaller but more private. Pizza Organic attracts a cheerful youngish crowd although early evenings and weekends it's big on families.

All the menu is organic excluding a few wines and soft drinks. Prices compare well with other high street pizza venues because of buying power, economy of scale and reduced margins. Other would be organic eateries, take note – it can be done!

The pizzas are excellent and for veggies there are two Margheritas and a roast veg to choose from. The vegetarian Calzone verdura of mushrooms, peppers, garlic, spinach, blue cheese and tomato topped with mozzarella and oregano is good and comes with salad. Omnivore choices are available.

Save room for dessert as there are a whopping nine organic desserts to choose from. The oaky organic Bonterra Chardonnay is highly sippable otherwise there's Freedom beer, organic rum, vodka, gin or fruit juice.

Pizza Organics are also at 75 Gloucester Road, SW7 (tel 020 7370 6575) and 100 Pitshanger Lane, Ealing, W5 (tel 020 8998 6878).

Pizza Organic
Italian, Fast Food

🖃	*75 Gloucester Road, SW7*
☎	*020 7370 6575*
🚇	*Gloucester Road LU*
🕐	*Mon-Thur & Sun 12noon-11.30pm, Fri-Sat 12noon-12midnight*

Organic ★★★★★
Vegetarian ★★★★
Taste ★★★★
Price £

Meals as per Pizza Organic review above.

HUGO's

Café - Bar - Restaurant
Specialist in Organic Food

Hugo's at Queens Park and Exhibition Road, Kensington are popular venues, specialising in organic meat and wine, there is also some fantastic veggie food on offer and they are famous for their breakfasts. Queens park has a full blown Jazz Club on Sunday evenings (Jamie Callum played there) with other musical evenings on offer and Kensington is the perfect venue for those on their way to or from the Albert hall or the Museums, with a fabulous summer terrace. Both are available for private hire and Hugo's also offers an outside catering service.

51 Prince's Gate
Exhibition Road
Kensington
020 7596 4006

25 Lonsdale Road
Queen's Park
London NW6
020 7372 1232
open
9.30am to 11.30pm

Planet Organic
Organic Vegetarian, International
🖃 *25 Effie Road, SW6*
☎ *020 7731 7222*
🚇 *Fulham Broadway LU (1 min walk)*
🕙 *Mon-Sat 9.30am-8.30pm, Sun 12noon-6pm*
🥕 *Vegan options*
🍼 *Child friendly*
i *Eat in (counter Service) & Takeaway*
✉ *Mail order available*

Organic ★★★★★
Vegetarian ★★★★★
Taste ★★★
Price £

This welcome addition to Fulham opened in June 2004 and is similar in layout but slightly smaller than the flagship store in Westbourne Grove. The meal choices are the same and are reviewed on page 173.

Thai Square South Kensington
Thai, Classic

Vegetarian ★★★
Taste ★★
Price £££

🗔 19 Exhibition Road, SW7
☎ 020 7584 8359
🚌 South Kensington LU
🕐 Mon-Sat 12noon-3pm & 6pm-11pm;
 Sun 12noon-3pm & 6pm-10.30pm

Attractive intimate venue. See food review Thai Square Trafalgar Square (page 29).

Yao Thai
Thai, contemporary

Vegetarian ★★★★
Price ££

🗔 8 Egerton Garden Mews, Knightsbridge, SW3
☎ 020 7584 7007
🚌 Knightsbridge LU (5 min walk)
🕐 Mon-Sat 12.30pm-2.30pm & 5pm-11pm, Sun 5pm-11pm
🔸 Vegan options
i Eat in (table service) & Takeaway

Formerly, Red of Knightsbridge, the Chinese vegan organic restaurant, it's now turned Thai. They retain the old Red menu for regulars, however, I suspect that in time they will eventually change over to the full Thai menu – so catch it while you can.

Set in a pretty average looking basement round a back mews close to Brompton Road, it's best reached via Yeomans Row. On arrival, tell them you are vegetarian and they'll see you straight. The Thai menu is omnivorous with ten veggie dishes and they will adapt the carnivore recipes for veggies if you wish.

Most people go to Yao Thai for the lunchtime buffet, a definite bargain in Knightsbridge, that's two courses for a fiver, 3 courses for £6.50 with a dozen dishes to choose from. It's mixed omnivore but with enough veggie choices to choose from.

The veggie Red à la carte is extensive with two courses setting you back about £16 per head. Yao Thai also does an evening buffet for £10 per head for two courses plus service. Unlike the old Red of Knightsbridge, the wines here are neither vegan nor organic. Some of the food is still organic but not all. Friday and Saturday nights are eat, drink and karaoke.

Zuma

Japanese, Modern

⌷ *5 Raphael Street, SW7*

☎ *020 7584 1010*

🚌 *Knightsbridge LU (5 min walk)*

🕐 *Lunch served Mon-Fri, 12noon-2.30pm, Sat & Sun 12.30pm-3.30pm;*
Dinner served Mon-Sat 6pm-11pm, Sun 6pm-10.30pm

✎ *Vegan options*

☀ *Outside seating*

Organic ★★★
Vegetarian ★★★★
Taste ★★★★★
Price £££££

Tucked away down a side street near Harvey Nichols and Harrods, Zuma is where the rich and famous and exquisite Japanese vegetarian cuisine intersect. With its relaxed, swish atmosphere and highly atten-tive service. This is the peachiest of places where the cost of a meal will devour your bank account. Expect £160 for two and dress down as if it's where you eat all the time although the suited and booted are in evidence at some tables.

As you go in there's a great bar and lounge, followed by an open kitchen surrounded by seats and dining tables. At the far back are two excellent private dining areas.

The menu is extensive and a nightmare to navigate. Those new to Zuma should call the manager, declare their vegetarianism and let him unlock the door to gastronomic paradise.

Dishes are small, beautifully presented, designed for sharing and mostly organic. To begin with Steamed Edamame, a traditional Japanese green bean dish is excellent. Kaiso Salad Goma Renkon Zoe, is one of the most scrumptious seaweed salads one will ever find and comes with sesame and lotus root. Home-made tofu with intensely flavoured condiments, Zara Dofu, is good but the Grilled Tofu is even better. Particularly good is the Barbecued Seasoned Rice shaped like a small veggie banger with a crispy crunchy texture and the Japanese grilled aubergines were outstanding. The Veggie Rolls of avocado, asparagus, ginger, hiso, cabbage, cucumber and carrot are wonderful. Seasonal Vegetable skewers of shitake mushroom, onion and courgette from the Robata Grill were also very good.

Desserts are of a high standard and the Green Tea and Banana cake with coconut ice cream and peanut toffee sauce is recommended. Steamed organic milk pudding is also available. The sake selection is enormous.

NOTTING HILL

Notting Hill is one of the most expensive parts of London and also one of the most fashionable. If you want to get a veggie snack in the company of the rich and famous you could try E&O. A little further east is the less fashionable but equally delicious Mandola and this area also has a branch of Ottolenghi for fine mediterranean cuisine in a stylish environment. To combine shopping and eating you can also find a branch of Fresh & Wild, Planet Organic and the unique Books for Cooks.

Restaurants

1) Books for Cooks p.163
2) E&O p.164
3) Fresh & Wild p.166
4) Mandola Café p.168
5) Ottolenghi p.169
6) Planet Organic p.170

Shops

a) Bliss p.247
b) Books for Cooks p.247
c) Fresh & Wild p.248
d) Green Baby p.249
e) Natural Mat p.249

f) Notting Hill
   Farmers' Market p.276
g) Planet Organic p.249
h) Portobello Wholefoods p.250
i) The Tea and Coffee Plant p.250

Books for Cooks
International, Classic and Modern

Organic ★★★★
Vegetarian ★★★★★
Taste ★★★★★
Price £

🖾 *4 Blenheim Crescent, W11*
☎ *020 7221 1992*
🚌 *Ladbroke Grove LU (5 min walk),*
   Notting Hill Gate LU (10 min walk)
🕐 *Lunch served Tue-Sat 12noon-2pm (or when the food runs out);*
   Coffee and cakes served Tue-Sat 10am-6pm
🖋 *Vegan options*
☀ *Outside seating*
🍸 *BYO*

Eat veggie recipes straight from the latest cookbooks at London's greatest specialist cookbook shop. It's an absolute bargain and one of the best kept secrets in vegetarian and organic London.

The formula is simple. They take a new book and cook some recipes from it and offer results to customers at a ridiculously low price. If it goes down well they order more books for the shop.

I struck gold the lunchtime I dropped in as the featured book was The Gate Vegetarian Book (from the much loved Gate restaurant in Hammersmith, see page 175 for eats review) by Adrian and Michael Daniel, published by Mitchell Beazley, £25.

The Hot and Sour soup, Thom Yam was a delicious starter and came with a quantity of egg noodles making it unavoidably slurpy with some lunchers resorting to spoon and fork to get it down. Accompanied by freshly baked foccaccia bread, for some it was a meal in itself. The main, Japanese Vegetable Terrine with Barley Miso dressing dazzled with some exquisite flavours. Four vegetarian desserts were on offer and the Citrus Almond Polenta cake was superb and the Torta Della Nonna even better. All this three courser costs is £7. So what's the catch? Well, there's isn't one except that there are only five tables.

The food is all prepared at the back of the bookshop by an excellent chef, (that day Sarah Benjamin) in what is not so much a restaurant but more a test kitchen of restaurant standard.

The atmosphere is friendly, informal and of course stuffed with foodies, both local and from afar. The menu changes every day with either a veggie starter or main and once a week there is both. Phone in the morning to see what's on offer and then make sure you are there well before noon as the food sometimes runs out by 12.15pm. On my visit, however, you could still get a table at 1.30pm. Books for Cooks bring out their own recipe book once a year too.

E&O

Vietnamese, Modern

Vegetarian ★★★
Taste ★★★★
Price £££££

🖃 *14 Blenheim Crescent, W11*
☎ *020 7229 5454*
🚌 *Ladbroke Grove LU (5 min walk),*
Notting Hill Gate LU (10 min walk)
🕑 *Mon-Sun 12noon-12midnight*
🌿 *Vegan options*
☀ *Outside seating*
i *Booking essential in evenings;*
Private dining room for parties up to 18

Although it looks like a bog standard black-painted corner pub on the outside, E&O is a supremely hip restaurant and bar catering to Notting Hill socialites, celebrities and wannabes. Here, savvy and attentive waiting staff serve a modern Pan Asian cuisine with a twist, mostly on small plates tasting menu style but with some big dish numbers too. Lunch will set you back something north of £30, dinner £50.

Inside, there's a small strip of a bar whilst the dining room is a spacious, white tableclothed affair where movers and shakers like celebrity vegetarian Stella McCartney book a booth.

Lunchtimes are okay for walk-ins, evenings require a reservation and allow two days to park if a non-resident. The short menu is Vietnamese with Thai, Malaysian, Japanese and Chinese influences, mainly veggie with some omnivore appeal. On the veggie dimsum, there is edame, soy and mirin or mushroom and waterchestnut green tea dumplings or roasted coconut and pomegranate betel leaf. The special Vegetable Phad Thai (£9.50) main is a biggie, delicious and sufficient without starter or dessert. Garam masala curry with tomato and aubergine makes another tempting choice.

" Vibrant produce, great breads, organic takeaway and juicebar and a huge selection of organic foods and natural remedies. "

Soho
69-75 Brewer Street
London W1F

Camden
49 Parkway
London NW1

Notting Hill
210 Westbourne Grove
London W11

Clapham Junction
305-311 Lavender Hill
London SW11

City
194 Old Street
London EC1V

Stoke Newington
32-40 Church Street
London N16

Clifton
85 Queens Road
Bristol

FRESH & WILD
THE REAL FOOD STORE

Fresh & Wild

Organic Vegetarian, International

🖭 *210 Westbourne Grove, W11*
☎ *020 7229 1063*
🚌 *Notting Hill Gate LU (7 min walk)*
🕐 *Mon-Fri 8am-9pm, Sat 8am-8pm, Sun 10am-7pm*
🥕 *Vegan options*
◔ *Child friendly*
☀ *Outside seating*
Mail order available
i   Eat in (counter service) & Takeaway

Organic	★★★★★
Vegetarian	★★★★
Taste	★★★
Price	£

Modern in-store cafeteria specialising in low priced veggie-organic, a bargain in West London's rich-kid playground. Set along the coolest Notting Hill shopping strip, it's a real local hangout for the quality organic cappuccino set with people-watchers and wannabe-seens languishing at pavement tables slurping health juice concoctions. Inside and upstairs, lunch and early evenings bustle with an amiable eco-aware, youngish crowd chilling out at café-style tables. Counter staff are friendly and obligingly arrange for kiddy buggies to be lugged up and down the stairs.

On self-service daily are two fresh organic vegan soups and one vegetarian – hearty lunchtime fillers. Hot mains, an eclectic mix of trad English, Indian and Thai are of variable looking quality. Vegetarian Chilli with steamed brown rice was spicy but disappointingly bland and came with a dried up sauce. Contrastingly, Parsnip, Cashew and Parmesan mock sausage with roast potatoes and broccoli came up trumps. Quiches and salads at the deli counter look quite sexy and are perhaps the best things here. There's a wide veggie and vegan cake selection including a delicious but crumbly Farmhouse Carrot cake.

Fresh & Wild

Mandola Café
Sudanese, Classic

Vegetarian ★★★★
Taste ★★★★
Price ££

🖾 *139 Westbourne Grove, W11*
☎ *020 7229 4734*
🚌 *Notting Hill Gate or Queensway LU (10-15 min walk)*
🕐 *Lunch served Mon-Fri 12noon-3pm & Sat-Sun 1pm-4.30pm;*
   Dinner served Mon-Sun 6pm-11pm (2 sittings 7.30pm & 9.30pm)
◊ *Child friendly but no highchairs*
♈ *BYO (£1 corkage)*
i *Eat in (dinner booking essential) & Takeaway*

An authentic Sudanese restaurant that wears its African heart on its sleeve and oozes personality. On the walls hang hand-weaves while around the floor stand enormous gourds and leather camel accoutrements. Bare wooden tables are tightly set together making for a bit of a squeeze but who cares – everyone here is friendly and up for a good night. Evenings draw a casually-garbed twenty to thirtysomething crowd most of whom bring their own bottle. Service is informal and friendly.

A meal of three acts opens with salad dips best mopped up with flame-heated pitta bread. The star performer is the Aswad Salad of tender lime juice marinaded aubergine slices ordered with a spiced yogurt called Mish and a rocket leaf garden veg mix called Kadra. A simpler approach, but equally filling is The Daqua Salad of cabbage and onions in a mild peanut sauce.

Main courses include a Lentil Stew with caramelised garlic, boiled beans dressed either with crushed falafel and feta or an exotic vegetable mix in a spicy tomato sauce. Either way, side-dish the meal with the memorable Spicy Rice.

Save room for the final act. You'll need it for one of ten desserts with Middle Eastern accents. The mouthwatering warm Date Mousse is enough for two. Finish the show with a Sudanese coffee, an Ethiopian mocha meets cinnamon, clove and ginger affair that arrives in a cutesy clay serving pot.

Ottolenghi

Mediterranean, Classic

🖂 *63 Ledbury Road, W11*

☎ *020 7727 1121*

🚌 *Notting Hill Gate LU (7 min walk)*

🕒 *Mon-Fri 8am-8pm, Sat 8am-7pm, Sun 9.30am-6pm*

◊ *Child friendly*

🍸 *No alcohol licence*

i *Eat in (counter service) & Takeaway*

Organic ★★★★
Vegetarian ★★★★
Taste ★★★★
Price *££*

Thumbs up to this stylish eaterie serving well-made vegetarian buffet salad choices to eat in or out. Opened in August 2002, it's a split level affair with an inviting front of house buffet and patisserie counter. The small downstairs dining area is decorated in ultra chic white with futuristic white chairs surrounding a single huge plastic table. Affluent mums & kids people the mornings here, followed later by designer-dressed ladies-who-lunch and solitary grazers keen for a chat or just a quiet read.

Everything is made on the premises, about 60% is organic and the menu changes every day with 10 vegetarian choices including two soups, salads and a main course such as roast veg, goat's cheese and parsley tart.

The top salad for regulars is the Roasted Organic Root Vegetable with mixed herbs and garlic which is great. Mixed Organic Beans in Plum Sauce is good too, whilst Fried Haloumi is pretty salty but comes balanced with yummy roasted peppers. The Organic Kohlrabi (an unusual turnip-like veg belonging to the cabbage family) comes sliced with a salad of spring onion, parsley and poppyseed in a lemon and olive oil dressing and is wonderfully tasty. All the salads work well together and when eaten in, come served on decent plates.

All the teas are organic. Luscombe organic ginger beer comes in bottles and is excellent and there's a selection of Innocent Smoothies too. The vegetarian pastries and cakes are visually enticing with the slices of cake big enough for two.

A second restaurant has opened in Islington that also serves evening meals. See page 105 for details.

Planet Organic
Organic Vegetarian, International

🖳 *42 Westbourne Grove, W2*
☎ *020 7727 2227*
🚌 *Bayswater or Queensway LU (5 min walk)*
🕐 *Mon-Sat 9.30am-8pm, Sun 12noon-6pm*
🥕 *Vegan options*
◊ *Child friendly*
i *Eat in (counter service) & Takeaway*

Organic ★★★★★
Vegetarian ★★★★★
Taste ★★★
Price £

Modern organic cafeteria that's fronts perhaps the best known organic supermarket in London. Beige, bland and big with comfortable wooden tables, this is real in-store dining with chatty checkout cashiers and shoppers queuing a stone's throw away.

There are eight salads on offer with a good choice of hot dishes all made on-site including Stir Fry Tofu, vegetarian lasagne or ratatouille. The hot Peanut Butter Curry and the Veggie Shepherds Pie made with lentils are two other flavoursome choices. The Celeriac Salad is one of their best dishes and the Kumquat salad makes an interesting change. Half the food is vegan.

The cafeteria is also a good organic tea-time venue. The vegan Pear and Pecan nut cake is delicious and the coffee quite acceptable, but those paper cups and plates for eat-in get the thumbs down. Hot porridge is available at breakfast. Planet Organic also features a good juice bar and continues to pull in many a wheatgrass fanatic from around London. See page 249 for shop review.

"the benchmark of all organic shops"
The Independent

Fruit & Vegetables • Groceries
Juice Bar • Health & Bodycare
Bread • Meat & Fish • Café

25 Effie Road, SW6 1EL
22 Torrington Place, WC1 7JE
42 Westbourne Grove, W2 5SH
General Enqs: 020 7221 7171
Mail Order: 020 7221 1345

PLANET ORGANIC

HAMMERSMITH & SHEPHERD'S BUSH

The price of property in Portobello and Notting Hill has been forcing the smart middle class into the surrounding neighbourhoods of Hammersmith and Shepherds Bush leading to a gradual process of gentrification. There are some great vegetarian restaurants in this part of London among the best being Blah Blah Blah and The Gate. For delicious Indian vegetarian cuisine there is the very smart Sagar and further west the renowned Woodlands.

Blah Blah Blah
International, Modern

	Organic ★★
	Vegetarian ★★★★★
	Taste ★★★★
	Price ££

🖼 *78 Goldhawk Road, W12*
☎ *020 746 1337*
🚌 *Goldhawk Road LU (1 min walk)*
🕐 *Lunch served Mon-Sat 12.30pm-2.30pm;*
  Dinner served Mon-Sat 7pm-11pm (bookings advised at weekends)
🍴 *Vegan options*
🍼 *Child friendly*
🍷 *BYO (corkage £1.25 per person)*

With a name like Blah Blah Blah you know you're in for something very different. Forget the décor, it's the food that matters at this rough-round-the-edges neighbourhood restaurant – modern, well-crafted, carefully presented and good value.

Outside, amusingly, above the burgundy painted entrance are two bulls' head sculptures – just the thing for a veggie eaterie. Inside, it's modern grot, rough wooden flooring, a chunky old Viennese style wall mirror, enormous TV studio lights hanging from the ceiling, odd chairs and wall seats in desperate need of recovering. That said, the open kitchen towards the back is clean and professional.

Set on two floors, the more private downstairs dining area is Moorish in feel. I prefer the ground floor for its sheer design nonchalance which grows on you the more you drink.

The short menu features just six starters, five mains and four desserts. The Plaintain Fritter starter consists of three small balls filled with raisins, ginger, sweet potato and coriander and comes on an attractive chilli and pineapple sauce, finished with a coconut lime coulis. Mushroom Polenta with cap, oyster and button mushrooms is even more delicious. The Baked Tostada main is a gorgeous layered tower of Mexican tortillas filled with refried beans, sweet potato gratin served with a jalepeno sauce and is recommended. Butternut Squash Gougère, also presented as a tower, is an enjoyable choux pasty filled with butternut squash and cauliflower gruyère with red pepper sauce. The Rhubarb and Apple Crumble dessert can come with a rather tough pasty casing and is bit heavy. The Roast Plum Crumble with vanilla custard, however, is delicious. Mains at lunchtime are £6.95 and £9.95 at dinner.

A much beloved dining spot for West Londoners, Blah Blah Blah, is a great vegetarian venue for partying. I love it!

The Gate

The Gate
Modern, International

Vegetarian ★★★★★
Taste ★★★★★
Price £££

⌧ *51 Queen Caroline Street, W6*
☎ *020 8748 6932*
🚌 *Hammersmith LU (5 min walk)*
🕒 *Lunch served Mon-Fri 12noon-3pm;*
    Dinner served Mon-Sat 6pm-11pm
🥕 *Vegan options*
👶 *Child friendly*
i *Booking advised especially weekends*

Outstanding modern vegetarian dishes so moderately priced they are worth beating a path to. The path in this case is from a conventional restaurant street entrance on a residential back street, through a court-yard and upstairs to a former art studio.

Iconic giant prints of Marilyn Monroe and Stan Laurel are set high up on the yellow walls whilst a diverse low volume mix of Iggy Pop and Sinatra re-inforces a cool creative retro-atmosphere. Dubbed the 'Disney canteen', lunchtimes are busy with nearby film studio folk and execs from Universal Pictures, Sony Ericsson and Harper Collins. Evenings attract a relaxed talkative eco-intelligent crowd of casually dressed thirty somethings. Service is friendly and attentive.

The short and informative menu is inviting and comprises eight starters, five mains and six desserts, which change every two months.

Complimentary olive bread and oil gets the meal off to an agree-able start and is followed by a delectable starter of Plantain Fritters, three deep fried green banana balls loaded with sultanas, carrot and pine nuts on a well-matched cream chilli sauce with a small side-salad. The Warm Root Vegetable Salad is a big starter, a tasty, well arranged mix of roast swede, parsnip and carrot, rocket leaves, crispy toasted pumpkin seeds and a mustard dressing. Haloumi Kibis, a tandoori-marinated cheese number served on a skewer deserves a mention as it's a firm favourite with regulars. The signature main dish however is the beautifully presented vegan Cashew Nut Roast with dried wild mushrooms and comes with roast veg and a marvellous cranberry compote. Aubergine Schnitzel, a successful modern twist on moussaka arrives as two large tender grilled aubergine slices layered with smoked mozzarella and French-styled creamy baked potato, fried kale and rounded off with horseradish sauce and tastes voluptuous.

Desserts make a big showing here and are generally large enough to be split. Pecan and Plum Crumble comes with crème anglaise and is recommended. Cranberry Sponge Pudding is likeable, and comes with Drambuie ice cream. Vegan ice cream and sorbet is made on the premises.

The Gate has an interesting choice of vegetarian and vegan wines including a recommendable mild oaky Argentinian Organic Vegan Chardonnay Buenas Ondas. Vegan dessert wine and port are also available. The Gate is one of the great vegetarian restaurants of London.

Queen's Head
British and Mediterranean, Classic

Vegetarian ★★★
Taste ★★★
Price ££

🖾 *13 Brook Green, W6*
☎ *020 7603 3174*
🚇 *Hammersmith LU (3 min walk)*
🕒 *Daily 12noon-11pm*
🥕 *Vegan options*
◊ *Child friendly*
i   *Counter service; Booking advised at weekends*

This comfy traditional pub does vegetarians proud with a menu of seven vegetarian snacks, three starters and two mains – well above average for London pubs these days.

The snack choices include Classic Pub Cheddar Ploughman's, Vegetarian Club Sandwich, Jacket Potato with Wexford Style Mushrooms and Stilton. Portions are generous, but for more substantial appetites, the Spinach, Red Pepper & Blue Cheese Terrine starter is not bad at £4.95. The Ultimate Chunky Vegetable Lasagne – £7.95, is their most popular veggie dish (and with a name like that it's not hard to understand why!). Each pub in the Chef & Brewer national chain, does veggie options and some blackboard specials that change weekly.

See also The Bull's Head, Chiswick (page 178), another Chef & Brewer pub.

Sagar
South Indian, Classic

Vegetarian ★★★★★
Taste ★★★★
Price £

⌨ *132 King Street, Hammersmith, W6*
☎ *020 8741 8563*
🚌 *Hammersmith LU (3 min walk)*
🕐 *Daily 12noon-11pm*
🥕 *Vegan options*
🍼 *Child friendly*
i *Eat in (table service) & Takeaway*
   Booking advised at weekends; Party catering available

Sagar opened in February 2003 and serves inexpensive homestyle South Indian vegetarian cuisine. One of the new wave of informal, modern designed vegetarian Indian restaurants, it's a welcome addition to Hammersmith's main street and gets busy from early evening with young couples and families building up to out-on-the-town goodtimers later on. Service, however, is efficient and the turn around on tables quick.

Inside, the décor is pleasant: coloured wooden walls with sections of panelling filled with dried flowers and South Indian paraphernalia set in lit wall recesses.

The menu is very well explained and offers great value for money. My wife and I split three starters: Idli (two sweet steamed rice cakes served with sambar and coconut chutney) and Sev Puri, a Bombay Chowpati speciality which was superb. These crispy poori are topped with chopped onion, tamarind, coriander, garlic chutney and sev and are delicious with the other chutneys. However, the Bhaji were disappointingly uncrunchy.

For the main course, we split the Rajdani Thali, and opted for mild sauces. The Veg Kurma, a creamy curry with cashew nuts tasted good as did the Channa Masala, a tomato curry with chick peas and the Mattar Paneer, a curry with cheese and peas. Chappathi, Aloo Gobi, Raita and Pilau rice were other enjoyable, well-executed dishes. To top up, we ordered spiced spinach with home-made cheese, Saag Paneer that went down well. Full, I tried the Thali's Vermicelli and Nut Sweet but didn't think much of it.

The Lunch Special is a real bargain for £4.95 and includes Masala Dosa, a whacking big fried pancake filled with mild flavoured potato and onions, rice of the day, veg curry, raitha, salad, sambar and chutney.

CHISWICK

The Bull's Head

British and Mediterranean, Classic

▫ *15, Strand on the Green, W4*

☎ *020 8994 1204*

🚇 *Gunnersbury LU, Kew Bridge Rail*

🕘 *Food served daily 12noon-10pm*

Vegetarian ★★★
Taste ★★★
Price £L

This pub is part of the Chef & Brewer chain and offers some good vegetarian choices. See review Queen's Head page 176.

"the benchmark of all organic shops"
The Independent

Fruit & Vegetables ● Groceries
Juice Bar ● Health & Bodycare
Bread ● Meat & Fish ● Café

25 Effie Road, SW6 1EL
22 Torrington Place, WC1 7JE
42 Westbourne Grove, W2 5SH
General Enqs: 020 7221 7171
Mail Order: 020 7221 1345

PLANET ORGANIC

Woodlands

South Indian, Classic

Vegetarian ★★★★★
Taste ★★★★
Price £££

- 12-14 Chiswick High Road, W4
- 020 7994 9333
- Stamford Brook LU (2 min walk)
- Daily 12noon-3pm & 6pm-11pm
- Vegan options
- Child friendly
- i Eat in (table service, booking advised) & Takeaway

Fine gracious vegetarian dining at one of the largest Indian restaurant chains in the world specialising in dosas and uthappams. This particular Woodlands opened in late 2002 and sports a relaxing medley of modern décor and classic vintage artifacts on the walls. The best tables to reserve for comfort and social posturings are the banquettes around the perimeter.

The menu is extensive and all the food and drink is well-presented. To start, Aloo Papdi Chaat, a snacky Mumbai street food, is wonderfully delicious with chopped potatoes on crushed pastry discs, green chillies and chutney immersed in yogurt with mixed spice. The London Royal Thali is a good way of trying a wide range of specialities in small amounts. It begins with two excellent steamed hot Idli (rice cakes) with sambar and coconut chutney. The Thali set comes with a good Masala Dosa, a small filled pancake filled with mild spiced potato, onions and snow peas and Uthappam (lentil pizza) topped with chilli. In the serving dishes a thick lentil souped Sambar, a Vegetable Korma, a tasty north Indian-styled Pilau rice, and Raita. I was too full to finish the small Sheera dessert of cream of wheat with nuts and ghee. The house red Syrah turned out to be a good choice. Service is more perfunctory than friendly but despite this people really do seem to enjoy themselves here.

Woodland Chiswick may be out of the way for some but is worth the trek. Other Woodlands are at Marylebone Lane, W1 (page 47), Panton Street, Piccadilly, SW1 (page 30) and Wembley, North London (page 150).

EALING

Carluccio's Caffé
Italian, Modern

🖳 5-6 The Green, W5

☎ 020 8566 4458

🕒 Mon-Fri 8am-11pm, Sat 9am-11pm,
  Sun 10am-10pm

🥕 Vegan options

☀ Outside seating

☗ Child friendly

i Booking advised in evenings; Outside catering (tel 020 7629 0699)

Vegetarian ★★★
Taste ★★★★
Price ££

See Carluccio's Caffé, St Christopher's Place for food review (page 35).

Pizza Organic
Italian, Fast Food

🖳 100 Pitshanger Lane, W5

☎ 020 8998 6878

🚌 Ealing Broadway (15 min walk)

🕒 Daily 11am-11pm

Organic ★★★★★
Vegetarian ★★★★
Taste ★★★★
Price £

See Pizza Organic review (page 158).

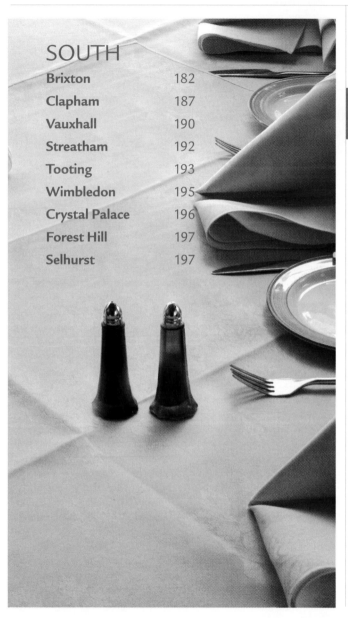

SOUTH

BRIXTON

Bug
International, Modern

Vegetarian ★★★
Taste ★★★
Price ££

🖃 *The Crypt, St Matthew's Church, SW2*
☎ *020 7738 3366*
✎ *www.bahhumbug.co.uk*
🚌 *Brixton LU & Rail (5 min walk)*
🕐 *Mon-Thur 5pm-11pm, Fri-Sat 5pm-11.30pm & Sun 5pm-11pm*
🥕 *Vegan options*
☀ *Outside seating*
♫ *Music (DJ)*

Much beloved by South London veggies as Bah Humbug, this hip underground music and food venue has been fine-tuned down to 'Bug' with great success. On a summer's evening people hangout in the churchyard eating and drinking but for my money the action is down in the vaulted crypt. This is not at all spooky but rather it is modern, with funky lighting and velvet sofas in the well-stocked cocktail bar that gets packed on Friday and Saturday nights. The restaurant oozes with gothic details old arches, brassy chandeliers, gilt mirrors and big fat candles dimly illuminating the place. Coupled with the house, hip hop and funk music playing it's likeably surreal. Midweek, even when there was no live music, the place was filled with a cheerful 18-30 crowd and at the back, the 'Cocoon' private dining room was in full swing with a party of 25.

The short eclectic omnivore menu created by chef Stuart Caldwell who joined Bug from Michelin acclaimed The Dining Room in Surrey, has three veggie starters and three veggie mains that change monthly. Starters may include a neat wrap of asparagus, buffalo mozzarella with red pepper essence or a well-presented oven roasted goats' cheese and beetroot with caramelised cider apples. Not surprisingly, given the locality, several of the main courses have Caribbean influences. Mango and Okra Curry with Pilau rice, pumpkin and plantain comes up mild and substantial with a delicious orange and chilli chutney. Cantonese Mock Duck, however, remains the all time veggie fave here and always features on the menu. It's one of those interactive dishes where you place cucumber and carrot batons on a pancake, add some crispy mock duck made from wheat protein, ginger and dipping sauce and then wrap the pancake up and eat it. Whilst quite delicious, tiny parts of the mock duck can be over crispy making it a bit hard to eat – a point to note when ordering.

Of the five vegetarian desserts two are organic. Bug's blackberry organic ice cream is made on the premises and is excellent whilst the Bourbon Vanilla and Wild Strawberry flavours are quite good too. There's a choice of organic white and red wine with Sangiovese/Montepulciano, Rosso Piceno Superiore (£18) proving to be a smooth match for our mains.

Bug has a fun atmosphere with friendly attentive service. Live music events usually take place on Thursdays, through to Sundays. Phone for details or log onto their website for future line-ups.

Bargain tip: become a Bug member and you get 25% discount off your food Sunday-Thursday 5pm-8pm.

Café Pushka
European, Mediterranean, African

	Organic ★★★
	Vegetarian ★★★★★
	Taste ★
	Price £

🖃 424 Coldharbour Lane, Brixton, SW9
☎ 020 7738 6161
🚇 Brixton LU & Rail (2 min walk)
🕓 Mon-Tue 11am-5pm, Wed-Sat 11am-11pm
🥕 Vegan options
i Evening booking advised

The neighbourhood may be loud and edgy but, on the day I visited Café Pushka was tranquil to the point of dullness.

The table menu included vegan and vegetarian breakfasts of home-made veggie sausages, beans, mushrooms and tomatoes or organic muesli with milk/yogurt, honey and banana for £4.95 as well as three types of toasted panini. The blackboard menu changes regularly with snacks and light meals, some with organic ingredients, served throughout the day for about £5. This rises to £7.50 in the evening when the food is served on better plates, the tables are candlelit and more organic choices are on offer. There are four organic whites, organic pilsner and juices like freshly squeezed orange juice .

The food itself was disappointing. The so-called Tasty Vegeburger of soya blended with mushroom and herbs was flavourless, while the bun tasted like cardboard. The Red Wine Moussaka of beans, rice, aubergine, red pepper, courgette and side salad was not much better although the salad is okay. At the time of writing this eaterie is up for sale hence perhaps the lacklustre experience. The good news is the landlord wants it to remain a veggie restaurant.

Eco Brixton
Italian, Fast Food

🖼 *4 Market Row, Electric Lane, SW9*

☎ *020 7738 3021*

🚌 *Brixton LU (5 min walk)*

🕐 *Mon-Sat 9am-5pm*

🥕 *Vegan options*

🍼 *Child friendly*

☀ *Outside seating*

i *Eat in (table service) & Takeaway*

Vegetarian ★★★★
Taste ★★★★
Price ££

The same pizzas and pastas as Eco Clapham, but in a smaller venue. For food review see Eco Clapham, page 189.

Eco

Clapham

Cicero's
International, Classic

🖵 *2 Rookery Road, SW4*

☎ *020 7498 0770*

🚇 *Clapham Common LU (2 min walk)*

🕐 *Daily 10am-6pm (Summer), 10am-4pm (Winter)*

🥕 *Vegan options*

🍼 *Child friendly*

☀ *Outside seating*

i *Eat in (table service) & Takeaway; Outside catering available*
Restaurant bookable for evening parties of 20-25

Organic ★★
Vegetarian ★★★★★
Taste ★★★
Price £

Vegetarian parklife venue popular with creative types, parents with kids, flies, pigeons and squirrels. Arriving by car, allow up to two days to find it, by tube and foot allow 5 minutes. Set on the east side of the Common, it's a former netball changing rooms with a glass mosaic adorning the outside and attractively lit with lanterns at night. Pick a fine day to sit outside but don't expect the Hanging Gardens of Babylon, instead it's traffic along a busy road.

Cicero's is an ideal venue for mums and dads to bring their offspring and there's a kids' playground adjacent. Facilities include high chairs and a kids' play gascooker. Folk are notably friendly and you may well end up in conversation with a local actor, photographer or artist. Come here regularly enough and everyone will know your name.

The food is all veggie with some organic elements such as rice, beans and pulses. The blackboard menu changes every few days, whilst regular choices such as veggie breakfast (£5.50), hot ciabatta sandwiches (£3.75), mushroom on toast, hummous, pitta and salsa get changed just once a year. There is always a vegan soup such as lentil curry soup and several cakes all of which looked as if they would go down well with the very good cappuccino.

Mains (£6) are oversized, enough for two and best split. Brie and Roast Veg Tart, a warm moderately tasty affair was filled with mushroom and artichoke with a pastry that was a bit overcooked. It came with a salad of couscous, rice, tomato, cucumber, beans and barley with green leaves that was a bit carb heavy (more green veg and bright coloured stuff would help). Children's portions are half price.

Esca

Eco
Italian, Fast Food

Vegetarian ★★★★
Taste ★★★★
Price ££

▢ *162 Clapham High Street, SW4*

☎ *020 7978 1108*

🚌 *Clapham Common LU (2 min walk)*

🕐 *Mon-Thur 12noon-4pm and 6.30pm-11pm,*
   Friday 12noon-4pm and 6pm-11.30pm,
   Sat 12noon-11.30pm & Sun 12noon-11.30pm

🥕 *Vegan options*

🍼 *Child friendly*

i *Eat in (table service) & Takeaway, booking advisable in evenings*

Contemporary, vibrantly designed pizza-pasta paradise serving ten vegetarian pizzas, four pizza bread sandwiches, pastas, calzones, and a big range of salads. Designed ten years ago by Anana Zenz (who also did Belgo in Chalk Farm), Eco has a modern décor with wavy plywood, asymmetric tables and bendy metal lighting. The atmosphere is upbeat and the staff alert and friendly. In the evenings there are often queues waiting for tables with lunchtimes much less manic.

Eco serves amongst the best pizzas in London. All their pizzas are made from scratch so they can build a pizza just as you like it. I can vouch for the Amore, a delicious array of chunky fresh artichoke, long roasted red peppers, green beans, aubergine, tomato sauce, garlic and olive oil. Take a spritz of their olive oil condiment – it's good. A mixed side salad here is a real treat.

The Eco team also own Esca, next door. Esca is a relaxed eaterie and deli with some organic fare. It's worth a visit if your in the area - see the review on page 190. A smaller Eco is in Brixton see page 184.

Esca

Mediterranean, Classic

Vegetarian ★★★★
Taste ★★★★★
Price £££

🏠 160 Clapham High Street, SW4
☎ 020 7622 2288
🚇 Clapham Common LU (2 min walk)
🕐 Mon-Fri 8am-8pm, Sat 9am-8pm
🥕 Vegan options
◊ Child friendly
i Eat in (counter service) & Takeaway

High quality deli counter with 7-8 vegetarian dishes that can be eaten at informal large tables at the back of house. Esca means 'bait' in Italian and its food certainly looks good enough to tempt people in off the street. Tomato, mozzarella and basil salad, roasted pumpkin with raisins and almonds, and spring beans, pine nuts with sesame and sundried tomato are appetising options. Some ready-made sandwiches at £2.60-£3.20 are available as are packs of organic dried fruit. For shop review see page 256.

Good Earth Express

Chinese, Classic

Vegetarian ★★★★
Taste ★★★★★
Price £££

🏠 116 St Johns Hill, SW11
☎ 020 7228 3140
🚇 Wimbledon LU & Rail(20min walk)
🕐 Daily 5.30pm-11.30pm
i Takeaway and delivery service only

See Good Earth Knightsbridge (page 155) for food review.

VAUXHALL

Bonnington Café

Japanese, French, German,
East European, Medieval, Classic

Organic ★★★
Vegetarian ★★★★★
Taste ★★
Price £

🏠 11 Vauxhall Grove, SW8
☎ 020 7820 7466,
🖃 www.bonningtoncafe.co.uk
🚇 Vauxhall LU & Rail (2 min walk)
🕐 Daily 7am-11pm
🍸 BYO (off licence opposite)
🥕 Vegan options
☀ Outside seating in summer

Communally, co-operative run vegetarian restaurant with different chefs cooking on different nights, an arrangement which accounts for the eclectic range of cuisines on offer. Thursday night is Vegan Night and that's the night I visited.

The café is on a residential backstreet and on the outside looks completely unappealing and derelict. The area is gradually going through the process of gentrification and in the last 20 years considerable improvements have been made. The community spirit is still strong and the café is near Bonnington Square and its delightful community gardens where diners relax in the summer before going to the café.

The diners are predominantly socially and eco-aware vegetarians. Vaz, an amiable shaven-haired vegan chef says, "Most vegetarians here are now eating it for health reasons. This has become a more important reason than animal welfare that was the principle concern several years ago. There's an interest in how our community has evolved. We get artists from all over London and visiting architects interested in the set-up here."

Inside the café the décor is down at heel. My chair seat was ripped, the knives and forks were old, and none of the plates matched. The table had a red plastic tablecloth that buckled a bit. Next to us, a young couple who lived nearby said they ate at the café regularly and supported the ideals of the place. On some nights the chef arranges cabaret, and that night we wished we were not being entertained by a lady tinkering on the piano and singing something obscure. Tarot readings take place on some nights. Candlelit, the atmosphere is intimate, everybody seems to know each other and one could be forgiven for feeling a bit of an outsider. However, any fears are allayed by our amiable waiter.

Most diners have a starter and main from the menu blackboard. The starter of Marinated Shitake tossed with brown rice and tamari with chives and roast sesame dressing looked quite good and was tasty. Mains come up big. The Broccoli and Leek bake in sage and cumin bread sauce was uneven in temperature and not all that great although the potato slices in paprika were good. The other main, Tart of Fennel Bulb and Chickpeas, came in a medium strong creamy mustard sauce on a buckwheat flour base along with a couscous and coriander mound, roasted garlic, rosemary and thyme and green salad. It was substantial and tasted fine.

The café's low prices are enshrined in its constitution and the place can get busy – proof that community eateries can really work.

STREATHAM

Whole Meal Café
International

	Organic ★
	Vegetarian ★★★★★
	Taste ★★★
	Price £

🖃 *1 Shrubbery Road, SW16*

☎ *020 8769 2423*

🚃 *Streatham Rail or*
   Streatham Hill Rail (5 min walk)

🕐 *Daily 12noon-10pm*

🥕 *Vegan options*

🍼 *Child friendly*

i *Eat in (counter service) & Takeaway*

A relaxed, neighbourhood, 100% vegetarian café with a 30% vegan menu. A stone's throw from Streatham High Street, the outside doesn't look much but inside it's bright and airy with white walls and polished tables. Lunchtime is busy with casually-dressed local business people, shoppers, bookworms and netties tapping wireless laptops.

The Main with Fruit Juice Set Lunches at £4.95 are filling and good value. The Homity Pie, a big slab of mashed potato, onion and garlic with a large mixed salad was okay but a bit bland. The vegan Tokyo Salad was tastier with miso-dressed lettuce, rocket leaves, crunchy beansprouts, peppers, rice and green beans. For less hungry bods, there are the usual baked potato choices, hummous salads, vegan soup and vegeburgers made with breadcrumbs, nuts and veg. Dessert lovers should leave room for the Banoffi Pie with cream and a dusting of chocolate that's good but probably not 'World Famous', as is claimed.

Evenings are candlelit. There's a short organic wine list of Petit Chablis, Sancerre, Pinot Grigio and Frascati Superiore and some organic beers although the non-alcoholic Red Grape Juice is delicious. Whole Meal is a great little place if you're in the Streatham area and wanting a low priced meal that's value for money.

TOOTING

Kastoori
Indian and East African

Vegetarian ★★★★★
Taste ★★★★
Price £££

⌨ *188 Upper Tooting Road, SW17*
☎ *020 8767 7027*
🚇 *Tooting Broadway LU or Tooting Bec LU (5 min walk)*
🕐 *Lunch served Wed-Sun 12.30pm-2.30pm;*
   Dinner served daily 6pm-10.30pm
🍴 *Child friendly*
🌱 *Vegan options*
i *Eat in (table service) & Takeaway*

Worth a trip to Tooting in its own right, this family run restaurant serves vegetarian Gujarati/East African cuisine. Set along a non-descript High Street in a predominantly Indian neighbourhood, Kastoori's interior is elegant and roomy with cool white walls adorned with white sculptures, comfortable chairs and bright yellow clothed tables. Evenings get very busy, lunchtimes are less so. The clientele are casually dressed locals and the occasional foodie from further afield. The menu is Indian home-style, so there aren't many Indian customers as they want a change from home-cooked meals.

The restaurant is run by the amiable Thanki family, dedicated vegetarians who themselves are Gujarati Jains who previously lived in East Africa. The menu has clear descriptions, the service is good and waiters offer helpful advice.

Spicy papadoms with a hot mix of coriander, ginger and peanut chutney, carrot and tomato pickle and a cooling raita was enjoyable. The Dahi Puri starters, a Thanki family creation, are attractively looking crispy cased puries the size of table tennis balls filled with veg and a mildly flavoured sauce. The trick is to bite into them and eat them in one gulp and it takes a bit of practice to avoid the sauce running down the chin. The signature Samosa starter richly filled with vegetables and accented with cinnamon is recommended whilst the Onion Bhaji is competent but not memorable.

There's a good selection of 13 curry mains and The Bhatura Bread fried with fennu (fennel and sesame) is to be recommended as an accompaniment, although the chapati here is good too. The Tomato Curry is novel, tasty but not as hot and spicy as the menu made out. The Kastoori Kofta, a herby, spicy curry sauce with chunky vegetable balls went down a treat. A handsome Panir Passanda of cheese pockets stuffed with coriander and mint in a nut and melon seed sauce is a good dish to share. There are 12 special mains, one of which is available each day. Kasodi, (Swahili sweetcorn) comes in coconut milk and peanut sauce and was delicious whilst the Green Banana Curry is well worth a try.

The usual dessert treats are here such as the sweetish Gulab Jambu, Khir (aromatic rice pud) and Kulfi (mango or pistachio Indian ice cream). To be recommended is the Shrikland – a spicy sweetish curd cheese sprinkled with nutmeg, with flavours of cardamom and saffron.

Much effort has been made to make the wine list match the cuisine. Echeverra Sauvignon Blanc turned out to be a good choice throughout our meal. Masala Tea, a spicy milky traditional finish completes the Kastoori dining experience.

Sakonis Vegetarian Restaurant
North and South Indian, Classic

Vegetarian ★★★★★
Taste ★★★★
Price £

  🖃 180-186 Upper Tooting Road, SW17
  ☎ 020 8772 4774
  🚊 Tooting Broadway LU (5 min walk)
  🕔 Tue-Fri 12noon-9.30pm, Sat & Sun 12noon-9.45pm
  🍼 Child friendly

This is run along the same lines as Sakonis in Green Street (see page 215 for food review) except no breakfasts are served here.

WIMBLEDON

Good Earth Express

Chinese, Classic

Vegetarian ★★★★
Taste ★★★★★
Price £££

- 🏠 *81 Ridgeway, SW19*
- ☎ *020 8944 8883*
- 🚆 *Wimbledon LU & Rail (20 min walk)*
- 🕐 *Daily 5.30pm-11.30pm*
- *i* *Takeaway and delivery service only*

See Good Earth, Knightsbridge (page 155) for food review.

Service-Heart-Joy

International, Classic

Organic ★★★
Vegetarian ★★★★
Taste ★★★
Price £

- 🏠 *191 Hartfield Road, SW19*
- ☎ *020 8542 9912,*
- 🚆 *Wimbledon LU & Rail (10 min walk)*
- 🕐 *Mon-Sat 9am-5pm (except Fri 9am-9pm)*
- 🍼 *Child friendly*
- ☀ *Outside seating*
- *i* *Eat in (counter service) & Takeaway; Outside catering available*

Small, bright looking pure vegetarian neighbourhood café serving breakfasts, lunches, speciality coffees and cakes. Its location is somewhat isolated away from the hustle and bustle of the main Wimbledon shopping area, but the café nevertheless draws in a fair share of locals. The place is smartly decked out with blue tables, yellow chairs, and there are books on meditation and incense sticks to buy.

Service-Heart-Joy offers a good selection of sandwiches, salads and pancakes. Organically, there's home-made cakes, ice cream, hot chocolate, herbal teas and coffee as well as soya milk and vegan margarine on request. Juice enthusiasts may be spoilt for choice but the Wimbledon Strawberry (£2.50) – a strawberry, banana, orange juice and bioyoghurt mix – is worth a try.

Main courses of lasagne, curry or quiche are about £5 a pop, soup is £2.50 and substantial. Takeouts include samosa, vegebacon and burgers, biscuits and cookies.

Tip: phone through to confirm the Friday evening slot as the night I went they had decided to close the place to do an outside catering function.

CRYSTAL PALACE

Domali Café

English and mediterranean, Classic

Vegetarian ★★★★
Taste ★★★
Price £

🖃 *38 Westow Street, SE19*
☎ *020 8768 0096*
🚃 *Crystal Palace Rail (10 min walk), Gypsy Hill Rail (5 min walk)*
🕐 *Mon-Sat 9.30am-11.50pm (last orders 11pm),*
   Sun 9.30am-10.30pm
🥕 *Vegan options*
🍼 *Child friendly*
☀ *Outside seating*
🎵 *Music (DJ)*

Domali is named after its vegetarian owners Dominic and Alison and is pretty well established on this main shopping street, having opened its doors in 1996. The vibe here is laid-back, veggie breakfasts served until 6pm whilst the main menu features a tempting array of upscale sandwiches, salads and hot main courses. Comfy living room leather sofas, informal tables and chairs, vibrant contemporary artwork-for-sale and friendly service, combine to create a bohemian-hip ambiance.

Evenings are candlelit and on the tables complimentary bowls of pistachios. Domali's attracts a pleasant casually dressed twenty-thirtysomething crowd of juice, wine and designer-lager drinkers not out to get smashed. At the back is a very popular garden with wooden benches and outdoor heaters.

Every five weeks, Sunday nights rev up a gear with live DJ's on the mixing deck playing a lively blend of Funk, Afrobeat, Latin and Soul. Weekday morning's it's a different kind of sound – that of mums and kids enjoying a spot of brekker. Children's portions and high chairs are available and there is a good range of breakfast options including homemade muesli and fresh fruit salad.

Recommended for lunch/early evening are the Weekday Deals (9.30am-6pm) which will get you any vegetarian special for just £3.90 instead of the usual £7.90. There are eight to choose from although many of the mains are heavily bread-based. The S.L.T –Veggie Sausage, tomato, lettuce and mayo – is huge and enough for two. The veggie sausage is fairly good and a better option than the bacon.

With its chilled out mood, Domali is a great place for a drink and there are several vegetarian and vegan wines, plus a good range of juices and smoothies for kids. Whilst there are organic wines by the glass only a few food items are organic as they want to keep their prices affordable for their price conscious Crystal Palace clientele. "Hopefully" says Alison, "if organic prices come down we'll make the switch. However, we do buy locally and use smaller suppliers that are in need of support."

Domali has some tempting vegetarian cakes including Chocolate and Raspberry Fudge, Carrot and Banoffi. A really likeable hang out.

FOREST HILL

Provender Wholefoods and Bakery
Organic Vegetarian, International

Organic ★★★★★
Vegetarian ★★★★★
Taste ★★★
Price £

▱ *103 Dartmouth Road Forest Hill SE22*
☎ *020 8699 4046*
🚃 *Forest Hill Rail*
🕐 *Mon-Sat 8am-6.30, Sun 10am-4pm*

Step inside Provender and you are greeted by the irresistible smell of freshly baked bread and a long table spread with a colourful, tempting array of home-baked organic breads, pastries and cakes. Originally just a shop (see page 261) Provender has expanded to accommodate a café. A rustic bench style seating area can be found at the back of the shop past the shelves of wholefoods where regulars can sit down and enjoy organic coffee or a herbal tea and also food. With an eco-aware policy Provender has twice won the Council's Business Environmental Excellence (BEE) Award, bronze in 2000 and gold in 2002.

SELHURST

Pepperton UK
European, Eastern, African, Classic

Organic ★★★
Vegetarian ★★★★★
Taste ★★★
Price £

▱ *25 Selhurst Road, SE25*
☎ *020 8683 4462*
🚃 *Selhurst Rail (5 min)*
🕐 *Tue-Sat 10am-10pm, Sun 12noon-10pm*
☀ *Outside seating*
🌱 *Vegan options*
i *Therapy rooms upstairs*

Opened August 2003, Pepperton UK is more than a neighbourhood veggie restaurant, it's a lifestyle venue and comes complete with displays of contemporary art and alternative therapy rooms. Décor-wise the place has a relaxed cool karma. The ground floor has immaculately polished wooden tables, stripped wooden floor, a comfortable sofa and when I visited the walls were lined with photographic images about the Sherwood Forest Tree Protesters and pictures of forest preservation by Maeve Tomlinson. This is a restaurant with a conscience and one concerned about local community welfare and healthy nutrition via vegetarian and vegan eating. Upstairs there are courses on various new age alternative regimes.

Pepperton UK is run by African vegetarian and former social worker Celestine Agbo who also gives talks on vegetarian food and art to local schools and at the time of writing was building a studio in the back garden for children to participate in art projects. Celestine also gives psycho-counselling sessions when the restaurant is closed and is a friendly smiling face always ready for a chat with customers.

The menu is an eclectic mix of salads, side dishes and mains. West African Stew looks good and is an enjoyable recipe of yam, plantain, black-eyed bean and Scotch Bonnet pepper and well worth £6.50 (the average price for mains here). The Brazilian Stuffed Peppers are filled with a flavoursome mix of aubergine, herby tomatoey goats' cheese, onion and garlic and is served with wild rice. Other choices include two penne pastas, a ricotta and spinach filo dish, a Mexican chilli and bean recipe and jacket potato with cheese or beans (£4).

Juices here are only £1 for a large glass and there are organic white and red wines, Utkins vodka, gin and beer. There's a tempting selection of desserts and all the cakes are vegan.

Pepperton UK is set on a small shopping parade a bit out of the way from things although it's opposite a pub much favoured by Crystal Palace Football supporters. Fans of Pepperton UK include the surrounding multi-ethnic community of East and West African, Chinese, Polish and English vegetarians. The place is also popular with the Croydon Vegan Society, who visited the day before me. Pepperton is well worth a visit for South East London vegetarians.

EAST LONDON

East

BRICK LANE & SPITALFIELDS

For a place that's cultivated a reputation of being London's No.1 Indian dining strip and a hip cool place to gravitate towards, it's a paradox that there isn't a single pure veggie Indian eaterie on Brick Lane. Most of the restaurants are run by Moslem (meat-eating) Bangladeshis who nevertheless recognise the need to offer a good vegetarian food selection. Competition for your money is cut throat with restaurant touts pestering passers-by on the street with 25% discount meal deals and a pint of lager thrown in! The area has a vibrant atmosphere and is always busy with tourists, students, foodies and locals. Amongst the best veggie-orientated eateries here are Shampan, Bengal Cuisine and Preem. Spitalfields is within five minutes walk of Brick Lane and has a great selection of international food bars at lunch-time and the long established Café Mediterraneo which offers a good Mezze.

Restaurants

1) Bengal Cuisine p.201
2) Preem p.202
3) Shampan p.202
4) Café Mediterraneo p.205
5) Spitalfields Food Market p.206

Shops

a) Ambala Foods p.263
b) Spitalfields Food Market p.277
c) Spitalfields Organics p.264

BRICK LANE

Bengal Cuisine
Indian, Classic

Vegetarian ★★★
Price £

🖃 *12 Brick Lane, E1*
☎ *020 7377 8405*
🚆 *Shoreditch LU or Liverpool Street LU & Rail (10 min walk)*
🕓 *Daily 12noon-12midnight*

A menu of classic vegetarian Indian dishes like mixed vegetable balti, vegetable dhansk, biryani, korma, and vegetable sizzler dishes.

Want to cook curry like the experts? Bengal Cuisine runs 'Cook Your Own Curry' sessions every Tuesday 6pm-9pm where the chef takes you to the kitchen and shows you how to do it. You choose starter, main, side, rice and bread. You get two drinks and the deal costs £25 per person. The cookery course takes 2-8 persons per session. The vegetarian business lunch of starter and main course is £6.95, while the Sunday buffet (from 12noon-7.30pm) offers 10 dishes for £5.95 (adults), or £3.95 (kids).

Bengal Cuisine

Preem Restaurant and Balti House

Indian, Classic

Vegetarian ★★★
Price £

🖃 *120 Brick Lane, E1*

☎ *020 7247 0397*

🚇 *Shoreditch LU or Liverpool Street LU & Rail (10 min walk)*

🕓 *Mon-Sat 12noon-2am, Sun 12noon-1am*

Veggies are well catered for here with a choice of seven veggie starters, twenty-four side dishes and main courses such as masala dosa, biryani, vegetable balti and vegetable masala balti. Budget for £7.50 per head excluding drinks and tip.

The Shampan Restaurant

Indian, Classic

Vegetarian ★★★
Price £

🖃 *79 Brick Lane, E1*

☎ *020 7375 0475*

🚇 *Shoreditch LU or Liverpool Street LU & Rail (10 min walk)*

🕓 *Sun-Wed 12noon-1am, Thur-Sat 12noon -2am*

i   Eat in (table service) & Takeaway

Traditional, upscale Bangladeshi and Indian restaurant that avoids the use of food colourings and artificial additives. The menu features six vegetarian starters, eleven vegetarian speciality mains including Vegetable Tikka Masala and several Bangladeshi specials of which Sag Uribessi Gatta (a dish with spinach and the seeds of Bangladeshi runner beans) makes an excellent choice for veggie diners. Vegetable Biriani and a vegetarian Thali are also available and there is a good selection of side dishes.

Bargain tip: there's 10% discount if you make a reservation for lunch or the weekend.

Shampan

Café Mediterraneo

SPITALFIELDS

Café Mediterraneo
Mediterranean, Organic Vegetarian

🖃 *Old Spitalfields Organic Market,*
   Honer Square, E1
☎ *020 7377 8552*
🚌 *Liverpool St LU & Rail (5 min walk)*
🕐 *Mon-Fri 8am-4pm & Sun 8am-5pm*
☀ *Outside seating*
👶 *Child friendly*
i *Eat in (counter service) & Takeaway*

Organic ★★★★
Vegetarian ★★★★
Taste ★★
Price £

For atmosphere it's best to catch this on a Sunday, organic market day at Spitalfields, although on weekdays it's popular with city workers. The décor's not much to write home about – think indoor-market basic. Go to the counter to admire the inviting Lebanese and Syrian mezzes, order then grab a table outside. The house special, the Pumpkin and Sesame salad is the best pick. a mixed meze here is only £4.50 and there's couscous, grilled aubergine and a huge array of mediterranean salads made with organic produce. They also do a reasonable Okra Salad and a broad bean dish that you dip garlic mayo into. Their own recipe hummous is top notch. on the hot choices there's veggie organic Moussaka and Lasagne both served with mixed salad and also a two skewer vegetable barbecue dish with rice It's a good pitstop also for organic coffee and soft drinks and has just a few meat dishes for carnivorous companions.

Spitalfields Food Market

Commercial Street, E1
Liverpool Street LU & Rail (5 min walk)
Main market Sun 8am-5pm, food stalls open daily 11am-3pm

For hungry market moochers, there's no better place to be than Spitalfields with its multitude of international cuisine food stalls. Eat one of their many meal deals as you stroll around the organic riches or chow down in the communal seating area, if you can find a space.

Popular, and with the longest queue, is **Indonesian Food** which serves tofu satay, veg noodle and spring rolls or for less wait, head for the Potato or Tandoori Hut. A big hit is **Falafels** whose speciality falafels look scrummy and with warm pitta bread cost just £2.70.

For a full-on organic slurp, **Jumpin' Juice** whisks a wicked smoothie of strawberry, raspberry, apple, orange, banana with cherry for £3.75 and a range of energy smoothies. Jumpin Juice is located amongst the organic food stalls and is there Sun 9.30am-5pm.

Nearby, is **Ash Green Organic Foods** grocery stand (Sun-Wed 10am-6pm). They have a colourful spread of fruit and veg and offer a free home delivery service throughout Kent. They're also at Greenwich Village Market 10am-5pm on Saturdays. **Cranberry** is a dried fruit and nut specialist with a selection that's half organic and also runs a stall at Borough Market. Check out the delicious figs, mangoes, pineapples and apricots.

Spitalfields Market's destination stall for organic tofu lovers is **Clean Bean**. Do try their free samples of smokey organic tofu, 5 spice or sesame and ginger – all delicious and made at 170 Brick Lane, E1. Their dipping sauce that's a tamari soya sauce, cider vinegar, sesame, garlic and vinegar combo is also most enjoyable. Clean Bean is at Spitalfields on Sundays 9am-5.30pm and at Borough Market on Saturdays 9am-4pm.

Celtic Breads have an awesome stall of organic breads. Based in Cricklewood, they bake it all themselves and now serve 20 markets and many London organic food shops. One of the most popular breads is the Sourdough Rye which is yeast and wheat-free for those worried about allergies. There's a good selection of gluten-free breads. Aidan's seeded sourdough Levain takes the prize for the sexiest looking bread.

Bliss Organic Ltd make their own organic cakes and sell 300-400 portions per week. Their apple, date, sultana and honey cake (£1.30/slice) is superb. Several are gluten-free and they do supply other wholefood stores in London. The stall is open Sun 9am-5pm and can also be found at Stoke Newington Farmers Market on a Saturday.

BETHNAL GREEN

Three to try: Wild Cherry, The Gallery Café and The Thai Garden, The first two have Buddhist affiliations although you would never guess it and there's also an organic shop, Friends Organic nearby.

The Gallery Café
International

🖃 *21 Old Ford Road, E2*

☎ *020 8983 3624*

🚌 *Bethnal Green LU (2 min walk)*

🕙 *Mon-Fri 8.30am-3.30pm (Tue closes at 3pm), Sat 10.30am-5pm*

🥕 *Vegan options*

🍼 *Child friendly*

☀ *Outside seating*

i *Eat in (counter service) & Takeaway*

Vegetarian ★★★★★
Taste ★★★
Price £

One of East London's best kept veggie secrets for daytime eating, drinking, chatting and chilling out. Outside, there's a charming small sitting area, inside it's an airy, long spacious room pleasantly windowed at both ends.

Like the nearby Wild Cherry (see page 209) and Friends Organic (see page 264) it's affiliated to the London Buddhist Centre, but is run by Western Buddhists and the food is a lot snackier. Expect soup and bread, bagels, pasta, flans, quiches, toasted ciabatta with veggie sausage, Spanish tortillas, green salads and stews woofed down by local charity workers, schoolteachers and a few mums with pushchairs.

Do check out the home-made 'traditional' German curd cheese cake which is like no other and quite reasonable although the diet-busting 'Nemesis' chocolate cake is more decadent. The coffee is organic.

The Thai Garden
Thai

Vegetarian ★★★
Taste ★★★★
Price £

🖃 249 Globe Road, E2
☎ 020 8981 5748
🚌 Bethnal Green LU (5 min walk)
🕐 Lunch served Mon-Fri 12noon-3pm;
    Dinner served Mon-Fri 6pm-11pm
🥕 Vegan options
🍼 Child friendly
i   Eat in (table service) & Takeaway

Award-winning neighbourhood traditional Thai restaurant with an extensive menu of forty vegetarian dishes, many of which are vegan. The Thai Garden actually calls itself 'meat-free' as the rest of the menu is seafood and it prides itself on being MSG-free and GM-free. Evenings are busy, lunchtimes quiet.

The place is filled with classic Thai ornaments and is properly table-clothed. Service is formal and attentive. Although it's non-smoking upstairs, downstairs has more atmosphere.

Worth trying is Tom Khar, a coconut soup with cauliflower and galanga flavour or the Gaeng Herd Woon Sen, a clear vermicelli soup with mixed veg. The noodle choice is huge and they only use Thai fragrant rice in their dishes. The veggie mock duck dish Gang Phed Ped Yang Jay comes with Thai aubergines, pineapples and beanshoots in red curry with coconut cream and is excellent.

A glorious dessert for waistline watchers is the Tropical Fruit Salad and for dietbreakers, Thai Custard, a yellow bean, egg and coconut cake.

Wild Cherry

International, Classic

   241 Globe Road, E2

   020 8980 6678

   Bethnal Green LU (5 min walk)

   Mon 11am-3pm, Tue-Sat 11am-7pm

   Vegan options

   Child friendly

   Outdoor seating in Summer

i   *Eat in (counter service) & Takeaway*

Organic ★★

Vegetarian ★★★★★

Taste ★★★

Price £

East

BETHNAL GREEN

Wild Cherry

A busy, bright, modern-looking canteen-style eaterie, associated with the London Buddhist Centre next door. Surprisingly, inside there's no in your face Buddhism at all, apart from a discreet mission statement referring to a commitment to spiritual growth and a few leaflets by the entrance. Instead, dotted around the walls are pictures exhibited by local artists, whilst the eating area is decked out with spic and span modern chairs and tables.

By 1.30pm it's packed with chatty local office types, social workers and student bookworms munching a choice of salads, jacket potatoes and sandwiches. Servings here are abundantly generous, especially the made-on-the premises bakes and casseroles that change daily. The Spinach and Chick Pea Curry with brown rice is massive on spinach, tasty but monotonous. Chicory and Butter Bean Bake with potato and chilli and nice sized mushrooms and a Thai Noodle Salad is a better choice as it gets progressively tastier the more one eats it. Desserts include vegan cakes with some sugar and wheat-free options and there are organic juices and teas, GM-free soya milk and herbals.

Traditional veggie breakfasts of fried egg, scrambled egg, veggie sausage, tomato, mushroom, potato, muesli, fruit salad, pancakes and organic maple syrup are available.

Although Wild Cherry does not open in the evenings, they do run one-off evening dinners, parties and special events and hire out the premises for functions.

Formerly called The Cherry Orchard, it's run by eight friendly Western Buddhist women. Their working ideals are based on the principles of non-violence, honesty and generosity and what is particularly significant is their aim to promote vegetarianism and provide home-cooked veggie meals to the local community.

A short walking distance away and connected with the Buddhist Centre are Friends Organic (page 264) and The Gallery Café (page 207).

VICTORIA PARK & HOMERTON

H ome to gentrified Hackney's famous organic pub and restaurant The Crown, with dining rooms that make great venues for organic wedding receptions, parties and functions. Or for a real laid back, chilled out ungentrified Hackney caff experience Pogo offers inexpensive all-vegetarian offerings that will suit all pockets.

The Crown

Organic, British,
Mediterranean, Modern

Organic ★★★★★
Vegetarian ★★★★
Taste ★★★★
Price £££

🏠 *223 Grove Road, Victoria Park, E3*

☎ *020 8981 9998*

🚌 *Bethnal Green LU, Stepney Green LU & Mile End LU (10 min walk)*

🕐 *Pub open Tue-Sun 10.30am-11pm, Mon 5pm-11pm;*
   Food served Mon 6.30pm-10.30pm, Tue-Fri 12.30pm-3pm &
   6.30pm-10.30pm, Sat 10.30am-3.30pm & 6.30pm-10.30pm,
   Sun 10.30am-4pm, 6.30pm-10pm

🍼 *Child friendly*

☀ *Outside seating*

This excellent organic pub, opened in May 2000 and is sister to the Duke of Cambridge (see page 99 for food review). It's only the second organic certified pub in the world and has an extensive organic wine list, with wines being offered at half price on Monday evenings when ordered with food. Of the 36 organic wines, nine are available by the glass with the Tempranillo and the Sauvignon Blanc being most popular.

The ground floor bar is spacious, with big wooden tables and a friendly atmosphere. Upstairs are two dining rooms with table service and a gastropub menu. The Crown's menu is about 30% shorter than the Duke's although essentially it's the same dishes just less of them. The place gets manic at weekends with families and kids when booking is strongly advised. In decent weather there is outside seating on the balconies with views of Victoria Park. The two dining rooms upstairs are ideal for a party, reception or functions featuring high quality organic food and drink.

POGO

International, Café

Organic ★★★
Vegetarian ★★★★★
Taste ★★★
Price £

🖳 *76a Clarence Road, Hackney, E5*
☎ *020 8533 1214*
🚌 *Hackney Central Rail (5 min walk)*
🕐 *Mon 1pm-6pm, Wed-Sat 1pm-9pm, Sun 10am-9pm (closed Tue)*
◍ *Child friendly*
✎ *Vegan options*
🍸 *BYO (£1 corkage per person)*
i *Eat in (counter service) & Takeaway*

Pogo is a neighbourhood hang-out offering value for money, home-made vegan café-style eats with good vegan cake and a selection of organic coffee. The café is located in a run-down enclave of Hackney and is situated opposite the ugly Pembury Estate, but inside the atmosphere is friendly and welcoming.

Opened in August 2004, this non-profit making worker's co-operative is on the former Pumpkins site and still has a couple of the old sofas, the same wooden dining tables, comfy chairs and books and games for children to play in a corner. The décor now is less colourful although Cool Jo's Art Show and works of other local artists spice the place up a bit – as does their varied Morrissey, Motown and New Order recorded playlist. Evenings are busier than lunchtimes and attract an 18-40 casually dressed crowd, although weekday lunchtimes get a few business suits and Town Hall folk.

The blackboard menu offers four vegan starters, five mains of Mediterranean, Mexican or British. Recipes are a mix of the staff's own and Pumpkins recipes such as the Cashewnut Burger (£3) that although a light meal is tasty and comes with chopped red cabbage, carrot and lettuce salad. More substantial is Pogo's own Smoked Tofu with aubergine, peppers and rye bread (£5) that tastes good too and goes down well with a Strawberry Soya Shake. Cakes here look good and the sweet and moist Banana Cake is to be recommended.

FOREST GATE

Forest Gate has a large and active Indian population and nowhere is this more evident than on Green Street with numerous Indian jewellery and sari outlets and, of course, lots of very good Indian eateries. Among the best outlets are Sakonis that does good Chinese options too and Vijay's Chawalla with its busy bakery. On nearby Romford Road there's City Sweet Centre and Juларam.

City Sweet Centre

Indian, Classic

Vegetarian ★★★★★
Taste ★★★
Price £

- 510-512 Romford Road, E7
- 020 8472 5459
- Woodgrange Park LU (7 min walk)
- Daily 10am-8pm (except Tuesdays)
- Vegan options
- Child friendly
- Alcohol-free zone
- i Eat in (table service) & Takeaway

Busy 100% veggie eaterie with all food made on the premises in their massive back kitchen. The big event here is the freshly made confectionery (see shop review on page 265) although there is a fair sized dining area with locals young and old keeping the place busy throughout the day. I can vouch for Bhel Puri, Pani Puri, Special Puri, Patis Chaat, Dahiwada, Samosas and Dhoharia as being very enjoyable. The Vegetarian Spring Rolls, however, lacked the pizzazz of most Chinese ones. There are just a couple of lassi and fruit juices and most diners opt for the commercial fizzy canned drinks.

Sakonis Vegetarian Restaurant
North and South Indian, Classic

Vegetarian ★★★★★
Taste ★★★★
Price £

⌦ *149-153 Green Street, E7*
☎ *020 8472 8887,*
🚌 *Upton Park LU (5 min walk)*
🕐 *Tue-Sun 12noon-9.30pm*
   (breakfasts served 9am-11am Sat & Sun only)
☖ *Child friendly*
i *Table and buffet service*

East · FOREST GATE

Great value Indian and Chinese buffet in this popular and voluminous canteen restaurant. The night we went we were the only non-Indian diners there but I felt totally at ease with the most amiable and helpful staff and genuine friendliness from the other diners. These are westernised Indians with kids that drink Coke and Fanta and put Heinz tomato ketchup on their uttapa! Mobile phones ring constantly as dad does a bit more business whilst the kids play on gameboys and mum enjoys a night off. Some of the women wear saris but otherwise it's all denims, baseball caps and trainers. The busiest time is 8pm-9pm.

Sakonis does an à la carte menu but everyone goes for the mighty eat-as-much-as-you-like buffet, that changes daily. The dinner buffet goes for £7.99 + 10% eat-in (recommended), while lunch is a cut down version of the dinner deal and comes in at £5.99. Drinkswise, sweet Mango Lassi here is good but the Fresh Lime Juice (Limbu Sharbat) is even better. Over at the buffet counter Aloo Papadi Chat, Bhaji, Sev Puri, Mogo Chips and Mysore Masala Dosa were all extremely good and served at the right temperature. After a break, try the four Chinese options and don't miss the excellent Paneer Chilli and the Szechuan Spicy Noodles. Next up, order a Sakoni Faluda, a rose flavoured shake drink with a straw and then spoon up the vanilla ice-cream. It's excellent. Me done, my partner opted for a sweet and satisfyingly tasty Gulab Jambu dessert.

Traditional dosa breakfasts are available at £2.99. At the entrance, is a small shop section Good Morning Panwalla (see page 266) worth checking out.

Altogether there are four Sakonis in London with the biggest at 119-121 Ealing Road, Wembley, Middlesex (tel 020 8903 9601) and a smaller one at 5-8 Dominion Parade, Station Road, Harrow (tel 020 8863 3399), and one in Tooting (see page 194 for details).

Vijay's Chawalla
Indian, Classic

Vegetarian ★★★★★
Taste ★★★
Price £

- ⌧ 268-270 Green Street, E7
- ☎ 020 8470 3535
- 🚌 Upton Park LU (3 min walk)
- ⊕ Daily 11am-9pm
- 🥕 Vegan options
- ⫟ Child friendly
- i Eat in (table service) & Takeaway

Popular Indian fast food vegetarian eaterie with separate shop counter selling Indian sweets, breads and snack takeaways. It gets particularly busy on Friday, Saturday and Sunday evenings although it's more mellow during the week. Inside, two TV sets at either end of the eaterie blare B4U Music Interactive while near the entrance are three relaxing fish tanks.

Most people start with a couple of vegetarian snacks and a main course or go for the Special Thali at £7. Mixed Bhaji is an enjoyable spicy pakora selection and the Aloo Papadi Chaat and the large samosa here are also tasty. The menu has useful illustrations and the Chole Bhatura, two deep fried breads with delicious spicy chick peas and small salad is just what you see in the pictures The Passionfruit juice is wonderfully gluggable whilst the Lime drink is quite good too. Save room for the desserts of which I can vouch for the Cassata Bombay, a colourful cashew nut rich tutti-frutti, with pistachio and mango ice cream. At 8.45pm they call last orders for food and at 9pm they are stacking chairs on the tables.

LEYTONSTONE

Taste
International

Vegetarian ★★★★★
Taste ★★
Price £

- ⌧ 676 Lea Bridge Road, E10
- ☎ 020 8539 3855
- 🚌 Walthamstow Central LU & Rail (15 min walk)
- ⊕ Mon 9.30am-3pm, Tue-Sat 9.30am-6pm
- 🥕 Vegan options
- ☀ Outside seating
- i Eat in (counter service) & Takeaway

Small modern good-looking neighbourhood vegetarian café serving inexpensive popular choices. Vegetarians Matt and Tracy originally opened Taste in April 2003 as a coffee and sandwich bar extending the menu later to include soups and dishes such as wild mushroom risotto, bean chilli wraps, mezzes, salads and jacket potatoes. The food is all pretty regular stuff although the red and white wine is organic. The home-made Veg Stew Dumpling comes with a baguette and is a murky soup mix of potato and vegetable suet, a good winter filler albeit one that tastes extraordinarily bland. Toasted Panini with Mediterranean Vegetables and Mozzarella is alright and on a par with those sold at the big coffee shop chains. The salad counter looks reasonable and they also do smoothies and shakes with soya milk on request. Sweet tooths should enjoy the good quality Coffee and Walnut cake.

Set on a nondescript shopping parade, Taste is more pit-stop than destination eaterie but with its new stripped pine floors, abstract artwork for sale, natty red plastic-backed chairs, chill-out sofas and inexpensive food, it plays well with the locals.

CANARY WHARF

Carluccio's Caffé
Italian, Classic

Vegetarian ★★★
Taste ★★★★
Price ££

🖃 *2 Nash Court, E14*
☎ *020 7719 1749*
🚌 *Canary Wharf LU & DLR*
🕓 *Mon-Fri 8am-11pm, Sat 9am-11pm & Sun 10am-10pm*
🖊 *Vegan options*
🍼 *Child friendly*
☀ *Outside seating*
i *Outside catering (tel 020 7629 0699)*

A great place to head for when in Canary Wharf. It's located in a prime position in Docklands' financial district with good outside seating to soak up the high-tech architectural atmosphere and Carluccio's Italian food. See Carluccio's Caffé, St Christopher's Place for meal review (page 35).

SHOPPING AREA INDEX

Shops

INTRODUCTION

The first organic food shop 'Wholefood' in Baker Street was conceived in 1965 by Mary Langman, one of the first organic farmers in Britain and a founder member of the Soil Association. It was supplied with organic produce from producers throughout the country and was the prototype for the development of the entire British organic food industry.

Organic produce was made available to a wider market in the 1980's at the suggestion of younger members of the Soil Association. At present, regulations for organic produce are strictly controlled by the UK Register of Organic Food Standards (UKROFS) and European Union (EU) legislation. UKFROS authorises ten organic certification bodies that monitor the proper maintenance of organic food production. Genuine organic products have packaging that displays the registration number of a UKROFS (eg UK2, UK5 etc) or an EU approved certifier. In the European Union overseas products must comply with EU legislation. However, with different levels of control procedure in different countries, especially in the USA what is and isn't organic can be confusing for the consumer to discern.

Availability of organic produce

Globally, levels of organic production are small fry. Just 2.2% of EU agricultural land is certified organic farmland. Consequently, when there's a run on a particular item at your local wholefood shop, demand can overwhelm supply especially outside the local growing seasons. Supermarkets and wholefood shops try to get the freshest produce they can but sometimes if the price on an item is sky high they may decide to give it a temporary miss. If you have trouble sourcing a particular item try Planet Organic, Fresh & Wild, Waitrose, Marks and Spencers, Tesco or ring around the many local places listed in this chapter.

Organic Perceptions

Certainly people tend to see organic food in a very good light. According to Professor Carlo Leifert of The Tesco Centre of Agriculture at the University of Newcastle 'Consumers do perceive organic food as healthier, more sustainable, better for the soil and tastier.' There has been some support for this view in a study in the respected scientific journal – Nature (Nature 410, 926-930, 2001), in which organic apple production was found to be more sustainable, and produced better tasting apples than conventionally grown apples.

The juice, the whole juice & nothing but the juice.

If we're honest, Grove Fresh isn't like other juices. It's squeezed from 100% organic fruit or vegetables making it healthier and extra delicious. It's also pure juice and not concentrate, which means there's no added water. Simply squeezed, for you to drink.

www.grovefresh.co.uk

Veggie and organic shopping trends

In London, a wholefood or organic shop is never far away. Many are small stores catering for neighbourhood needs and invariably provide a more personal service than big retail chains like Waitrose and Tesco. However these chains do offer a huge variety and as more and more of their smaller units pervade London, organic food will become even more accessible. The Fresh & Wild organic supermarket chain and the three Planet Organics also provide good choice for discerning organic customers.

In the event that you need home delivery there are several specialist firms providing this service and these too are listed in this chapter. Alternatively, there are also online organic delivery services offered by the main supermarket players.

In this chapter, organic shops and wholefood shops have been grouped together as there is a certain amount of overlap. Also, of note are the many Indian vegetarian sweet shops often overlooked by veggies. These offer delicious arrays of traditional confectioneries and snacks. Anyone who has yet to try them can always ask for a small mixed box. Once you've tasted, you'll be hooked.

Many of the hottest things on the organic and vegetarian retail scene have been at the expensive end of the spectrum. Stella McCartney's store in Bruton Street sells a wonderful range of designer shoes and clothes for vegetarians, Aveda in Covent Garden offers top hairdressing with organic products with a great on-site organic café, whilst Green Baby has everything for a baby's organic needs. A new men's organic skincare and grooming range has been launched by Jurlique. There's even organic interior decorating products at Texture in Stoke Newington. Welcome to the veggie and organic shops of London!

CENTRAL LONDON

BLOOMSBURY

Alara Wholefoods
Organic foods, drinks, eats, bodycare, household items

⌂ *258-260 Marchmont Street, WC1*
☎ *0207 837 1172*
🚇 *Russell Square LU (1 min walk)*
🕐 *Mon-Fri 9am-6pm, Sat 10am-6pm (Thur till 7pm)*
✉ *Mail order available*

Large neighbourhood vegetarian, health food and alternative remedy shop that's strong on organic hot and cold foods, juices, smoothies and hot drinks. See restaurant review on page 12.

Established in 1979 it was taken over in 1999 by vegetarian husband and wife Xavier and Pary, both of whom are passionate about organic food. Xavier is particularly knowledgeable and will direct you to some very interesting products. At Alara Wholefoods they import funky Odwalla bars from the USA and Joseph's sugar-free organic cookies suitable for diabetics. Fresh organic fruit and veg are delivered every day.

What is noticeable with Alara Wholefoods is the sheer range of goods they carry with just a few of each line that quickly get replenished. Consequently they have a good range of tofu, honey and juices and a huge selection of seeds and dried fruits.

Alara Wholefoods should not be confused with Alara Foods, a long-standing organic and gluten-free muesli manufacturer. However, this shop does stock Alara Foods' Soil Association certified cereals. Currently there are six different types of Alara Muesli with a very tempting Organic Branberry with dried strawberries and blueberries and a high fibre content to kickstart your day healthily.

Bargain tip: check out the back of the shop for special promotions.

Planet Organic
Organic food, drink, eats

🏠 *22 Torrington Place, WC1*

☎ *0207436 1929*

🚇 *Goodge Street LU (5 min walk)*

🕐 *Mon-Fri 9am-10pm, Sat 11am-6pm & Sun 12noon-6pm*

Popular with nearby London University students and affluent Fitzrovians, this is the second organic supermarket from Planet Organic. See Planet Organic, Westbourne Grove branch for review (page 249).

COVENT GARDEN & HOLBORN

Aveda Institute
Hairdressing, beauty therapy, environmental lifestyle store, organic café

🏠 *174 High Holborn, WC1*

☎ *0207 7350 7350*

🚇 *Tottenham Court Road LU or Holborn LU (5 min walk)*

🕐 *Mon-Fri 9.30am-7pm, Sat 9am-6.30pm*

i   Drivers phone for special deal with nearby NCP car park

Eco-conscious Aveda are committed to certified organic ingredients and petrochemical avoidance where possible in their extensive hair, beauty and fragrance product ranges. About 97% of ingredients are organic, the remaining 3% being there to preserve shelf life.

Urban Retreat is a cool hair and beauty salon with very well-trained staff. The Environmental Lifestyle Store is Aveda's showcase for their pure flower and plant essences, hair and beauty products and a range of complimentary holistic services including stress relieving treatments, make-up applications and classes. The institute implements principles of Ayureveda, the ancient Indian healing art.

Mycafé, Aveda's organic café is excellent, for review see page 25. There are further branches of Aveda in Westbourne Grove (tel 020 7243 6047) and Marylebone High Street (tel 020 7224 3157).

TASTE OUR IMAGINATION

Blending cultural influences, quality ingredients and contemporary cooking, Cauldron produces tasty and convenient vegetarian and organic foods.

✓ **AWARD-WINNING**
✓ **NON-GM**
✓ **SOIL ASSOCIATION CERTIFIED**
✓ **VEGETARIAN SOCIETY APPROVED**

Find Cauldron's range in organic supermarkets and health foods stores throughout London.

cauldron

www.cauldronfoods.co.uk

Central COVENT GARDEN & HOLBORN

Monmouth Coffee Company

Coffee beans, drink, eats

🖃 27 Monmouth Street, WC1

☎ 020 7645 3560

🚇 Covent Garden LU (10 min walk)

🕘 Mon-Sat 9am-6.30pm

Coffee cognescenti can choose from five certified organic coffees from Brazil, Peru, and Uganda plus the company's own organic espresso blend. The tasting area at the back is now a tiny wooden hideaway café for revelling in these awarding winning cuppas.

They have a larger sister shop just outside Borough Market at 2 Park Street, SE1 (tel 020 7645 3585), as well as a stall inside the market on Friday and Saturday near the fruit and veg people.

Neal's Yard Remedies

Organic beauty, skincare, gifts, herbs and therapies

🖃 15 Neal's Yard, WC2

☎ 020 7379 7222

🚇 Covent Garden LU (5 min walk)

🕘 Mon-Sat 10am-7pm, Sun 11am-6pm

A vast choice of organic products to pamper yourself with and a key destination for those choosing alternative remedies.

MARYLEBONE, MAYFAIR & BAKER STREET

Stella McCartney
Designer clothes

🖼 *30 Bruton Street, W1*
☎ *020 7518 3100*
🚌 *Bond Street LU (5 min walk)*
🕐 *Mon-Sat 10am-6pm (Thur till 7pm)*

Upscale designer store in four storey Georgian townhouse opened in 2003 by Stella McCartney, leading fashion designer and a patron of the Vegetarian Society. Dress to impress when you come as there's security on the door. Once you're inside however the atmosphere is relaxed and the service slick and sophisticated.

All the clothes and shoes are suitable for vegetarians and the perfume range is organic. Through the elegant hallway is a drawing room adorned with a wall of marquetry panels. On display are accessories, sunglasses, handbags and don't forget to peruse the marquetry drawers that can be be pulled out to yield a further array of products.

Next on is a glasshouse garden with a beautiful maple tree surrounded by works of art and furniture. At the rear of the ground floor is the Shoe Room which houses a circular display of exclusive shoes completely suitable for vegetarians.

Ready to Wear Collections are on the first floor and at the rear is a Lingerie Boudoir. Further upstairs is a bespoke tailoring service supervised under the watchful eye of a Savile Row master tailor.

Total Organics
Organic and vegetarian food store, lunchtime eats

🖼 *6 Moxon Street, Marylebone, W1*
☎ *020 7935 8626*
🚌 *Baker Street LU (10 min walk)*
🕐 *Mon-Sat 10am-6.30pm, Sat 10am-6pm, Sun 10am-3pm*

This welcome addition to Marylebone Village opened in September 2004 and is run along the same lines as their highly popular Borough Market concession (see page 65 for food review). The store is pleasantly modern in look with a well-stocked deli counter, a help-yourself muesli bar, a good selection of soya, quinoa, rice and quality pastas as well as freshly delivered sprouted mung beans and alfalfa. Food savvy American students from the nearby college hit the juice bar either for wheatgrass or the 'Sticky Gingers', a carrot, apple and ginger energy boosting juice.

Service here is friendly, knowledgeable and there are 14 high stools with tables at the back to enjoy summer salads or winter soups, casseroles, paella and Marcel's Spanish omelettes. Fresh cakes, many gluten and dairy-free, gorgeous breads made by Flour Power and canned soft drinks are available but at the time of writing not coffee – somewhat of a surprise for this café area.

The 'Pots for Tots' organic baby food range, a selection of organic household items and vegetarian Christmas Puddings are also available.

Marylebone Farmers' Market

▱ *Cramer St car park (off Marylebone High Street), W1*
🕐 *Sun 10am-2pm*
🚌 *Bond St and Baker St LU*

See page 275 for more information about London Farmers' Markets.

SoHo

Country Life

Wholefood shop, takeout snacks

▱ *3-4 Warwick Street, W1*
☎ *020 7434 2922*
🚌 *Piccadilly LU (5 min walk)*
🕐 *Mon-Thur 10am-6pm, Fri 10am-2.30pm*

Small mainly vegan food and natural products shop with some dairy items. Stocks takeout sandwiches, salads, small cakes and pies with some pre-packed organic items. It has its own vegetarian cook book for sale and they can order you in other veggie cookbooks if required. Tey also have an impressive basement vegan restaurant, see page 51 for review.

On Thursdays, Dr Clemence Mitchell, a vegan GP is available for consultation. The doctor advises on obesity and high blood pressure and offers nutritional and natural remedies. A small charity donation is normally asked for this service.

Fresh & Wild

Food, Drink, Eats

▱ *69-75 Brewer Street, W1*
☎ *020 7434 3179*
🚌 *Piccadilly LU (1 min walk)*
🕐 *Mon 7.30am-9pm, Sat 9am-9pm, Sun 11.30am-6.30pm*

Shop organic on the Soho wildside. See Notting Hill branch for food review (page 168) and organic shop review (page 248).

Peppercorns
Food, drink, eats, health products

🗐 2, Charlotte Place, W1

☏ 020 7631 4528

🚌 Goodge Street LU (3 min walk)

🕓 Mon-Sat 9am-7pm

Tucked away down an alleyway in Fitzrovia, Peppercorns is a natural and organic food mini-market with a large stock of Solgar vitamin and mineral products, pre-packed vegetarian and vegan takeaways including sandwiches, cakes and a contacts and campaigns noticeboard with leaflets.

SOUTHWARK & WATERLOO

Borough Market
🗐 Southwark Street, SE1

A huge food event with all manner of fine produce on offer from organic wines to farm produced cheeses. See pages 64 & 277 for details.

Coopers
Organic food and vegetarian café

🗐 17 Lower Marsh, SE1

☏ 020 7261 9314

🚌 , Lambeth North (5 min walk), Waterloo LU &Rail (5 min walk)

🕓 Mon-Fri 8.30am-5.30pm

A fair-sized wholefood shop, Tim Cooper, who runs it, is a passionate vegetarian with a real interest in organic produce. The shop has a selection of organic and biodynamic breads, nuts, soup mixes and vitamins. The snack café has been running since 1984, see page 66 for review.

HOXTON & SHOREDITCH

The Beer Shop
Organic beer shop and brewery

🗐 14 Pitfield St, N1

☏ 020 7739 3701

🚌 Old Street LU & Rail, exit 2 (3 min walk)

🕓 Tue-Fri 11am-7pm, Sat 10am-4pm

Mega selection of organic wines, ciders and beers. Their own Pitfield Brewery makes seven organic brews with all bottled beers being vegan. The stout was awarded Champion Organic Speciality Beer in 2001 but my preference is the Wheat Beer, served at The Crown (see page 211).

Fresh & Wild (City)
Organic food, drink

- 194 Old Street, EC1
- ☎ 020 7250 1708
- Old Street LU & Rail (1 min walk)
- ◷ Mon-Fri 9.30am-7.30pm, Sat 10.30am-5.30pm

See Notting Hill Gate shop review on page 248. However, there's no restaurant or juice bar here at the Old Street branch.

The Organic Delivery Co.
Organic food delivery service

- 70 Rivington Street, EC2A
- ☎ 020 7739 8181
- ◷ Mon-Fri 10am-5pm
- ✎ www.organicdelivery.co.uk

Registered with the Soil Association, this firm supplies a wide range of organic products from fruit and veg to organic drinks and bread. Check out their website for a full product listing. There is no minimum order, with a £2.95 delivery charge for orders below £14, but all larger orders are free throughout London. They run an organic vegetable and fruit box scheme that starts from £9.95 including daytime and evening delivery in London. Their organic box delivery service has been highly commended by The Soil Association.

People Tree
Organic clothes
- Unit 7, 8-13 New Inn Street, EC2A 3PY
- ☎ 0845 450 4595
- www.peopletree.co.uk
- ✉ Mail order (free catalogue)

A company with a conscience, People Tree campaigns for consumers to wear organic cotton to help prevent the chronic health problems and deaths of tens of thousands of people associated with the use of agricultural pesticides. Whilst they don't have a shop of their own they do have an office unit (five minutes walk from Old Street tube) which is their nerve centre for their mail order enterprise. Here, from time to time they also run sales from the previous season's collections with up to 50% discount off. Telephone to find out details of their next sale.

People Tree clothes are modern casual urban basics, plain or simply patterned and very affordable. A selection is available at:

Selfridges
- The Contemporary Collection, 400 Oxford St, W1A
- ☎ 0870 8377377

Ganesha
- 3 Gabriel's Wharf, 56 Upper Ground, SE1
- ☎ 020 7928 3444

Co-op
- 168-176 Eltham High St, SE19
- ☎ 020 8850 2631

CLERKENWELL

Rye Wholefoods
Wholefood & organic food
- 35a Myddleton Street, EC1
- ☎ 020 7278 5878
- 🚇 Angel LU (10 min walk)
- 🕐 Mon-Fri 9am-5pm, Sat 1pm-5pm

A quaint, small, 80's-style vegetarian, vegan and organic provisions shop with a couple of tables for eating in. For eats review see page 91.

NORTH LONDON

ISLINGTON

Green Baby
Baby clothes and products
- 🏠 *345 Upper Street, N1*
- ☎ *0207 359 7037*
- 🚇 *Highbury and Islington LU & Rail (20 min walk)*
- 🕐 *Mon-Fri 10am-5pm, Sat 10.30am-6pm*
- ✉ *Mail order available (tel 0870 240 6894)*

Organic clothes and products for babies (up to six years) and mums. Products are either 100% organic or primarily organic and include nappies, baby clothing, wraps, underwear, pyjamas, eco-friendly washing products and nursery furniture. An excellent mail order catalogue is available.

Green Baby's organic clothing range for babies is made at a fair trade project in India, whilst their organic skincare range is made in Britain. Other items are European-made in countries such as Germany where organic cotton is quite commonly used.

Green Baby wholesales to 250 independent retail outlets and is the first organic clothing range to be stocked in Debenhams, Oxford Street. An even bigger branch is at Notting Hill, see page 249 for details.

Islington Farmers' Market
- 🏠 *Essex Road (opposite Islington Green), N1*
- 🕐 *Sun 10am-2pm*
- 🚇 *Angel LU*

See page 275 for more information about London Farmers' Markets.

Camden Town & Primrose Hill

Ambala Foods
Specialist pickles and chutneys, Indian sweets

📖 *Head Office and Shop, 112-114 Drummond Street, NW1*

☎ *020 7387 7886*

🚇 *Euston LU & Rail (2 min walk)*

🕐 *Daily 9am-9pm*

Opened in 1965, this modern upscale store sells a stylishly packaged range of pickles and chutneys, savouries, snacks and an inviting sweet selection. It is run as a franchise with some branches owned by the company.

Braintree Hemp Store
Hemp clothes for men and woman

📖 *Unit 9 East Yard, Camden Lock, NW1*

☎ *020 7267 9343*

🚇 *Camden or Chalk Farm LU (10 min walk)*

🕐 *Daily 10am-6pm*

Nothing to do with Braintree in Essex, this is the London branch of a large Australian chain selling organic hemp trousers, shirts, t-shirts, blouses and skirts. About 20% of the range is completely hemp whilst the rest of the stock is about 55% hemp mix with non-organic cotton.

Fresh & Wild
Food, drink, eats

📖 *Camden Town, 49 Parkway, NW1*

☎ *020 7428 7575*

🚇 *Camden Town LU (2 min walk)*

🕐 *Mon-Fri 8am-9pm, Sat 9.30am-9pm and Sun 11am-8pm*

See Notting Hill branch for eats review (page 168) and organic shop review (page 248).

Gupta Confectioners (London) Ltd
Indian sweets, takeaway snacks and savouries

📖 *100 Drummond Street, NW1*

☎ *020 7380 1590*

🚇 *Euston LU & Rail (2 min walk)*

🕐 *Daily 11am-7pm*

Small shop with good vegetarian sweet selection and street nosh. I enjoyed the fried aubergine snack whilst walking along the street! Their main shop is in Hendon (see page 241).

Sesame
Organic food, drink

🏠 *128 Regent's Park Road, NW1*
☎ *020 7586 3779*
🚇 *Chalk Farm LU (5 min walk)*
🕐 *Mon-Fri 9am-6pm, Sat 10am-6pm, Sun 12am-5pm*
🍴 *Vegan choices*

Friendly service is a hallmark of this 30 year old neighbourhood store that's 90% organic and virtually all vegetarian. Whilst fresh fruit and veg, several breads and cheeses are in evidence of real note is the impressive range of honeys and oils. Takeaways of hot soups such as lentil, leek and carrot, rice stir-fry and salads are popular with lunching local business people and it's a great stock-up point for an idyllic summer picnic on Primrose Hill opposite.

FINSBURY PARK

Fabulous Foods
Wholefood delivery service

🖃 *53 Lancaster Road, N4*

☎ *020 8920 6916*

Currently wholesale delivery only but with plans to extend to home delivery service in 2005. Phone for details.

Just Organics
Organic food delivery service

🖃 *113 Wilberforce Road, N4*

☎ *020 7704 2566*

Has been delivering organic fruit and veg boxes since 1994 and is registered with the Soil Association. Subscribers choose a £10 or £15 box. There is some flexibility as to what you get, and the company tries to find substitutes if customers don't like particular things. The produce mainly comes from Riversford Farm in Devon, although an alternative organic wholesaler is sometimes used providing the diversity people require. Just Organics get all their produce on Monday and all deliveries are made by Thursday to ensure freshness. Unfortunately, they do not currently deliver in South London.

HIGHBURY

Highbury Park Health Foods
Organic food, baby and household goods, supplements

🖃 *17 Highbury Park, N5*

☎ *020 7359 3623*

🚆 *Highbury or Finsbury Park LU & Rail*

🕐 *Mon-Sat 10.30am-7pm*

Unpretentious neighbourhood store selling pre-packed organic foodstuffs, supplements, and baby products. Good on general organic items but somewhat uninspiring for foodies.

CROUCH END

Ambala Foods (Turnpike Lane)
Specialist pickles and chutneys, Indian sweets

- *Wood Green, N8*
- *020 8292 1253*
- *Turnpike Lane LU*
- *Daily 9am-9pm*

See Ambala Drummond Street for review (page 233).

Fresh & Wild
Foods, drink, eats

- *44-52 Coleridge Road, N8*

Planned opening 2005

Haelen Centre
Wholefood, food supplements and homeopathic remedies

- *41 The Broadway, N8*
- *020 8340 4258*
- *www.haelan.co.uk*
- *Finsbury Park LU & Rail (Bus W7)*
- *Mon-Sat 9am-6pm, Sun 12noon-4pm*

Well-established wholefood and organic provisions store with newly refurbished herbal dispensary and homeopathic pharmacy upstairs. The ground floor shop is crammed with breads (many gluten and wheat-free), inexpensive organic fruit and veg, takeaway eats, convenience foods as well as organic baby foods and formulas. All the food is vegetarian and free from artificial flavourings, colourings and preservatives. Also stocks organic practitioner strength tinctures. Check out their website for their mission statement and more details.

STOKE NEWINGTON

Food For All
Organic herbs, vegetarian wholefood and snacks

🖼 *3 Cazenove Road, N16*

☎ *020 8806 4138*

🚌 *Stoke Newington Rail (1 min walk)*

🕐 *Mon-Wed 9am-6pm, Thur-Fri 9am-7pm,*
Sat 10am-6pm, Sun 10am-3pm

This is organic herb central. A community health store since 1975 it sports a jaw-dropping selection of 250 organic and wild harvested herbs all stored in big brown paper bags crammed onto a wall display unit. Also eco-friendly body care products, organic and allergy-free foods, medicinal remedies and food supplements. Worth a visit just to see the herbs.

Fresh & Wild
Organic food, drink, eats

🖼 *32-40 Stoke Newington Church Street, N16*

☎ *020 7254 2332*

🚌 *Stoke Newington Rail (10 min walk), 73 bus passes*

🕐 *Mon-Fri 9am-9pm, Sat 9am-8.30pm, Sun 10am-8pm*

✉ *Mail order*

Of all the organic supermarkets in London this is where you'll find the edgiest looking staff – full-on goths and hippies. This is the best organic grocery store in Stokey and the eaterie is a good hang-out zone. See Notting Hill branch for eats review (page 168) and organic shop review (page 248).

Mother Earth Organic Market
Food, drink, eats, toiletries

🖼 *5 Albion Parade, N16*

☎ *020 7275 9099*

🚌 *Highbury and Islington LU & Rail, 73 bus passes by*

🕐 *Mon-Sat 9.30am-8pm, Sun 10am-7pm*

Cluttered old-style wholefood shop with about 80% organic products. There's a small organic fruit and veg section, organic Celtic cakes and breads and some patisserie products. At back of house locals fill their own bottles with purified water at 20p a litre. Organic soup and organic coffee are available to takeaway and there are sandwiches, rolls and samosas made by Hare Krishna people.

Stoke Newington Farmers' Market

⌗ *The Old Fire Station, Leswin Road, N16*

☎ *Kerry Rankine (Growing Communities) 020 75092 7588*

🕔 *Sat 10am-2.30pm*

✎ *www.growingcommunities.org*

See page 275 for more information about London Farmers' Markets.

Texture
Fabrics, clothes, paints

⌗ *84 Stoke Newington Church Street, N16*

☎ *020 7241 0990*

🚃 *Stoke Newington Rail (10 min walk),*
Highbury and Islington LU & Rail (20 min walk)

🕔 *Tue-Sat 10am-5.30pm, Sun 12.30pm-4.30pm*

✉ *Mail order available*

An organic haven specialising in cotton fabrics and home décor. Popular with London's eco-conscious, art and fashion students, the shop is centred around the premise that normal cotton uses 25% of the world's insecticides whilst organic cottons avoid it. They stock organic cotton bedlinen, bathrobes and towels as well as soft buckwheat pillows, helpful for people allergic to feathers. Curtains and blinds, natural-shaded paints, classic casual clothes and babywear are all here too and they do an attractive gift box range that make great prezzies.

Two Figs
Wholefood & organic food, eats

⌗ *101 Newington Green, N1*

☎ *020 7690 6811*

🚃 *Canonbury Rail (3 min walk), 73 bus passes by*

🕔 *Mon-Thur 8.30am-7pm, Fri-Sat 9am-5pm*

Small is beautiful at this food boutique where there are interesting home-made deli choices and foods from small specialist suppliers. See restaurant review (page 143) for wholefood and organic produce details.

HOLLOWAY & TUFNELL PARK

Bumble Bee Natural Food
Organic fruit, veg, breads, takeaway eats, wine and beer

- 🏠 *30, 32 & 33 Brecknock Road, N7*
- ☎ *0207 607 1936*
- ✑ *www.bumblebee.co.uk*
- 🚇 *Kentish Town LU & Rail or Tufnell Park LU*
- 🕐 *Mon-Sat 9am-6.30pm (Thur till 7.30pm)*
- ✉ *Mail order*

Established in 1980, Bumble Bees has grown into a collection of three stores and a natural remedy shop (see below) to compliment the food shops. The three food outlets are hot on veggie foods including dried fruit and nuts, herbal teas, organic coffees and for those on the tipple more than 100 organic beers and wines. Emphasis here is on fresh fruit and veg with freshly baked bread delivered daily. Whilst the three stores are structurally separate, customers can fill up at all three and pay at the end of the shop. Remedies and non-food products are at:

Natural Remedies
Remedies & Alternative Healthcare Clinic

- 🏠 *35 Brecknock Road*
- ☎ *020 7267 3884*
- 🕐 *Mon-Sat 9am-6.30pm*

The Organic Health Food Store
Dietary foods, bodycare, kosher snacks

- 🏠 *766-768, Holloway Road, N19*
- ☎ *020 7272 8788*
- 🚇 *Archway LU (5 min walk)*
- 🕐 *Mon-Fri 9am-9pm, Sat 9am-8.30pm & Sun 10am-8pm*

Run by devoutly religious group called the Black Hebrew Jews that are strongly eco-conscious. Of special interest are the organic kosher take-away food snacks that include their own vegetable spring rolls, fruit cake and crumbles. There's a good selection of breads, fruit wines as well as branded organic foods and fresh fruit at front of house of this double fronted modern shop which stays open till late. It has an big organic skincare section. Unusual for a strict jewish shop, it stays open Friday evenings. Apparently according to Genesis they say it's okay.

pomona

❋ *Daily deliveries of freshly baked bread, sandwiches, prepared meals, fresh fruits, salad & vegetables*

❋ *Extensive wine selection*

❋ *Award winning meals*

❋ *Wide range of chilled, frozen products*

❋ *Large grocery section*

"no one excelled her in love of the garden"

179 Haverstock Hill, Belsize Park, NW3
020 7916 2676

Eco13

Clothes, accessories, household products,

🖃 *13 Brecknock Road, N7*

☎ *020 7419 1234*

🚌 *Tufnell Park tube (10 min walk), 253 or 29 buses run nearby*

🕓 *Tue and Wed 10am-4.30pm*

Opened in August 2004, this green and sustainable lifestyle products store has a good range of organic clothing, hemp T-shirts, vegetarian shoes and leather-alternative belts and bags. Situated in the same building as the veggie-organic café and deli (see page 122 for food review), Organic13, the store, is modern, large and decked out with islands of shelving units. They sell a wide range of items from organic beauty and skincare products to biodegradable vegan condoms. Eco13 offers a range of eco-paints and DIY and there are also organic cleaning products such as floor cleaner that can be refilled here. Eco13 specialise in renewable energy technology and re-cycled and renewable materials. They stock green stationary and office products – their own stationary is printed using vegetable based ink on 100% recycled paper.

They hope to extend their opening times as things progress.

HAMPSTEAD & SWISS COTTAGE

Peppercorns
Food, drink, eats, health products
- 193-195 West End Lane, West Hampstead, NW6
- 020 7328 6874
- West Hampstead Rail (10 min walk)
- Mon-Sat 9am-7pm West

Natural and organic food market, smaller and busier than their sister West End branch. See Peppercorns, Charlotte Place for details (page 229).

Pomona
Food, drink, eats
- 179 Haverstock Hill, Belsize Park, NW3
- 020 7916 2676
- Belsize Park LU (2 min walk)
- Mon-Fri 8am-9pm, Sat 8am-7pm, Sun 8am-6pm

This slick, modern organic provisions store is just the place for stocking up on organic gourmet items and also boasts an excellent selection of organic wines, some at bargain discounts and with several vegetarian and vegan options. I have it on authority that Tues, Thurs and Fri are the very best days for grocery freshness. They also stock organic Celtic breads and a good selection of gluten-free products for those with special dietary requirements. About 70% of the stock is organic.

Swiss Cottage Farmers' Market
- 02 Centre Car Park, Finchley Rd, NW3
- Wednesdays 10am-3pm
- Finchley Road and West Hampstead LU
  West Hampstead and Finchley Road Rail

See page 275 for more information about London Farmers' Markets.

HENDON

Gupta Confectioners (London) Ltd
- 262 Watford Way, NW4
- 020 8203 4044
- Colindale LU
- Tue-Sun 10am-6pm Colindale LU

See Euston branch for review (page 233).

Kilburn

Olive Tree
Organic fruit, veg, bread and general food provisions,
supplements and natural cosmetics

🏠 *84 Willesden Lane, NW6*
☎ *020 7328 9078*
🚇 *Kilburn LU*
🕐 *Mon-Fri 9am-7.30pm, Sat 9am-6pm*

A small shop with a surprisingly wide selection of whole and organic
foods and other health products. Of note is their fresh fruit and veg,
and their fresh bread which is delivered three times a week. A great
little place.

Vegetarian & Vegan
Dog and Cat Food

VeggiePets.com

- Happidog Crunchy Nuggets
- Yarrah Vegetarian Organic
- Yarrah Vegetarian Pate
- Ami Vegan Cat Food
- Herbal Remedies
- Digestive Enzymes
- Vegan Biscuits & Chews

Delivered to your door!

Buy online: **www.veggiepets.com**
or call 0800 542 9707 for Mail Order forms

We accept these cards

Write to VeggiePets.com 6 Southbrook Close, Havant, PO9 1RW

FINCHLEY & GOLDERS GREEN

Temple Health Food
Vitamin & mineral supplements, beauty products, takeout eats

- 17 Temple Fortune Parade, NW11
- 020 8458 6087
- Golders Green LU (10 min walk)
- Mon-Fri 9am-6pm, Sat 9am-3pm and Sun 10am-4pm

The product range here divides evenly between mineral and vitamin supplements and upmarket organic beauty products including skincare and haircare products such as the very affordable Green People organic beauty and grooming range. Temple Health Food does a brisk lunchtime takeout trade in pre-packed vegetarian sandwiches, samosas, organic ice cream and organic drinks. They also stock a good range of organic dried fruits.

NEW SOUTHGATE

Jaaneman Sweet Centre
Vegetarian Indian, classic

- 170 Bowes Road, N11
- 020 8888 1226
- Arnos Grove LU or Bounds Green LU (5 min walk)
- Tue-Sun 11am-6pm
- Vegan choices

Road raging round the North Circular? Pull over and tank up on veggie energy at this gem of an Indian sweet shop. Locals have been popping in since '86 for this great selection of 100% vegetarian sweets such as barfi, halwa and coconut ice that are milk-based and cooked with cholesterol-free vegetable oil. All the sweets are made on the premises. For veggie TV addicts there's also Bombay Mix, Rice Chewdo, Tikha Gathia and a large selection of biscuits. For savoury snack attacks samosas and kachori-dal are on hand.

WEST LONDON

KNIGHTSBRIDGE, KENSINGTON & CHELSEA

Chelsea Health Store
General organic and wholefood provisions

⌨ *402 King's Road, SW10*
☎ *0207 352 4663*
🚌 *Sloane Square LU (then Bus 11 or 22)*
🕐 *Daily 9am-7pm*

Neighbourhood fill-up store just a few doors along from the Organic Pharmacy (page 245). It offers organic muesli and oats as you walk in, followed by a good selection of general and health remedy products.

Fushi
Herbal remedies, beauty products and juice bar

⌨ *55 Duke of York Square, Sloane Square, SW3*
☎ *020 7730 4000*
🖉 *www.fushi.co.uk*
🚌 *Sloane Square LU*
🕐 *Mon-Sat 9am-7pm, Sun 12noon-6pm*

A cool, ultra modern setup selling its own brand herbal extracts and tinctures, hair and skin products. The coffee is organic and fair trade. Fushi has a concession on the ground floor of the Harvey Nichols store in Knightsbridge.

Here
Organic supermarket

⌨ *125 Sydney Street, Chelsea Farmer's Market, SW3*
☎ *0207 351 4321*
🚌 *Sloane Square LU (10 min walk)*
🕐 *Mon-Sat 9.30am-8pm, Sun 10am-6.30pm*
✉ *Mail order available*

This modern well-designed organic store received a 'Highly Commended Shop' Soil Association Award in 2001. It has a very good fruit and veg section, and an extensive selection of skincare products. Surprisingly, there is a paucity of veggie eateries in this area but 'Here' fills the gap with a range of organic sandwiches. They also specialise in biodynamic foods and run a mail order service.

The Organic Pharmacy
Natural and organic medicines and beauty products

- *396 King's Road, SW10*
- *020 7351 2232*
- *Sloane Square LU (then Bus 11 or 22)*
- *Mon-Sat 9.30-6pm, Sun 12noon-6pm*
- *Mail order available*

Looks like a regular pharmacy but isn't. The dispensary here is only herbal and homeopathic (so don't take your penicillin prescriptions in). They also freshly make skin care and beauty products by hand, using certified organic cold pressed oils and essential oils and botanicals. The shelves are well stacked with upscale organic beauty products such as the Dr Hauschka range. Downstairs are a clinic and beauty rooms for their 'signature facial. A firm favourite of celebrities'. They also produce an informative booklet listing potential carcinogens in certain products.

Pimlico Farmers' Market

🔲 *Orange Square (corner of Pimlico Road and Ebury Street), SW1*
🕐 *Saturdays 9am-1pm*
🚌 *Sloane Square LU, Buses 211, 11 & 239*

See page 275 for more information about London Farmers' Markets.

Planet Organic

Organic food, drink, household items

🔲 *25 Effie Road, SW6*
☎ *020 7731 7222*
🚌 *Fulham Broadway LU (1 min walk)*
🕐 *Mon-Sat 9.30am-8.30pm, Sun 12noon-6pm*
✉ *Mail order available*

Opened in June 2004 this is the third Planet Organic supermarket in London. Although smaller it offers the same great choice as the flagship store in Notting Hill. See Planet Organic, Westbourne Grove (page 249) for review.

Space NK

Environmentally friendly skin, haircare and baby products

🔲 *307 King's Road, SW3*
☎ *020 7351 7209*
🚌 *Sloane Square LU (2 min walk)*
🕐 *Mon-Sat 10am-6pm, Sun 12noon-5pm*

An upscale apothecary with outlets throughout London. The highly desirable products on offer here include the Erbaviva range of organic baby oil, nappy cream and baby massage oil and the Ren brand which, whilst not labelled organic, uses only 100% natural fragrance and is free from synthetic colours, petrochemicals, sulphates and animal ingredients. Space NK also stocks Jurlique, a high quality product range that is environmentally friendly but not yet organic certified. For mail order or branch locations telephone 0870 168 9999.

Notting Hill

Bliss
Food, vitamins, herbal medicines, books, footwear and health clinic

🔲 *333 Portobello Road, W10*

☎ *020 8961 3331*

🚌 *Ladbroke Grove LU*

🕐 *Mon-Fri 9am-9pm, Sat 9am-6pm and Sun 11am-7pm*

✉ *Mail order available*

Stylish store with white walls and concealed lighting, a stark contrast to the homely appearance of most health food shops. Bliss offers a good range of packaged foods, all organic, although no food is prepared on-site. Their health clinic offers acupuncture, reflexology and massage and sells an extensive range of vitamins, aromatherapy oils and herbal remedies.

Books for Cooks
Vegetarian and organic cookery books and courses

🔲 *4 Blenheim Crescent, W11*

☎ *020 7221 1992*

🚌 *Ladbroke Grove LU (5 min walk)*
   Notting Hill Gate LU (10 min walk)

🕐 *Tue-Sat 9.30-6pm*

Salivate at this treasure trove of 300-400 vegetarian cookery books with about another 8000 cookbooks if you are hungry for more. Upstairs you can extend your cooking expertise further on one of the veggie cookery courses they run. Has friendly, super-knowledgeable staff who can help find any vegetarian books you may be looking for worldwide. Depart with a pile of vegetarian cookbooks and maybe having tasted a recipe too (see page 163 for their tasting kitchen/restaurant review).

Fresh & Wild

Organic food, drink, eats

- 210 Westbourne Grove, W11
- 020 7229 1063
- Notting Hill Gate LU (7 min walk)
- Mon-Fri 8am-9pm, Sat 8am-8pm and Sun 10am-7pm
- Mail order available

Vegetarian Society Best Retailer of the Year 2003 offering 6000 Soil Association certified organic products. Of particular note is an amazing tofu range, attractively displayed veggie-deli foods, breads, speciality cheeses, upscale vegetarian and vegan wines. Where items are not organic the policy is to offer the highest quality alternative. There's a good kiddy section too, with organic nappy range, eco-friendly washing powders and cleaning products.

The store is community-spirited rather than being a big, impersonal chain supermarket. The atmosphere is relaxed and friendly with very helpful enthusiastic staff who are switched-on and knowledgeable. Star gazers can join the checkout queue behind local A-list celebs such as Madonna, Geri Halliwell, Jude Law, Kate Winslet and Gwyneth Paltrow. Stop press... Gwynnie now sends her 'personal shopper' instead. Oh well, you can't have everything! For restaurant review see page 168.

Green Baby
Baby clothes and products

⌨ *Elgin Crescent, W11*
☎ *0207 792 8140*
🚌 *Notting Hill Gate LU (5 min walk)*
🕓 *Mon-Fri 10am-5pm, Sat 10am-6pm and Sun 11am-4pm*
✉ *Mail order available*

See review for Green Baby, Islington branch (page 232).

Natural Mat
Natural bedding for babies and kids

⌨ *99 Talbot Road, Notting Hill, W11*
☎ *020 7985 0479*
🚌 *Notting Hill Gate LU (8 min walk)*
🕓 *Mon-Sat 10am-5pm*
✉ *Mail order available*

Whilst not organic certified this mattress specialist uses organic constituents in their mats for cribs. Natural fibres allow mattresses to breathe, preventing overheating and helping to keep them clean.

Notting Hill Farmers' Market

⌨ *Car park behind Waterstones, access via Kensington Place, W8*
🕓 *Saturdays 9am-1pm*
🚌 *Notting Hill Gate LU, Buses 12, 27, 28, 52, 70, 94, 328*

See page 275 for more information about London Farmers' Markets.

Planet Organic
Organic food, drink, eats, household items

⌨ *42 Westbourne Grove, W2*
☎ *020 7727 2227*
🚌 *Bayswater LU or Queensway LU (5 min walk)*
🕓 *Mon-Sat 9.30am-10pm, Sun 12noon-6pm*
✉ *Mail order available*

A popular destination for organic householders, with an attractive display of fruit and veg and big selections of organic breads, tofus and wines. Planet Organic also stocks its own label products such as olive oil, pulses, nuts and seeds. Baby foods and nappies can be tracked down in the Children's section, along with some products from the Green Baby, Baby Basic range. Stocks organic non-vegetarian products as well.

See eats review on page 170. Other branches are in Torrington Place WC1 and Fulham SW6.

Portobello Wholefoods
Vegetarian and organic food

▢ *266 Portobello Road, W10*

☎ *0208 960 1840*

🚇 *Ladbroke Grove LU*

🕐 *Mon-Sat 9.30am-6pm and Sun 11am-5pm*

Petite, classic wholefood store with 20 years' pedigree and popular with Notting Hill locals for its healthy food selection and varied choice of breads. It's well-stocked with supplements and natural remedies too.

The Tea and Coffee Plant
Specialist coffee retailer and wholesaler

▢ *180 Portobello Road, W11*

☎ *020 7221 8137*

🖰 *www.coffee.uk.com*

🚇 *Ladbroke Grove LU (10-20 min walk), near Blenheim Crescent*

🕐 *Mon-Sat 8.15am-6.30pm, Sun 9.30am-4.30pm*

✉ *Mail order available*

A funky new coffee shop selling some 30 coffees, of which 12 are organic and Soil Association certified. The company claims to carry the largest range of organic and/or fair traded coffee in the UK and their bestsellers are the Mexican Organic and their Organic House Blend. The place has a sweeping bar and a further counter selling boxes of coffee and tea. They also supply numerous organic restaurants and caterers. The coffee is roasted twice a week at their roastery in Spitalfields and delivered daily to their Notting Hill premises.

HAMMERSMITH & SHEPHERD'S BUSH

Buchanans Organic Deli
Wholefoods, organic produce, café

⌑ *22 Aldensley Road, Hammersmith, W6*

☎ *020 8741 2138*

🚌 *Hammersmith LU (10 min walk)*

🕓 *Mon-Sat 7am-6pm and Sun 7am-7pm*

A small traditional deli that manages to cram a good deal into its limited floor space with a well-stocked organic deli as well as a café offering all kinds of delicious organic snacks and coffee. The deli has a good selection of organic produce from fresh fruit and veg to cheeses, frozen goods and organic cooked meats. Since its opening in 1979, Buchanans has become a firm favourite with locals and has a genuinely friendly atmosphere. A great little shop.

Bushwacker Wholefoods
Wholefoods, natural remedies

⌑ *132 King Street, Hammersmith, W6*

☎ *020 8748 2061*

🚌 *Hammersmith LU (5 min walk)*

🕓 *Mon-Sat 9.30am-6.30pm (Tue 10am-6pm)*

Set along a busy high street, the shop's noticeboard campaigns against GMO and highlights food and health issues. The shop itself stocks vegetarian, vegan and organic products including fresh organic fruit and veg, soya drinks, first aid remedies and books. Conveniently opposite Sagar Vegetarian Restaurant (see page 177 for meal review).

The Fresh Food Company Ltd
Organic delivery service, food drink, recycled cleaning, personal and baby care products

⌑ *The Orchard, 50 Wormholt Road, Shepherds Bush, W12*

☎ *020 8749 8778*

✐ *www.freshfood.co.uk*

Online and telephone organic food delivery service founded in 1989 and running a nationwide delivery scheme for organic fruit, veg, herbs and salads. Most customers take out a subscription for their boxes which are delivered either weekly or fortnightly. The company employs full and part-timers with a familiarity of organic food and basic cooking techniques and also maintains a very useful database of fruit and veg recipes.

Maida Vale

The Organic Grocer
Organic provisions and delivery service
- 🏢 *17 Clifton Road, W9*
- ☎ *020 7286 1400*
- 🚇 *Warwick Avenue LU (3 min walk)*
- 🕐 *Mon-Sat 8.30am-8.30pm, Sun 10am-7pm*

This small shop makes up for its lack of space with ingenious displays and a contemporary, simple style of décor. The store sells the full selection of organic products including fresh fruit and veg, bread, freezer foods, beers and wines, organic baby products and even has a deli counter. The shop also offers a local delivery service.

Chiswick

Apotheke 20-20
Beauty products
- 🏢 *Natural Health & Wellness Centre,*
  296 Chiswick High Road, W4
- ☎ *020 8995 2293*
- 🚇 *Turnham Green LU (5 min walk)*
- 🕐 *Mon, Tue & Fri 10am-6pm, Wed & Thur 10am-8pm,*
  Sat 9.30am-6pm and Sun 11am-5pm

Just next to the Jurlique Day Spa (see page 253), this flagship retail shop stocks the whole Jurlique range and offers natural health consultations. Whilst not Soil Association certified yet 95% of the herbs are grown on Jurlique's own certified farms in South Australia. The Jurlique Herbal Shaving Gel feels great and the Face and Body Moisturising Lotion is wonderfully light and suitable for oily skins. All Jurlique products are suitable for vegetarians and they have just launched a new men's range that is 98% organic and biodynamic.

As Nature Intended
Remedies, organic produce, household provisions
- 201 High Street, W4
- 020 9742 8838
- Turnham Green LU
- Mon-Fri 9am-8pm, Sat 9am-7pm and Sun 10am-5pm

Huge health store similar to Planet Organic stocking just about every conceivable type of wholefood and with enough range for customers to be able to get their entire week's shop under one roof. The organic cereals, breads, meat and fish are particularly noteworthy and there are pastries, fresh fruit and veg as well. Also stocks natural remedies and organic baby items. A great store and well worth checking out.

Chiswick Farmers' Market
- Car Park Pavilion, Dukes Meadows, off Edensor Road, W4
- Contact Kathleen Healy 020 8747 3063 (Chiswick Farmers' Market)
- Sunday 10am-2pm

See page 275 for more information about London Farmers' Markets.

The Jurlique Day Spa and Sanctuary
Spa treatments using natural and organic products
- Holly House, 300-302 Chiswick High Road, W4
- 020 8995 2293
- Turnham Green LU (5 min walk)
- Mon-Fri 10am-8pm, Sat 9.30am-6pm and Sun 11am-5pm

Organic beauty and de-stressing treatments popular with local looks-conscious women. Since May 2003 men have been able to get a slice of the action with a new range of treatments designed for 'Metrosexual' man and featuring quality organic facial treatment, revitalisers and flotation therapy.

The Natural Foodstore

Organic, natural & Fair-Trade products; grains, pulses, nuts & dried fruit; natural cosmetics, supplements, fresh bread and cakes

⌨ *41 Turnham Green Terrace, Chiswick, W4*

☎ *020 8995 4906*

🚇 *Turnham Green LU*

🕐 *Mon-Fri 9.30-6pm, Sat 9.30am-5.30pm*

A very popular store catering for the Chiswick crowd. Although small, it packs in a wonderful array of goods with shelves stretching to the ceiling. Products are carefully picked and the natural skincare section includes Dr Hauschka, Living Nature and Trilogy. The store does a good trade in frozen organic baby foods and offers an impressive choice of food supplements including Solgar and Biocare. A great local store offering everything from 'yogi Teas' to yoga mats.

KEW & RICHMOND

Oliver's Wholefood Store

Organic nuts, produce and breads, dried fruit, honey and pulses

⌨ *5 Station Approach, Kew Gardens, Richmond TW9*

☎ *020 8948 3990*

🚇 *Kew Gardens or District Line*

🕐 *Mon-Sat 9am-7pm, Sat 10am-7pm*

This beautiful airy shop has an excellent range of fresh organic produce, including organic seasonal fruit and vegetables delivered daily, together with well-stocked shelves heaving with organic groceries and specialist deli items such as oils, honey, bread, nuts and cereals. As well as a large choice of organic fish and meat, Oliver's is a destination for vegetarians, vegans and those on special diets. The store offers an extensive range of dairy free, gluten free and wheat free products. Oliver's also stock a large range of supplements and body care products. Nutritionists and skin care specialists are available to give free advice, seven days a week and are friendly and knowledgeable.

The winner of numerous awards, including Richmond Business of the Year 2003 and Soil Association Community Shop of the Year 1999, Oliver's has recently doubled it's shop size and also opened it's own natural health and beauty rooms.

Esca

SOUTH LONDON

BRIXTON

Brixton Whole Foods
Food, drink, eats, cosmetics, herbs
🏠 *59 Atlantic Road, SW9*
☎ *020 7737 2210*
🚇 *Brixton LU*
🕐 *Mon 9.30am-7pm, Tue-Thur & Sat 9.30am-5.30pm,*
    Fri 9.30-6pm

General organic fruit, veg and grocery provisions and some items for babies and children. The 'serve yourself' culinary organic herbs and spices section has over 300 to choose from. Somewhat more decadent delights await in the freezer in the form of Green and Black's organic ice cream whilst beauty in a bottle is available with a selection of cruelty-free cosmetics.

CLAPHAM & WANDSWORTH

Esca
Mediterranean, classic
🏠 *160 Clapham High Street, SW4*
☎ *020 7622 2288*
🚇 *Clapham Common LU (2 min walk)*
🕐 *Mon-Fri 8am-8pm, Sat 9am-8pm*

Has a good selection of high quality pre-packed deli items including organic honey, jam, chutneys, dried fruit, coffee and beer. Also has freshly made vegetarian salad items some ingredients of which are organic. For café review see page 190.

Dandelion
Vegetarian take-away and food supplements
🏠 *120 Northcote Road, SW11*
☎ *020 7350 0902*
🚌 *Clapham Junction Rail (4 min walk)*
🕐 *Mon-Sat 9am-6pm*

With Northcote Road becoming a smart shopping area swamped with wholefood stores, Dandelion has downsized its stock in response to fierce competition. Now it concentrates on high quality vegetarian and vegan takeaways coupled with a comprehensive selection of supplements and natural remedies.

Fresh & Wild
Organic food, drink and eats
🏠 *305-311 Lavender Hill, SW11*
☎ *020 7585 1488*
🚌 *Clapham Junction Rail (2 min walk)*
🕐 *Mon-Fri 9am-8pm, Sat 8.30am-7.30pm and Sun 12pm-6pm*

See Notting Hill branch for eats review (page 168) and organic shop review (page 248)

Esca

Kelly's Organic Foods

Organic food, drink, deli, sandwich and juice bar

🖭 *46 Northcote Road, SW11*

☎ *020 7207 3967*

🚆 *Clapham Junction Rail (5 min walk),*
   Clapham Common LU (20 min walk)

🕐 *Mon-Thur 9am-8pm, Fri-Sat 9am-6pm*

Kelly's is especially good for organic fruit and veg. In the summer, there are four marble tables outside at which to enjoy their home-made sandwiches and juice bar concoctions. The deli counter offers some good veggie choices and they also sell organic wines beers, bread and cakes. A good independent organic shop.

VAUXHALL

Farm-a-round Ltd

Organic food home delivery service

🖭 *Office B143, New Covent Garden Market, Nine Elms Lane, SW8*

☎ *020 87627 8066*

🖮 *www.farmaround.co.uk*

Provides Londoners with home delivered organic fruit and veg as well as other staples like eggs, fruit juice, olive oil and pasta. Most customers order a weekly delivery which can be arranged over the phone or via their website.

TOOTING

Ambala Foods

Specialist pickles and chutneys, Indian sweets

🖭 *48 Upper Tooting Road, SW17*

☎ *020 8672 8773*

🚆 *Tooting Bec LU*

🕐 *Daily 9am-9pm*

See their head office, Ambala Foods Drummond St for review (page 233).

Wimbledon Farmers' Market

🖭 *Wimbledon Park First School, Havana Road, SW19*

🕐 *Saturdays 9am-1pm*

🚆 *Wimbledon Park LU*

See page 275 for more information about London Farmers' Markets.

Kelly's Organic Foods

PLUMSTEAD

Ambala Foods
Specialist pickles and chutneys, Indian sweets
- 🏠 *62a High Street, SE18*
- ☎ *020 8317 0202*
- 🚉 *Plumstead Rail*
- 🕐 *Daily 9am-9pm*

See head office, Ambala Foods Drummond Street for review (page 233).

BLACKHEATH

Blackheath Farmers' Market
- 🏠 *Blackheath Rail Station Car Park, 2 Blackheath Village, SE3*
- 🕐 *Sundays 10am-2pm*
- 🚉 *Blackheath Rail, Buses 54, 89, 108, 202, 380*

See page 275 for more information about London Farmers' Markets.

Salt of the Earth
Organic clothing and natural skin products
- 🏠 *125 Lee Road, SE3*
- ☎ *020 8318 3133*
- 🚉 *Blackheath Rail*
- 🕐 *Tue-Sat 10am-5.30pm*

Fairly new business selling organic children's clothes and natural skin products for both adults and kids. Also stocks bio-degradable nappies.

Well Bean Health Foods
Organic food, household items and supplements
- 🏠 *9 Old Dover Road, SE3*
- ☎ *020 8858 6854*
- 🚉 *Blackheath Rail and 108 bus*
- 🕐 *Mon-Fri 9am-6pm, Sat 9am-5.30pm*

Vegan speciality neighbourhood shop, split 50/50 between food and supplements. Sells wholemeal breads, rice cakes, Green & Black's organic chocolate, hazelnut and peanut butter, ice-cream and soya vegetarian sausages.

GREENWICH

Greenwich Organic Food
Organic food
- 86 Royal Hill, SE10
- ☎ 020 8488 6764
- ✐ www.greenwichorganic.co.uk
- 🚃 Greenwich Rail and DLR
- 🕓 Mon-Sat 10am-6pm
- i Delivery service

Small store offering a wide selection of organic food including fresh fruit and veg, fresh bread, organic frozen goods as well as organic wines and beers. Although the store is conveniently located just off the main Greenwich High Street they can also arrange home delivery.

DULWICH & FOREST HILL

Health Matters
Natural cosmetics, supplements, vitamins, natural remedies
- 47 Lordship Lane, East Dulwich, SE22
- ☎ 020 8299 6040
- 🚃 East Dulwich Rail
- 🕓 Mon-Fri 9am-6.30pm, Sat 9am-6pm

Complementary health centre offering various alternative treatments, reference library and oodles of free leaflets. As well as selling supplements and natural remedies it also stocks Dr Hauschka and Living Nature products.

Provender Wholefoods and Bakery
Wholefood, drink, eats, organic bakery, homeopathic remedies
- 103 Dartmouth Road Forest Hill SE23
- ☎ 020 8699 4046
- 🚃 Forest Hill Rail
- 🕓 Mon-Sat 8am-6.30, Sun 10am-4pm

Provender sells a wide range of home-baked breads and pastries, and organic fruit and vegetables, which are used in the café's recipes (see page 197). They stock organic dairy products, herbal teas, spices, wholefoods, ecological body care and washing products and a new line of Provender's own brand of vitamins and supplements. They also provide an organic fruit and veg box service.

HERNE HILL

Abel and Cole Ltd
Organic food, household items

- 8-15 MGI Estate, Milkwood Road, SE24
- 020 7737 3648
- www.abel-cole.co.uk
- i   Home delivery service only

Excellent organic food delivery service that was awarded Organic Retailer of the Year 2004 by the Soil Association. Offers free delivery to your door providing you exceed the minimum organic food order of £6. Based in Herne Hill, they cover the whole of South London and most of North London. About 80% of their customers are families or couples who opt for the weekly organic mixed vegetable box scheme consisting of a selection of fresh organic produce based on what is seasonally available and costing £13.80. Other boxes are available to suit individual needs and their exclusion service enables customers to customise their own box. All the boxes are suitable for vegetarians. Recipes and food storage advice is available on their easy to navigate website.

Abel and Cole also deliver organic wines all of which are suitable for vegetarians as well as Ecover cleaning products and various books. They are also involved in the Crisis FairShare scheme that donates surplus food to local London charities for the homeless.

Four Way Pharmacy
Organic and natural products for children and mothers

- 12 Half Moon Lane, SE24
- 020 7924 9344
- Herne Hill Rail
- Mon-Fri 9am-7pm, Sat 9am-6pm

Small NHS pharmacy strong on organic baby foods, herbal teas and eco-friendly baby products. It imports bio-degradable, disposable nappies from Germany attracting eco-aware shoppers from outside London. In 2002 Four Way won Mother & Baby Magazine 'Child-friendly Pharmacy of the Year Award'.

EAST LONDON

BRICK LANE & BETHNAL GREEN

Ambala Foods (Brick Lane)
Specialist pickles and chutneys, Indian sweets

🏠 *55 Brick Lane, Aldgate East, E1*

☎ *020 7247 8569*

🚇 *Shoreditch LU or Liverpool Street LU & Rail (10 min walk)*

🕐 *Daily 9am-9pm*

See Ambala, Drummond Street for review (page 233).

Broadway Food Market E8

🕐 *Sat 8am-5pm*

🚇 *Bethnal Green LU (then bus)*

About a third of all stalls at this street market are dedicated to fresh food with many local organic producers selling their wares.

Friends Organic
Organic and vegetarian food, drink, eats

- 83 Roman Road, Bethnal Green, E2
- 020 8980 1843
- Bethnal Green LU (5 min walk)
- Mon-Thur 10am-6.30pm (Tue opens 10.30am),
  Fri 10am-7pm, Sat 10am-6pm

This modern neighbourhood shop set in Globe Town has seen an increase in local elderly customers buying organic fruit and veg for health reasons and as an alternative to the local market stall traders. They also like the social chat with staff and informative advice. The shop stocks an inviting locally produced sandwich range plus breads, skin care items and health remedies. Friends Organic, formerly Friends Foods, is associated with the London Buddhist Centre just up the road.

Spitalfields Food Market

- Commercial Street between Folgate and Bushfield Street, E1
- Liverpool Street LU and Rail
- Sun 11am-3pm

A good selection of organic fruit and veg, and fresh cakes and pastries. See page 206 for more details.

Spitalfields Organics
Organic and wholefood, health and beauty

- 103a Commercial Street, E1
- 020 7377 8909
- Liverpool Street LU & Rail (5 min walk)
- Daily 9am-7pm

Full-on organic shop store with grocery, health and beauty products and nutritional supplements. It's also a totally vegetarian wholefood oasis stocking all the leading brands as well as a reasonable selection of dried foods, provisions, organic breads and freezer goods. The shop is popular with city workers looking for a healthy lunch, but does not have the fresh fruit and veg and other fresh foods to be found at larger stores.

FOREST GATE

Ambala Foods (Green Street)
Specialist pickles and chutneys, Indian sweets

🖃 *284 Green Street, E7*

☎ *0208 472 6004*

Upton Park LU (5 min walk)

🕒 *Daily 9am-9pm*

See Ambala, Drummond Street for review (page 233).

also at

🖃 *253 Greens Street, Forest Gate, E7*

☎ *0208 470 4946*

City Sweet Centre
Indian, classic

🖃 *510-512 Romford Road, E7*

☎ *020 8472 5459*

🚍 *Woodgrange Park LU (7 min walk)*

🕒 *Daily 10am-8pm (except Tuesdays)*

Join the queue at this busy sweet shop that offers an informative and friendly service. Notably enjoyable choices are the Mawa Peras a sweet made with flavoured milk and pistachios, Triveri Barfi, a triple flavoured milk sweetmeat, Jalebi (orange coloured batter twirls soaked in a syrup) and Ladu (fried chick pea flour balls soaked in syrup). It also sells Farsan such as Fafadi, Bombay mixes and biscuits and Indian fast food (see restaurant review on page 214).

Eastern Foods
Indian vegetarian sweet shop

🖃 *165 Green Street, E7*

☎ *020 8472 0030*

🚍 *Upton Park LU (5 min walk)*

🕒 *Daily 9am-7pm*

i   Outside catering

Indian sweets suitable for those allergic to cows' milk. Their recipes use Buffalo milk which has 58% more calcium, 40% more protein and 43% less cholesterol than cows' milk. The Burfi fudge here is quite good and is colourant-free. Also sells samosa, pakora, aloo tiki and julab jamun.

Good Morning Panwalla

North and South Indian, classic

🏠 *at Sakonis Vegetarian Restaurant, 149-153 Green Street, E7*

☎ *020 8472 0960*

🚌 *Upton Park LU (5 min walk)*

🕐 *Tue-Sun 12noon-9.30pm*

Sells Mukhwas, Baklawa mix, cashew nuts, Methi Kari, Masala Kari and Sesame Balls. Also sell Pan (an after meal digestive) at 70p, or the addictive tobacco version at £1. I tried the Pan, a betel leaf stuffed with lime paste, nuts and spices chewed after meals as a digestive and breath freshener. The size of a mini-samosa and looking ornately attractive, it had an enjoyable coconut-minty flavour with a mild stimulating kick to it.

Mishtidesh

Indian vegetarian savoury and sweet shop

🏠 *278 Green Street, E7*

☎ *020 8472 9505*

🚌 *Upton Park LU (5 min walk)*

🕐 *Daily 10am-7pm*

A wide selection of Punjabi, Gujarati and Bengali foods, including Rosmalai yogurt and rasgulla (flour balls in syrup).

LEYTON

Ambala Foods (Leyton)

Specialist pickles and chutneys, Indian sweets

🏠 *680 High Road, E10*

☎ *020 8558 0385*

🚌 *Leyton LU*

🕐 *Daily 9am-9pm*

See Ambala, Drummond Street for review (page 233).

MANOR PARK

Jalaram Sweetmart
Vegetarian sweet shop

🖃 *649 Romford Road, E12*
☎ *020 8553 0894*
🚃 *Woodgrange Park Rail (5 min walk)*
🕙 *Daily 9.30am-7pm*
i *Outside catering*

Small traditional homestyle Gujarati Indian sweet and fast food shop. Specialising in curries and savouries such as Pata Gatia (a kind of crisp) and a good selection of sweets, breads and other Indian nosh.

WALTHAMSTOW

Ambala Foods
Specialist pickles and chutneys, Indian sweets

🖃 *480 Hoe Street, E17*
☎ *020 8539 6695*
🚃 *Walthamstow LU*
🕙 *Daily 9am-9pm*

See Ambala, Drummond Street for review (page 233).

Second Nature Wholefoods
Organic vegetarian food, wholefoods and organic provisions

🖃 *78 Wood Street, E17*
☎ *020 8520 7995*
🚃 *St James Street Rail (8 min walk)*
🕙 *Mon-Sat 9am-5.30pm*

Set along a very long shopping street and some distance from Walthamstow Market, everything on sale at this well-established neighbourhood wholefood shop is vegetarian. Organic fruit and veg can be bought throughout the week and their policy is to only buy from organic suppliers that don't handle conventionally grown produce.

Second Nature is hot on avoiding GM ingredients, foods with additives and products tested on animals. It sells a wide range of food and drink including organic chocolates, skincare products, sunblocks and biodynamic wine. They deliver all over East London with no minimum order and to the rest of London with an additional carriage charge. Service is friendly and knowledgeable – an excellent place.

ALCOHOLIC DRINK FOR VEGETARIANS

There are lots of pitfalls for vegetarians wanting to enjoy alcoholic drink without consuming animal products in the process. Below are details of what to look out for when looking for vegetarian alcoholic drink. The choice for those seeking organic drink is far wider and easy to identify with a wide selection of alcoholic and soft drinks on shop shelves. Look out for the Soil Association symbol which guarantees the organic nature of the product.

Wine

It is during the fining process that animal products are added to wine. Among the ingredients that may be used in this process are isinglass, gelatin, egg albumen, modified casein, chitin or on rare occasions ox blood. The use of such animal derived products is not necessary with plenty of alternatives such as bentonite, kieselguhr and kaolin used for the same purpose. Most organic wines avoid using animal products, but some do. Thorsons Organic Wine Guide by Jerry Lockspeiser and Jackie Gear is a good reference to check the veggie credentials of most wines. For a list of organic wine merchants visit www.infolondon.ukf.net/organic/

Beer

Cask-conditioned ales use isinglass to clear the remnants of fermentation. Bottled naturally conditioned beers will not always use isinglass. Lagers and Keg Beers are pasteurised and usually passed through Chill Filters. This also applies to canned beers and some bottled beers.

Cider

The main brands of cider have been fined using gelatine. Scrumpy ciders are usually not fined using animal products, but always check to be sure.

Spirits

Vegetarians have less worries when choosing a spirit, most of which are made without using animal products. There are exceptions such as some Malt Whiskies and blended whiskies and Spanish Brandies which may have been contaminated with animal contaminants from the cask. Another pitfall are certain Vodkas which may have been passed through a bone charcoal filter

Fortified Wines

With the exception of crusted port, all ports use gelatin in the fining process. There are brands of sherry which do not use animal products, but the majority use animal products for fining.

Colourants

The main animal based colourant is E120 which is derived from insects and is used in a limited number of red wines, some soft drinks and Campari.

For goods approved by the Vegetarian Society visit their website *www.vegsoc.org*

VINTAGE Roots
the organic wine specialists

Freephone **0800 980 4992** for a free copy of our latest mail order wine list

Vegetarian and **vegan** organic wines, beers, ciders, spirits, juices, oils and chocolates

touchstone
merlot

www.vintageroots.co.uk

269

HIGH STREET CHAINS

HIGH STREET SUPERMARKETS

All the major supermarkets in London stock organic products. They also offer home delivery, internet ordering and have a rapid turnover of stock. They have made a major contribution to organic consumption in London and have helped to bring organic within everyone's reach.

ASDA
www.asda.com

This huge supermarket chain has a good array of vegetarian items with a nice choice of organic breads and dairy products. Their website is informative and is worth clicking on as it tells you if a product has Vegetarian Society approved ingredients and also has a lifestyle section informing the customer if an item is GM free.

MARKS AND SPENCER
www.marksandspencer.com

Does excellent quality fruit and veg, ready-made meals, and juices of which the Organic Apple and Cranberry is delicious. M&S sandwiches are superb with the best selection at the Marble Arch branch. Veggies who enjoy a tipple should zoom to their wine counter where over 70% of the wines and all the beers and spirits are vegetarian-suitable. All ingredients in the veggie products are from all non-GM sources and M&S meticulously assess cross contamination risks from non-vegetarian ingredients.

M&S is the largest purchaser of organic produce in the UK but they also buy in from all over the world so that their products will always be available. They have recently introduced Organic Extracts, their new range of organic beauty and skincare products which contain a minimum of 70% organic ingredients. These high quality goodies include bathtime treats like Rose Geranium, Apple and Lavender Floral Bath Essence and skincare staples like daytime protective moisturiser with Jojoba Oil and Green Tea. For a winter reviver try inhaling the Clarifying Facial Steam Essence, instead of mentholatum.

SAINSBURY'S

www.sainsbury's.co.uk

Always has a great selection of vegetarian products with a wide range of organic produce and branded products dotted around the aisles rather than in a special section. However, the hunt is worth it. Sainsbury's has a good cheese section suitable for vegetarians and does takeaway sandwiches of which the Egg and Cress Sandwich (reduced fat) is a healthy choice if not all that tasty. Sainsbury's has 38 vegetarian wines and 11 organic whites and 15 organic reds.

Sainsbury's is a good starting point for new converts to vegetarianism. Their website has a useful Vegetarian Cuisine Guide in the Food Feature section that gives lots of ace ideas on veggie home cooking. Newcomers are recommended to begin with classic recipes that have never relied on meats to be satisfying such as Mediterranean mezzes, Thai and vegetable curries with rice. Other seasonal recipes are available for old hands looking for more creative inventions.

Online-shopping is available with about 60 individual vegetarian products and 160 organic lines listed with a delivery charge of £5 or free depending on whether they've got a special offer on.

To combat the stresses and strains of urban living, Sainsbury's offer the Organic Blue health and beauty range that's Soil Association approved. Some of these use certified organic ayurvedic herbs which are claimed to have quite noticeable results.

TESCO

www.tesco.com

This supermarket giant offers over 1200 organic lines. The larger Tesco stores have dedicated organic counters where customers can readily buy branded organic products, including a good selection of breakfast cereals including Organic Weetabix and bran flakes, Organic Duchy Original Biscuits, numerous organic juices and their own Tesco organic brand which includes organic peanut butter.

Customers can pick up organic refrigerated products such as the Cauldron food range although the deli counter is yet to stock any organic items. Tesco stocks several low-priced vegetarian sandwiches of which the egg and onion and cheese sandwiches are okay but nothing special. Better are the takeaway ready-to-eat pasta salads and bean based meals. They also do vegetarian submarines that are worth splashing out on.

Of the 113 Tesco stores in London, 24 are Tesco Metro stores, smaller mini-market shops offering a selection of vegetarian and organic items. For motorists on the go the Tesco Express format at petrol stations offers a convenient way of picking up essential items when other shops may be closed in an area. The small Metro stores and garage forecourts, however, tend not to stock much organic.

Tesco's organic range can be home-delivered by logging onto their website which gives product information, availability and details of how to order from your local store. Tesco also stock a range of organic foods for cats and dogs.

WAITROSE
www.waitrosedeliver.com

This food specialist supermarket chain carries a thousand lines of organic fresh produce, ready-made meals, biscuits, wines, drinks and more than 30 fair trade products. Stores tend to be situated in affluent areas where discerning customers are less worried about prices and more concerned about excellent quality. Waitrose often source produce from small specialist suppliers who offer something a bit different from the mainstream.

At Waitrose, the vegetarian selection is massive and includes a good range of delicious takeaway sandwiches and ready-meals. Their fresh patisserie counter is also vegetarian.

Their website and online shopping service has a detailed list of products with useful information so you can browse the Braeburn organic apples, cantaloupes and Bonterra wines before you buy.

HIGH STREET CHAIN RESTAURANTS

PIZZA EXPRESS

www.pizzaexpress.com

Pizza restaurants remain a firm favourite for many vegetarians looking for an enjoyable and relatively inexpensive meal out. Pizza Express has 101 restaurants in London serving a tried and tested menu which includes seven vegetarian starters and four vegetarian pizzas, of which the Margherita and Veneziana are of a good standard. The parmesan used on some other dishes is made with animal rennet and is therefore not suitable for vegetarians although all the pizza bases are suitable and they can adapt dishes if you request.

For those wanting live jazz, the Pizza Express Club (Soho) books some top line acts and is open 364 days of the year. For further details see page 59. For Pizza Express locations see their website for details.

PRET A MANGER

www.pret-a-manger.com

This popular upscale looking coffee and sandwich bar chain offers a selection of eight vegetarian sandwiches of which the Hummous and Oven Roasted Tomato is quite tasty and suitable for vegans. The coffee here is consistently enjoyable. Whilst not officially organic, their approach 'to avoid obscure chemicals and additives that are in so much prepared and fast food', is nevertheless commendable.

Also serves vegetarian baguettes with two made specially for kids as well as four good veggie soups and a vegetarian sushi. Pret does a wide selection of vegetarian cakes, croissants and doughnuts, desserts, juices and organic chocolate.

Their website will tell you your nearest shop and there's free delivery if you spend over £20.

FARMERS' MARKETS

armers' Markets are a relatively new arrival to these shores but in the last decade the idea has proved a great success and provided a vital life line for struggling British farmers. The markets are for farmers selling their own produce direct to the public. No produce is bought in and all food sold at the markets is from within 100 miles of the M25.

For vegetarians and those interested in quality organic produce these markets are a great place to find quality naturally grown seasonal produce. It also affords visitors the opportunity to talk with the farmers that grow the food and share some of the enthusiasm they clearly have for their work. One farmer at Pimlico Farmers' Market proudly showed off his diabetic jam which he developed to cater for a regular customer. You don't find that kind of enthusiasm at your local supermarket!

Below is a list of all the current markets run by the organisation known as London Farmers' Markets, as well as contact details for the organisation. Their website is a useful resource and will give you up-to-date information about any changes.

London Farmers' Market

☎ *Contact 020 7704 9659*
✐ *info@lfm.org.uk*
✐ *www.lfm.org.uk*

List of London Farmers' Markets below:

Blackheath SE3

▢ *Blackheath Rail Station Car Park, 2 Blackheath Village*
☉ *Sundays 10am-2pm*
🚌 *Blackheath Rail, Buses 54, 89, 108, 202, 380*

Ealing W13

▢ *Leeland Road, West Ealing*
☉ *Saturdays 9am-1pm*
🚌 *Ealing Broadway LU (then bus), West Ealing Rail*

Islington N1 (see map, page 94)

▢ *Essex Road, opposite Islington Green*
☉ *Sundays 10am-2pm*
🚌 *Angel LU, Bus 38, 73, 56*

Marylebone W1 (see map, page 34)
🖼 *Cramer Street car park, corner Moxon Street, off Marylebone High Street*
🕐 *Sundays 10am-2pm*
🚇 *Baker St or Bond St LU*

Notting Hill W8 (see map, page 162)
🖼 *Car park behind Waterstones, access via Kensington Place*
🕐 *Saturdays 9am-1pm*
🚇 *Notting Hill Gate LU, Buses 12, 27, 28, 52, 70, 94, 328*

Peckham SE15
🖼 *Peckham Square, Peckham High Street*
🕐 *Sundays 9.30am-1.30pm*
🚇 *Peckham Rye and Queens Road Rail, Buses 12, 36, 171, 345*

Pimlico Road SW1 (see map, page 68)
🖼 *Orange Square, corner of Pimlico Road and Ebury Street*
🕐 *Saturdays 9am-1pm*
🚇 *Sloane Square LU, Buses 211, 11 & 239*

Swiss Cottage NW3
🖼 *02 Centre Car Park, Finchley Rd*
🕐 *Wednesdays 10am-3pm*
🚇 *Finchley Road and West Hampstead LU,*
West Hampstead and Finchley Road Rail

Twickenham TW1
🖼 *Holly Road Car Park, Holly Rd (off King St), Twickenham*
🕐 *Saturdays 9am-1pm*
🚇 *Twickenham Rail*

Wimbledon Park SW19
🖼 *Wimbledon Park First School, Havana Road*
🕐 *Saturdays 9am-1pm*
🚇 *Wimbledon Park LU*

Other London Farmers' Markets

Chiswick W4
🖼 *Car Park Pavilion, Dukes Meadows, off Edensor Road*
☎ *Contact Kathleen Healy 020 8747 3063 (Chiswick Farmers' Market)*
🕐 *Sunday 10am-2pm*

Stoke Newington N16 (see map, page 136)

▢ *The Old Fire Station, Leswin Road*

☎ *Contact Kerry Rankine 020 75092 7588 (Growing Communities)*

🕐 *Saturday 10am-2.30pm*

✎ *www.growingcommunities.org*

A local farmers market specialising in organic and bio-dynamic produce.

All UK Farmers' Markets

For a national list, send SAE to
National Association of Farmers' Markets,
PO Box 575 Southampton, SO15 or visit www.farmersmarkets.net

Other Food Markets

There are other markets which also offer farmers' the opportunity to sell direct to the public, the only difference being that they are not exclusively open to farmers and allow other food traders to sell their wares. The best of these markets are:

Borough Market SE1 (see map, page 64)

▢ *Southwark Street*

🚇 *London Bridge LU and Rail*

🕐 *Fri 12noon-6pm, Sat9am-4pm*

A huge food event with all manner of fine produce on offer from organic wines to farm produced cheeses. See page 64 for more details.

Spitalfields Food Market E1 (see map, page 200)

▢ *Commercial Street between Folgate and Bushfield Street*

🚇 *Liverpool Street LU and Rail*

🕐 *Sun 11am-3pm*

A good selection of organic fruit and veg, and fresh cakes and pastries. See page 206 for more details.

Merton Abbey Mills SW19

▢ *Off Merantun Way, behind the Savacentre, South Wimbledon*

🚇 *Colliers Wood LU*

🕐 *Sat-Sun 10am-5pm*

Several good food stalls are to be found here at the weekend.

Broadway Market E8

🕐 *Sat 8am-5pm*

🚇 *Bethnal Green LU (then bus)*

About a third of all stalls at this street market are dedicated to fresh food with many local organic producers selling their wares.

CATERERS

CENTRAL LONDON

Organic Express Caterers
International, Classic and Modern, Organic

⌨ *17 Ansell Road, SE15 2DT*

☎ *020 7277 6147*

✐ *www.organic-caterers.com*

The only Soil Association accredited caterers in the UK, Organic Express specialise in upscale catering from small private parties with canapés to corporate buffets to wedding receptions with organic food. Both directors are vegetarians with a passion for organic and whilst they offer a UK-only menu to support local producers they also do a wide range of international food and have a South American and an Irish chef.

Most of their clients are in Central London and their kitchen is based in Battersea. However, they are quite happy to work on-site either in the client's kitchen or they can set up a kitchen.

The Place Below
International, Classic

⌨ *St Mary-le-Bow Church, Cheapside, EC2V 6AU*

☎ *020 7329 0789*

Vegetarian catering service available and the crypt can be booked for weddings, confirmations and parties.

Futures!
International, Classic

⌨ *8 Botolph Alley, Eastcheap, EC3*

☎ *020 7623 4529*

Vegetarian catering service from weddings and functions to office party canapés.

NORTH LONDON

Manna
Mediterranean, International, Modern and Organic

⌧ *4 Erskine Road, Primrose Hill, NW3*

☎ *020 7609 3560*

Expert inventive vegetarian and organic food that will dazzle your guests.

The Psychedelic Dream Temple
Mediterranean, International, Classic and Organic

⌧ *Unit 21/22 Stables Market, Camden Town, NW1*

☎ *020 7267 8528*

This dreamscape designed café can be booked for catered parties or they will do on-site catering subject to availability. See page 118 for venue and food review.

Anupam Caterers
Vegetarian Indian, Classic

⌧ *129 Bowes Road, Palmers Green, N13*

☎ *020 8889 9112*

This family business does 100% vegetarian catering from 50 to 2000 people with hundreds of dishes to choose from. Their repertoire extends to veggie burgers and sausages too!

Their Vegetarian Meals on Wheels service costs from £5 per meal per person and the company runs a free home delivery service in the surrounding 5 mile radius and offers group discounts.

Jaaneman Sweet Centre
Vegetarian Indian, Classic

⌧ *170 Bowes Road, New Southgate, N11*

☎ *020 8888 1226*

Pure vegetarian catering for parties and functions from this sweet and snack specialist that also has its own restaurant (see page 146) and shop (see page 243).

SOUTH LONDON

Service-Heart-Joy
International, Classic

☐ *191 Hartfield Road, Wimbledon, SW19 3JH*

☎ *020 8542 9912*

This south London café does French, Italian and Indian food for weddings, birthdays and other small functions.

EAST LONDON

City Sweet Centre
Indian, Classic

☐ *510-512 Romford Road, Forest Gate, E7*

☎ *020 8472 5459*

As well as being speciality confectioners, the City Sweet Centre also cater for weddings, parties and all other functions. Contact Mr Jethalal Damji Thanki for personal service. See their restaurant review (page 214) and shop review (page 265).

Eastern Foods
Indian, Classic

☐ *165 Green Street, Forest Gate, E7*

☎ *020 8472 0030*

Specialising in foods that use buffalo milk instead of cows' milk, Eastern Foods cater for all kinds of special occasions from weddings to vegetarian corporate events. They also support local community activities such as the annual Waltham Forest 'Green Fayre'.

Jalaram Sweetmart
Indian, Classic

☐ *649 Romford Road, Manor Park, E12*

☎ *020 8553 0894*

Tends to cater for small functions such as birthday parties and religious occasions in people's homes.

ORGA CONTACT GROUPS

VEGETARIAN CONTACTS

Brian and Julie's Vegan London

✎ *www.veganlondon.co.uk*

They are involved in London Vegans arranging monthly meetings and restaurant visits and their informative website includes information on events, accommodation, restaurants, animal rights and books.

Curvenetics

☎ *020 8550 0916*

✎ *www.curvenetics.com*

Vegetarian nutritional and dietary advice with effective gentle non-impact exercise technique giving excellent results in just ten hours. Established 25 years ago, classes are held at the Curvenetics Centre, 2 minutes from Oxford Circus. Nutritional advice is given by yours truly, Veggie and Organic London's author, Russell Rose, whilst the exercises are taught by ballet-trained Tracy Rose. Personal nutritional and exercise sessions can be tailored to individual requirements.

Gay Vegetarians and Vegans

▭ *BM Box 5700, London, WC1N 3XX*

☎ *020 8470 1873*

Established in 1979, this is now a small group of mainly lesbians in their 60's-70's who meet and eat informally and socially every Sunday for lunch in East London. The group produces a twice yearly magazine called 'Green Queen' for which they are delighted to accept contributions in the form of letters, articles, news on vegetarianism, and animal rights as well as fiction and poetry.

International Jewish Vegetarian Society

▭ *Bet Teva, 853/855 Finchley Road, London NW11*

☎ *020 8455 0692*

🕓 *Office hours: Mon-Thur 10am-4pm*

Advocates vegetarian ideals designated in Genesis and the Torah with meetings and functions at their Golders Green HQ. Altogether, there are nearly 3000 members of all ages in London and the rest of the country. Set up in 1966, there is a good social element to the organisation but they do also campaign on serious matters. The Society gives lucid advice in the form of a quarterly magazine 'The Jewish Vegetarian', which has detailed articles on international vegetarian issues, recipes, nutritional health information, compassion for animals features, gardening tips and is a useful source of vegetarian and vegan contacts.

At HQ, there's a big selection of books many of which are half-price. Visitors are welcome for a browse and coffee but do phone through first.

Lesbian Vegans

Contact: Kat

☎ 020 7243 8225

Affiliated to the Vegetarian Society, it's also open to vegetarian and bisexual women. Meets monthly for a chow down at restaurants in and around the London area.

London Vegans

▱ *7 Deansbrook Road, Edgware, Middlesex*

☎ *020 8931 1904*

⌂ *www.londonvegans.freeserve.co.uk*

Meetings are held on the last Wednesday of every month (apart from December) at Millman Street Community Rooms, Millman Street, London WC1, near Russell Square.

Also arranges walks in and around the London area, restaurant visits and outings. For schedule, log onto their website which also features a useful accommodation listing for vegetarians.

Muslim Vegan Vegetarian Society

▱ *Contact: Rafeeque Ahmed,*
  59 Brey Towers, 136 Adelaide Road,
  Camden, London, NW3 3JU

☎ *020 7483 1742*

A campaigning organisation which meets occasionally at vegetarian and vegan restaurants in or near Camden. Publishes an 'Islam and Vegetarianism' booklet.

Vegan Society

Donald Watson House, 7 Battle Road,
St Leonard-on-Sea, East Sussex, TN37 7AA

☎ *0845 4588244*

www.vegansociety.com

This campaigning organisation produces the Vegan Magazine, books and pamphlets on veganism, animal rights and animal-free lifestyles.

Vegetarian Society

Parkdale, Dunham, Altrincham, Cheshire, WA14 4QG

☎ *0161 925 2000*

www.vegsoc.org

A wonderful registered charity dedicated to extolling the virtues and dissemination of veggie diet info. The Vegetarian Society defines a vegetarian as a person who eats no meat, poultry, game, fish, shellfish or crustacea. Vegetarians also avoid the by-products of slaughter such as gelatine or rennet.

According to their surveys there are 3 million vegetarians in the UK with 2000 people a week in the UK dropping meat completely from their diets. As Vegetarian Society Patron and style guru Stella McCartney says, "Welcome to the most delicious, most talked about, fastest growing food trend of the new millennium – vegetarianism."

The Vegetarian Society produces a magazine 'The Vegetarian', that's free to all members and also have a tremendously informative website.

Vegetarian and Vegan Gay Group

WGG, 86 Caledonian Road, London, N1

☎ *020 7713 9063*

www.vvgg.freeserve.co.uk

Log on to their website for details of events, restaurant visits, veggie picnics, cookery demos, marches, festival visits, picnics at people's homes. The group usually meets twice a month and gets together for an indoor picnic from 6pm on the last Sunday of every month at London Friend, King's Cross. Sometimes has campaign meetings pertaining to ethical issues and animal rights.

Vegetarian Social Club

Contact: Helen Buckland

☎ *020 8688 6325*

Eats, walks, theatre trips and days out organised by this London based veggie club.

Young Indian Vegetarians

✉ *Contact: Nitin Mehta,*
   226 London Road, West Croydon, Surrey, CR0 2TF

☎ *020 8681 8884*

✎ *www.indian-vegetarians.org*

Campaigning group, founded in 1978, to promote animal rights and 'Ahisma' (respect for all living creatures). There's no formal membership, you don't have to be Indian and participants range in age from 10 years old to 50 years young!. Events include an annual vegetarian picnic in Hyde Park and visits to some great Indian restaurants including Kastoori in Tooting and Rani in Finchley. Young Indian Vegetarians also give talks at schools and colleges and join marches. The group also is involved in the Mahavir Medal Award for people who have done great work to end animal cruelty, promote animal rights and further vegetarianism.

ORGANIC CONTACTS

Biodynamic Agricultural Association (BDAA)

Painswick Inn Project,
Gloucester Street, Stroud, Gloucestershire, GL5 1QG
☎ *01453 759501*
✑ *www. biodynamic.org.uk*

Organisation that aims to promote biodynamic farming and arranges conferences, produces information literature and helps enthusiasts to find a job on a biodynamic farm.

Biodynamic food, drinks and products are pesticide and chemical-free. Produce is grown according to the principles of Rudolf Steiner at specific cycles of the moon and times of the day. Adherents to the Steiner approach envisage the farm as a self-contained organism, a carer of health, synergising soil, crops, stock and farmer in a cycle of virtuosity. Conceived in the 1920's biodynamic farming is the forerunner of organic farming today.

Certified biodynamic and organic produce can be found at Fern Verrow Vegetables in Borough Market (see page 64-65) while biodynamic beauty brands include Dr Hauschka, Waleda, Just Pure and Talya.

Friends of the Earth

26-28 Underwood Street, London, N1 7JQ
☎ *020 7 490 1555*
✑ *www.foe.co.uk*

Environmental pressure group that is represented in 58 countries.

Organic Research

✑ *www.organic-research.com*

Organic research and news with a database of 130,000 abstracted research articles accessed by subscription only. However, there are some free resources which include events, jobs, courses, farm lists and legal information.

Green Events

☐ *13, Brecknock Road, London, N7 0BL*
☎ *020 7424 9100*
⌨ *www.greenevents.fsnet.co.uk*

Alternative magazine giving details of forthcoming environmental, holistic and animal rights events and festivals. Given away free at vegetarian cafés and restaurants around the capital. The website also includes features.

Greenpeace

☐ *Canonbury Villas, London, N1 2PN*
☎ *020 7865 8100*
⌨ *www.greenpeace.org.uk*

Campaigning organisation which actively opposes the release of GM foods into the environment based on the premise that the risks are unpredictable and irreversible. Informative website.

Local Food Works

⌨ *www.localfoodworks.org*

A useful site that provides information for schools, hospitals and other groups who wish to source organic food and produce from local farmers. Covers useful issues on organic food and healthy eating. The organisation is a project involving the Soil Association and the Countryside Agency.

Soil Association

☐ *Certification Ltd, Bristol House,*
40-56 Victoria Street, Bristol, BS1 6BY
☎ *0117 914 2411*
⌨ *www.soilassociation.org*

The largest UK organic certification body. Their excellent website gives lucid information as to what constitutes organic, recipes, news, issues and events. Also answers many queries on organic certification.

Sustain

🖃 *94 White Lion Street, London, N1 9PF*

☎ *020 7837 1228*

🖝 *www.sustainweb.org*

Based in Islington, Sustain is an alliance of organisations campaigning for better food and farming. It is an advocator of agricultural and food policies and practices that improve the health and welfare of people and animals and improve the living environment.

Their Grab 5! campaign aimed to promote the eating of five portions of fruit and veg per day. Check out their website for information packs on growing schemes and ideas to encourage children to eat more fruit and veg in schools and its importance to their health.

Also runs London Food Link, a project to help producers, consumers and retailers make positive choices about sustainable and local foods.

VEGETARIAN COOKERY COURSES

Books for Cooks

🖃 *4 Blenheim Crescent, W11*

☎ *020 7221 1992*

Runs several vegetarian cookery courses during the year at their upstairs tuition kitchen.

ORGANIC GARDENING & FARMING COURSES

London South Bank University

Department of Applied Science, FESBE,
103 Borough Road, London, SE1 0AA
☎ *020 7815 7815*

LSBU have launched a new course in Organic Food Studies. Described as the first 'post harvest degree course in the UK', it's a development generating interest amongst retailers and manufacturers.

HDRA

Ryton Organic Gardens,
Ryton on Dunsmore, Coventry, CV8 3LG
☎ *01203 303517*

HDRA, the Henry Doubleday Research Association, researches, demonstrates and campaigns for environmentally safer gardening. It runs one day courses at its headquarters in Ryton to help you become an environmentally friendly gardener and how to create small scale edible gardens. HDRA also have gardens in Yalding in Kent.

Wye College

University of London, Wye, Ashford, Kent, TN25 5AH
☎ *01273 476286*

Runs an M.Sc course in Sustainable Agriculture. For further details contact the above address.

ORGANIC GARDENING PROJECTS

Brockwell Community Greenhouses
Organic gardening

▢ *Brockwell Park, SE24*
☎ *020 7622 4913*
🕐 *Wed, Thur & Sunday 2pm-5.30pm*
🚌 *Herne Hill Rail, then buses 3,196, 37*

An organically run garden with orchard, vegetable garden, medicinal herbs and a pond. It's open to the public and a good place to while away a couple of hours. Produce such as runner beans, kale, spinach and garlic are available to buy. School parties visit on educational trips. The place is run by volunteers, some of whom put in as many as four days a week although many are just Sunday people; volunteers are a mix of unemployed, retired and those needing a therapeutic antidote to the stresses of Brixton life.

Centre For Wildlife Gardening
Organic gardening

▢ *28 Marsden Road, Peckham, SE15 4EE*
☎ *020 7252 9186*
🖉 *www.wildlondon.org.uk*

Does gardening demonstrations, herb gardening, nursery of wild flowers. Has lots of raised bed and organic vegetables. Volunteers learn organic techniques and the trust also does good work for people with special needs, learning disabilities. Gets lots of school groups. Those working in the gardens get to to take home their produce so there is a real end product to it.

For those just wanting to relax and do nothing, one can come along and spend a pleasant couple of hours in the gardens and visitors centre.

Culpepper Community Garden
Organic garden with allotments and community activities

▢ *1 Cloudsley Road, Islington, N1*
☎ *020 7833 3951*
🚇 *Angel LU (5min walk)*
🕐 *Open during daylight hours – but telephone first to confirm*

Applies completely organic gardening principles to the development and upkeep of this pretty colourful, community garden for locals. Has

Contact Groups GARDENING PROJECTS

monthly workdays for volunteers and provides 46 plots for people without gardens. Allotment holders live within a half mile of the garden and in return help out with community activities. Culpepper supports many community projects such as playgroups, a mental health gardening group and a learning disabilities group.

Culpepper is tucked away behind Sainsbury's car park and by the children's playground. It has a good social atmosphere with plots of organic flowers, herbs and vegetables. Visitors can bring their own sarnies and drinks and eat at the tea hut. A swell place for organic gardening enthusiasts to visit.

Postal enquires to:
Clare Sutton, Culpepper Community Garden,
35 Batchelor Street, London N1 0EG

East London Organic Gardeners

□ *43 Arbour House, Arbour Square, E1 0PP*
☎ *020 7265 8257*
℮ *www.elog.org.uk*

East London Organic Gardeners (ELOG) is a voluntary group with monthly meetings throughout the year. During the summer they attend fairs and shows in East London. Their aims are to promote and advise on natural gardening that avoids synthetic chemicals and to promote the recycling of waste via composting. ELOG's secretary, Francis Schwartz, is a mine of useful information and can tell you lots about the local organic allotment scene.

Meeting topics have included a compost day, organic food, and a 'year in the life of a seed merchant'. It's a good opportunity to meet organic gardeners and to network. All their activities are free and very useful to anyone new to organic gardening.

Federation of City Farms and Community Gardens

□ *The Greenhouse, Hereford Street, Bristol, BS3 4NA*
☎ *0117 923 1800*

A useful contact for anyone interested in starting a city farm or allotment. The London contact number is 020 7485 5001.

GARDENING PROJECTS Contact Groups

Forest Farm
Organic allotment projects, educational, medical research, refugee social work

🖃 *Contact: Barry Watson*

　　Hazelbrock Gardens, Hainault, Essex

☎ *020 8592 8941*

🚌 *Hainault LU (5min walk)*

🕓 *Mondays only at present*

Forest Farm is a project recently set up by Barry Watson who previously organised Becontree Organic Growers in Dagenham. There are seven organically grown allotments and a 'peace garden', a forest garden is also being planned. They carry out environmental projects in schools and hope to run a 'Young Shoots' project, where children can plant and follow the growth of their own tree right through to their teenage life as part of an educational scheme. There will also be an organic medicinal herbal garden of 2500 herbs in conjunction with East London University. One of the herbs is a garlic derivative that may potentially be helpful in combating MRSA infections. Jenny Grutt also runs a national allotment project working with refugees who have been tortured. Interested volunteers should ring Jenny on 020 7435 4416.

Organiclea
Organic allotments

🖃 *c/o Hornbeam Environment Centre, 458 Hoe Street, E17 9AH*

☎ *07786 657713 for details*

🖉 *www.organiclea.org.uk*

Workers' co-operative on formerly abandoned allotment in Chingford. Attracts organic gardening volunteers from Hackney, Haringay, Redbridge and Walthamstow with a core group in their 20's-30's. Whilst not Soil Association approved organic methods are used and 'chemical-free' fruit, veg and herbs are grown here.

Has some conventional beds, a polytunnel and a forest garden that recreates a forest ecosystem producing edible and useful plants. There are pear and fig trees and some unusual plant varieties as well as herbs, rhubarb, Jerusalem artichokes and garlic.

Organiclea's open days for volunteers and visitors are on the 2nd and 4th Sundays of each month. Those who want to get stuck in with a bit of spade work will get some great hands-on training about organic gardening, environmental friendliness and network with the community growers of the Lea Valley. Participation is free of charge and any food harvested is divided up with surplus food given to the community.

Growing Communities
Organic fruit and vegetable box scheme, organic market
The Old Fire Station

🖃 *61 Leswin Road, Stoke Newington, N16 7NY*

☎ *020 7502 7588*

🖉 *www.grow.communities.com*

Social enterprise promoting organic sustainable agriculture founded in 1994. They run a local organic box scheme for about 180 households in Hackney and also run an organic market of 11 organic food stalls on Saturdays 10am-2.30pm.

All the produce is certified organic and some is grown locally in Hackney with three farms with Soil Association certified organic land near Stoke Newington. Whilst also a commercial proposition, it also enables people to meet and co-operate together – linked by the food on their plates.

Although called a box scheme, produce is packed in bags and collected by customers from one of three locations. Various fruit and vegetable bags are ordered and picked up weekly from Stoke Newington, Lower Clapton and Hackney City Farm. All the food comes from no further than 70 mile from the centre of London.

Various bag deals are available with a monthly trial period. A Standard Veg Bag contains 9 items of seasonal produce at £8.50 per bag or £5 for a smaller one.

Collection points

The Fire Station

🖃 *Leswin Road, N16*

🕐 *Wednesdays 4pm-9pm*

Staffed pick up and Urban Farm shop
4pm-7.30pm, Thur & Fri 8am-9pm

Fruit Basket

🖃 *Clapton*

🕐 *Wednesday 6pm-7pm, Thur & Fri 9am-7pm*

Hackney City Farm

🕐 *Wed 6pm-7.30pm, Thur & Fri 10am-4.30pm*

For Subscribers that are homebound they will do their best to organise a pick up for you, and encourage shared pick-ups.

Spa Hill Allotment Society Limited
Friendly community run organic allotment
and gardening club

⌨ *180 Spa Hill, SE19 3TU*

☎ *020 8653 5636*

✍ *www.spahill.org.uk*

🕐 *Office hours: Sat and Sun only 10am-12noon*

On the south west side of Crystal Palace Hill there are 300 allotments many of them organic but not all, with some plots having been in the same family for 3 generations. Novices to organic gardening get practical advice from experienced members and Spa Hill Training, which is run jointly by the Allotment Society and SHOGG, provides formal instruction in basic techniques. They run one day basic courses five times a year that attract up to 45 people at a time.

The Spa Hill Organic Gardening Group (SHOGG) meets at Spa Hill at 8pm on the third Wednesday of each month (except January and August). They run seed exchanges and give demonstrations at local shows. Also publishes a magazine, newsletters, organic gardening booklets, recipes and does educational visits to schools.

Spitalfields City Farm
Organic farm, community projects

⌨ *Weaver Street, E1 5HJ*

☎ *020 7247 8762*

✍ *www.spitalfieldscityfarm.org*

🕐 *Tue-Sun 10am-5pm*

🚌 *Shoreditch LU (3min walk), Liverpool Street LU & Rail (10min walk)*

Runs the women only Coriander Club project for 20-25 Bangladeshi women to cultivate plants. At Spitalfields City Farm there are polytunnels where kodu gourds are grown. There is also a young offenders project. Community volunteers are welcome to pitch in and get to know more about organic gardening and farming. Sells a selection of seasonal vegetables and herb as well stocking home garden composters.

On Sundays, it's a place to chill out for an hour or so and has a good display of flowers including marigolds and dahlias but unfortunately no café although there are farm animals for the kids. Spitalfields City Farm is situated at the end of Pedley Street, E1.

Stepney Stepping Stones

⌨ *Contact Lynne Bennet*
   Stepney Way, E1 3DG
☎ *020 7790 8204*
🕐 *Tue-Sun 9.30am-6pm (open bank holidays, Christmas & Boxing Day)*

Stepney Stepping Stones is an urban farm with eight allotments. They provide 84 growing boxes to financially hard-up people without gardens. Most are local community on the Ocean Estate and they grow Bengali vegetables in an organic way.

Located at the junction of Stepney Way and Stepney High Street, there's a garden centre, shop and café serving tea, coffee and biscuits. Whilst not organically certified because of the certification costs they do employ organic techniques. The garden centre is a source of income and sells runner beans, pumpkins, tomatoes and in future wild flowers too. The farm, began about 25 years ago and has piglets, cows, sheep, donkeys and is run by volunteers.

Willing Workers on Organic Farms

⌨ *PO Box 2675, Lewes, Sussex, BN7 1RB*
✍ *www.wwoof.org.uk*

WWOOF is a non-profit making organisation and produces a bi-monthly UK newsletter complete with members' letters, calls for volunteers, campaign updates, job vacancies in green and organic lines of work, funding, contacts, international news and classified ads. The annual subscription is £15.

Formerly called Working Weekends on Organic Farms, the organisation puts people who want to volunteer on organic farms in touch with organic farms, gardens and smallholdings who want volunteer workers. Volunteers stay for a weekend (or longer if you want!). In return for your help you receive meals, accommodation and the opportunity to learn. It may be hard graft but the payback is that you get to learn stacks about organic farming in beautiful rural countryside, eat food that you have helped produce and maybe meet some interesting like-minded folk. All the work is voluntary and you have to bring your own sleeping bag, wellington boots gloves etc, longer term WWOOFers can expect bedding.

HOTELS & APARTMENTS

CENTRAL

City Inn Westminster
Hotel   ★★★★

🖽 *30 John Islip Street, SW1*
☎ *020 7932 4600*
🚌 *Pimlico LU or Westminster LU (10min walk)*
◊ *Child friendly*
Al fresco dining on their 'Side Street'

The place for the discerning vegetarian traveller, the City Inn, serves superb vegetarian cuisine, from breakfast through to lunch and dinner (see page 69) and boasts chic, state-of-the-art bedrooms, complete with plasma TV, music system and – a nice touch this – an extra wide safe, in which to leave a laptop. There is an abundance of conference rooms and the hotel does seem more geared to the business traveller that those in search of holiday luxury. At £225+vat excluding breakfast, it isn't cheap but they do offer a good weekend deal of £99 per night.

The modern snazzy bar on the first floor stays open as long as hotel guests want and was busy at 11pm when I visited. The Inn hosts its own art exhibitions – well, it is near Tate Britain.

The Halkin Hotel
Hotel   ★★★★

🖽 *Halkin Street, SW1*
☎ *020 7333 1234*
🚌 *Hyde Park Corner LU (10min walk)*
Vegan choices

Fabulously, sophisticated boutique hotel catering for the highly affluent with vegetarian requirements. Through the opulent lobby is a lounge bar and the excellent Nahm restaurant serving exquisite vegetarian Thai food (see page 73 for review). Upstairs each floor is colour themed according to a different element: water, air, fire and sky. Each room is superbly furnished and equipped to the hilt. The Halkin is popular with film stars and celebrities. A double room starts at £310 a night but the service is impeccable and together with a meal at Nahm makes for an unforgettably luxurious experience.

The Lanesborough

★★★★★

Hotel

⬛ *1 Lanesborough Place, Hyde Park Corner, SW1*

☎ *020 7259 5599*

🚌 *Hyde Park Corner LU (30sec walk)*

Conveniently located on Hyde Park Corner this is an ideal place for well-heeled vegetarians who want top class accommodation, service and ambience. High quality vegetarian food is available 24 hours per day with individual nutritional requirements willingly catered for.

The hotel is in a grand style where guests are graciously received as if they were in a private home. The Library is one of the best bars in London and regularly has a high celeb count. The Conservatory is a marvellous destination for breakfast, lunch, tea and dinner (see restaurant review page 71).

The rooms are superb and come with complimentary butler service to take care of guests' unpacking and packing and to help co-ordinate social and business itineraries.

Inside the rooms there's lots of wooden panelling, beautiful swathes of luxurious curtaining not only for the windows but also the bed and the bath. All rooms have an imposing classic writing desk and book selection for those in pensive literary mood or who just want to send a postcard to the folks back home.

Phone through to see about special deals. The rate for an Executive Double is £475, The Buckingham Suite with three piece suite, dining room table and chairs £1950! However, a stay at the Lanesborough is something you (and your bank account) will remember forever.

West Street Hotel
Hotel

New (no ratings yet)

⌨ *13-15 West Street, WC2*
☎ *020 7010 8600*
🚌 *Leicester Square LU (5min walk)*

Has just three rooms of sophisticated modern design. In summer these offer particularly good value as the prices are slashed by 50%. The Loft is £225, the Stone Room complete with terrace is £175, and the somewhat smaller White Room is £125. Prices include a full breakfast but exclude VAT.

The hotel's restaurant East@West has an excellent vegetarian tasting menu (see review on page 19) and if you let the hotel know you are vegetarian they will take care of any special requests for breakfast you may have.

NORTH LONDON

Liz Heavenstone's Guest House
Apartment

⌨ *Contact Liz Heavenstone*
  Regent's Park Road, Primrose Hill, NW1
☎ *020 7722 7139*
🚌 *Chalk Farm LU (2min walk)*
Booking essential

The first organic bed and breakfast in London, it's a pleasant apartment set on two top floors of a Regency terrace just along from the Primrose Hill dining strip. There's a self-service vegetarian, mostly organic, breakfast, a communal table and a nice kitchen with basic self-catering cooking facilities at other times.

Breakfasts include organic cereals, yogurts and soya milks with tea, coffee and herbal drinks are available at all times. Bedlinen is natural fibre but not organic. A minute away is vegetarian restaurant, Manna (see page 116) and Café Seventy Nine (see page 109) for eats, as is Sesame the local wholefood shop. Liz asked me not to give out the street number as she doesn't want casual passerbys calling without appointments and waking up just arrived jet-lagged guests, so do telephone first.

The larger room is £65 per night (up to two people sharing, £75 for three) whilst the smaller is £55 (continental breakfast is included). The big plus with this place is that it becomes a self-contained apartment if both rooms are taken.

VEGGIE & ORGANIC LONDON HOTLIST

Outstanding Veggie Cafés

Café Seventy Nine, Primrose Hill	p.109
Wheatley Vegetarian Café, Exmouth Market	p.92
Whole Meal Café, Streatham	p.192

Traditional Veggie Cuisine

Kastoori, Tooting	p.193
Mildreds, Soho	p.57
Sabras, Willesden	p.148
Woodlands, Chiswick, Haymarket, Marylebone, Wembley	p.179

Modern Veggie Cuisine

The Gate, Hammersmith	p.175
Morgan M, Islington	p.104
Manna, Primrose Hill	p.116
Nahm, Hyde Park Corner	p.73
Plant, Soho	p.59
Roussillon, Sloane Square	p.74
Sketch, Mayfair	p.45

Low Budget Veggie Cuisine

Beatroot, Soho	p.49
Food for Thought, Covent Garden	p.22
Eateas, Soho	p.52
The Greenery, Farringdon	p.90
Indian Veg Bhel-Poori House, Islington	p.101

Medium Budget Veggie Cuisine

The Gate, Hammersmith	p.175
Kastoori, Tooting	p.193
Manna, Primrose Hill	p.116
Mildreds, Soho	p.57
Peking Palace, Archway	p.130
Rasa, Stoke Newington	p.141

Luxury Veggie Cuisine

The Lanesborough, Hyde Park Corner — p.71
Morgan M, Islington — p.104
Roussillon, Sloane Square — p.74
Sketch, Mayfair — p.45

The Hip List

The Bar & Grill, West Smithfield — p.86
Domali, Crystal Palace — p.196
Eat and Two Veg, Marylebone — p.40
E&O, Notting Hill — p.164
Fifteen, Hoxton — p.83
Nahm, Hyde Park Corner — p.73
Sketch, Mayfair — p.45
Zuma, Marylebone — p.161

Romantic Restaurants

Getti, Marylebone — p. 43
Nahm, Hyde Park Corner — p.73
Sarastro, Covent Garden — p.27
Whole Meal Café, Streatham — p.192
Zuma, Marylebone — p.161

Partying on a Low Budget

Domali Café, Crystal Palace — p.196
Gallipoli, Islington — p.96
The Psychedelic Dream Temple, Camden — p.118
Indian Veg Bhel-Poori House, Islington — p.101

Partying on a Medium Budget

Blah Blah Blah, Hammersmith — p.173
Café Pacifico, Covent Garden — p.17
El Pirata, Mayfair — p. 42
Mildreds, Soho — p.57
Sarastro, Covent Garden — p.27

Partying on a Big Budget

City Café, Westminster — p.69
The Lanesborough, Hyde Park Corner — p.71

Restaurants With a View

Restaurants For Al Fresco Dining

Restaurants For Mock Carnivore Veggie Food

Best Buffets

Recommended Pubs Serving Veggie Choices

Vegetarian Fast Food

Outstanding Organic Cafés

Organic Restaurants

Organic Pubs

Outstanding Organic Juice Bars

Organic Fast Food

Best Restaurants By Nationality

African/Caribbean
Mandola

American/Californian
Eat and Two Veg

Central America
Café Pacifico

British
Living Room (West Smithfield)

Chinese
Good Earth (Knightsbridge)
Mulan
Peking Palace

Eastern European and Jewish
Isola Bella
Milk 'n' Honey

French
Morgan M
Roussillon

Indian
Chai Pani
Deya
Kastoori
Mela
Sabras
Sagar
Sakonis
Woodlands

Italian
Carluccio's
Fifteen and Trattoria
Getti
Pizza Express
Pizza on the Park

Japanese
Wagamama (inexpensive)
Zuma (expensive)

Middle Eastern
Isolabella
Özer

Spanish/Portugese
El Pirata

Thai
Nahm
Thai Garden
Thai Square (Trafalgar Square)

Polish
Daquise

303

Index

Index

Order our other Metro Titles

The following titles are also available from Metro Publications. Please send your order along with a cheque made payable to Metro Publications to the address below. Postage and packaging is free (please allow 14 days for delivery).

Alternatively call our customer order line on **020 8533 0922** (Visa/Mastercard/Switch), Open Mon-Fri 9am-6pm

Metro Publications
PO Box 6336, London N1 6PY
metro@dircon.co.uk
www.metropublications.com

London Architecture
Author: Marianne Butler
£**8.99** ISBN1-902910-18-4

Bargain Hunters' London 3rd ed
Author: Andrew Kershman
ISBN 1-902910-15-X £**6.99**

Museums & Galleries of London
3rd ed Author: Abigail Willis
£**8.99** ISBN 1-902910-20-6